Retrieving the Big Society

WILEY-
BLACKWELL

Contents

Retrieving the Big Society

Edited by
Jason Edwards

Wiley-Blackwell
In association with *The Political Quarterly*

This edition first published 2012
© 2012 The Political Quarterly Publishing Co. Ltd except for editorial material

Blackwell Publishing was acquired by John Wiley & Sons in February 2007. Blackwell's publishing programme has been merged with Wiley's global Scientific, Technical and Medical business to form Wiley-Blackwell.

Registered Office
John Wiley & Sons Ltd, The Atrium, Southern Gate, Chichester, West Sussex, PO19 8SQ, United Kingdom

Editorial Offices
350 Main Street, Malden, MA 02148-5020, USA
9600 Garsington Road, Oxford, OX4 2DQ, UK
The Atrium, Southern Gate, Chichester, West Sussex, PO19 8SQ, UK

For details of our global editorial offices, for customer services, and for information about how to apply for permission to reuse the copyright material in this book please see our website at www.wiley.com/wiley-blackwell.

The rights of Jason Edwards to be identified as the editor of the editorial material in this work has been asserted in accordance with the Copyright, Designs and Patents Act 1988.

Wiley also publishes its books in a variety of electronic formats. Some content that appears in print may not be available in electronic books.

Designations used by companies to distinguish their products are often claimed as trademarks. All brand names and product names used in this book are trade names, service marks, trademarks or registered trademarks of their respective owners. The publisher is not associated with any product or vendor mentioned in this book. This publication is designed to provide accurate and authoritative information in regard to the subject matter covered. It is sold on the understanding that the publisher is not engaged in rendering professional services. If professional advice or other expert assistance is required, the services of a competent professional should be sought.

Library of Congress Cataloging-in-Publication Data
Edwards, Jason, 1971 Oct. 3-
  Retrieving the big society / edited by Jason Edwards.
    p. cm.
  Includes bibliographical references and index.
  ISBN 978-1-118-36878-7 (pbk.)
  1. Great Britain–Politics and government. I. Title.
JN318.E38 2012
320.520941–dc23
                            2012015777

Front cover image: William Hogarth, *Beer Street*, engraving, 1751.

Set in 10.5/12pt Palatino by Anne Joshua & Associates, Oxford
Printed in the UK by Charlesworth Press

1   2012

Contents

Notes on Contributors

Louise Bamfield is editor of *Impact* and a Visiting Research Fellow at the Department of Politics, University of Oxford.

Rodney Barker is Emeritus Professor of Government at the London School of Economics and Emeritus Professor of Rhetoric at Gresham College.

Johnston Birchall is Professor of Social Policy in the School of Social Sciences, Stirling University, and a Leverhulme Fellow.

Robert Crowcroft is Lecturer in Contemporary History at Edinburgh University.

Jason Edwards is Lecturer in Politics at the Department of Politics, Birkbeck, University of London and Co-Director of Birkbeck's Centre for the Study of British Politics and Public Life.

Alan Finlayson is Professor of Political and Social Theory in the School of Political, Social and International Studies, University of East Anglia.

Maurice Glasman is Reader in Political Theory and Director of the Faith and Citizenship Programme at London Metropolitan University. He was made a Labour peer in 2011.

Jose Harris is Emeritus Professor of Modern History at the University of Oxford and a Fellow of the British Academy.

Jeremy Jennings is Professor of Political Theory at Queen Mary, University of London.

Paul Kelly is at the Department of Government, LSE.

Richard Kelly is Head of Politics at Manchester Grammar School.

Adam Leeder is a PhD student in the Department of Politics, Birkbeck, University of London.

Deborah Mabbett is Professor of Public Policy in the Department of Politics, Birkbeck, University of London.

Jesse Norman is MP for Hereford and South Herefordshire and author of *The Big Society*.

Alan Ware is Professor and Tutor in Politics, Worcester College, University of Oxford.

Ben Williams is PhD candidate and postgraduate researcher at the Politics Department of the University of Liverpool.

© 2012 The Authors. The Political Quarterly © 2012 The Political Quarterly Publishing Co. Ltd
Published by Blackwell Publishing Ltd, 9600 Garsington Road, Oxford OX4 2DQ, UK and 350 Main Street, Malden, MA 02148, USA

Introduction
Retrieving the Big Society

JASON EDWARDS

THE SIGNIFICANCE of the formation of the coalition government in the United Kingdom in 2010 was not limited to it being the first such administration since 1945. The official coalition programme that emerged from negotiations between the Conservatives and Liberal Democrats proclaims a commitment to end the days of 'big government', to deal with the failure of 'centralisation and top-down control' by distributing 'power and opportunity to people rather than hoarding authority within government'.[1] While this was certainly not the first time an incoming government had pledged to take power out of the hands of the state and put it in the hands of 'the people', no previous postwar administration has advertised the intention with such fanfare. More remarkably, the substantive terms of this undertaking differ significantly from the dominant discourse of politics in Britain over the last thirty years: it is composed in the language of the 'Big Society'—the key motif that informed the policy agenda of the Conservatives after David Cameron's election as leader in 2005.

The idea of the Big Society has provoked bafflement in some quarters and cynicism in others. The contributors to this volume are united in thinking that the Big Society is more than bombast or window dressing for the coalition's deficit reduction programme. Its prominence at the heart of government marks an important shift in political attitudes in Britain to the relationship between the state and society. Until the financial crisis of 2008, Conservative and Labour governments had followed the neoliberal orthodoxy established under Margaret Thatcher's premiership. Neoliberals professed the virtues of the small state and the allocative efficiency of the market, yet over the past thirty years the state and its agencies have been strengthened while the general predilection for market deregulation contributed directly to present economic troubles. The idea of the Big Society was conceived prior to the present crisis, yet it was informed by anxieties regarding neoliberal government that had amounted over the decades: the lack of democratic control over managerialist bureaucracies in both the public and private sectors, and the socially dissociative effects of the pursuit of free-market economics and consumer capitalism.

But Big Society thinking is not just novel because it poses a challenge to the philosophical tenets of neoliberalism (even though its critics would argue that in certain policy matters—that is, with regard to the extension of private sector provision of public services—it constitutes a continuation of the neoliberal agenda), but because in doing so it asserts the value of an historical

Published by Blackwell Publishing Ltd, 9600 Garsington Road, Oxford OX4 2DQ, UK and 350 Main Street, Malden, MA 02148, USA

perspective on our current predicament. The Big Society laments a world that has been lost; a world where strong local politics, voluntary public service, and mutual and cooperative civic associations were at the heart of Britain's social and economic life. The years since 1945 have seen the gradual decay of this civil society, with its functions taken up by the state and, since the late 1970s, various quasi-public organisations and private companies licensed and contracted by the state. For Big Society thinkers, the combination of centralised state administration and Thatcherite 'free markets' has failed to provide the conditions for economic innovation and has created a 'broken society' where large number of citizens are left marginalised, idle, and dependent on social security benefits. The Big Society thus appears as an exercise in retrieval (and this is the first sense of the word to which the title of this volume points). The civil society we have lost must be retrieved and the responsibility for its resuscitation lies with the state.

The difficulty for many observers has been to discern the precise form of this retrieval. The frequently depthless political pitching of the Big Society disguises more substantial ideas. In his contribution, Paul Kelly shows that Cameron's vision of the Big Society owes a good deal to a particular understanding of liberal conservatism. Its liberalism resides in an embrace of the liberal norms and social pluralism of modern Britain. Of course, this is partly a strategic move for any political party concerned with pursuing power will look hopelessly old-fashioned should it campaign on a policy of turning the clock back to a 'nostalgic version of Britain in the 1950s'. However, Cameron's liberal conservatism concerns more than electoral appeal or the courting of (*Orange Book*) Liberal Democrat support. As is evident in the work of a key Big Society thinker, Jesse Norman, it also draws on the ideas of important twentieth-century political philosophers, including Friedrich Hayek and Michael Oakeshott. The latter's influence on this brand of liberal conservatism is particularly significant as it promotes the value of civil association while defending the notion of state neutrality with regard to questions of the good life. Accordingly, Kelly sees the Big Society as 'not merely an attempt to downsize the state and replace centralised provision with localism and mutualism', but as concerned with the construction of a 'free society that does not dominate'. Thus if the Big Society is the attempt at the retrieval of a lost civil society based on voluntary service, localism and mutualism, it is not so—at least not in Cameron's vision—because it seeks to return to a socially homogenous and conservative society.

The 'modernism' of the Big Society is also highlighted by Alan Finlayson. Yet this modernism is a reflection of a contemporary anti-establishment 'structure of feeling'. The architects of the Big Society are part of a generation who venerate the creative and socially entrepreneurial leader committed to 'social action'—the model of whom Finlayson takes, tongue only partly in cheek, to be the ubiquitous global rock star-cum-activist Bono. 'Bono-ism' consists of impatience with the formality of the 'system' and the manner in which it stifles the energy of the social entrepreneur in his or her efforts at social action. It emphasises the potential creative capacity of all people, and strives to set it free. For Finlayson, this mentality, which is a 'mélange of moral, political and aesthetic sensibilities', is 'a philosophical expression of a class formation: those whose labour is not directly productive but is also not wholly intellectual and whose income is derived from the production, manipulation and circulation of symbolic forms'. Cameronism channels its Bono-ism to an anti-statist commitment to the 'Post Bureaucratic Age'—an idea embraced by Cameron's chief political advisor, Steve Hilton. Yet as Finlayson suggests, the anti-statism of Cameronism does not involve a rejection of the idea that the lives of the (non-creative) individual should be governed, but seeks the transference of this task to a new 'creative' class of managers. The Big Society on this view remains a 'managerial problem'. Yet the new class of creative Bono-ist managers cannot see that while their outlook is 'very much in tune with the times [it] is, of course, a product of the times and not an account of them'.

Kelly and Finlayson thus ground the Big Society in particular strains of modern liberal-conservative political thought and the modern social sensibilities of the governing elite. This provides us with an important insight into the character of the kind of society that Big Society thinkers are interested in retrieving. In one important respect—in its apparent embrace of pluralism—it may appear that, as Rodney Barker puts it, the Big Society has stolen the democratic heritage of the left. Yet as Barker argues, pluralism is not and has not always been the property of the left. Whether a particular pluralism is of the right or the left is of less significance than the matter of 'exactly what kind of pluralism is being proposed, who benefits, who is in control and who is being controlled'. Like several other authors in the volume, Barker sees behind the Big Society's call for non-state providers of public services no surrender of the idea that the state should remain firmly in charge of the regulation and funding of such provision. There is nothing automatically attractive or convincing about the idea that non-state organisations are better than the state at delivering goods to citizens, for as Barker claims: 'If the social collectives from which the life of any individual is derived are varied, then groups are a resource for the citizen, not a defining community.' Without a comprehensive description of the character and role of the much-vaunted 'little platoons' of the Big Society, there is no reason to think that the pluralism it implies offers a convincing solution to our current predicament.

Barker suggests that the Big Society is thus in an important respect an empty concept, an idea pursued further in Jose Harris's account of various conceptions of 'society' in British political thought. A voluntarist and self-regulatory view of society held sway for much of the nineteenth century, but was challenged by more comprehensive and collectivist approaches that can be traced through the work of Tom Paine, Robert Owen and Tories such as Thomas Carlyle and John Ruskin. This tradition emphasised the civic aspects of social membership in a way that might seem to anticipate the Big Society, perhaps most obviously in the work of a figure such as Hilaire Belloc.

Belloc's attack on Edwardian social reform in his famous book, *The Servile State*—as Harris points out, often cited by Big Society thinkers such as Phillip Blond as a key influence—objected to the 'New Liberalism' as ruinous of the independence of civic institutions. Yet as Harris suggests, there has never been a consensus on the meaning of 'society' in modern British thought—in contrast to the meaning of the 'state' as the public power—and between these different views of society there 'seems no possibility of any shared ground'. Big Society thinkers often appear as wanting to reconcile a notion of society as a self-regulating contractual order (Adam Smith's 'Great Society') with the more comprehensive conception pointed to by Belloc. Whether this is an achievable reconciliation is, given the history Harris describes, highly questionable.

Harris contrasts the largely voluntarist conception of society in Britain in the nineteenth century with the more universalist idea characteristic of continental European thought. However, in his contribution Jeremy Jennings reminds us that one of the principal figures of mid-nineteenth century European political thought—Alexis de Tocqueville—was much exercised with the question of English society. More specifically, Tocqueville questioned the capacity of England to retain its system of aristocratic and local self-government, while in contrast he saw in America—notwithstanding the potential dangers posed by 'democratic despotism' to liberty—the basis of a free society in the power of civil association. Indeed, Jennings takes Tocqueville's work, in the context of nineteenth-century liberalism, as providing the grounds for 'a critical appraisal of the associational and participatory dimensions of the Big Society'. The associational life of America was sustained by a combination of the 'spirit of religion and the mores of liberty'; yet for Jennings these conditions are absent from contemporary British society. There is no 'spirit of religion', in the sense of substantive shared civic values, that could inspire people to social action, and the 'mores of liberty' have been subverted by the materialism of consumer capitalism.

Accordingly, Jennings is sceptical about claims for the social basis of the Big Society, a view shared by Alan Ware. Ware sees the Big Society as a certain supplement to the New Right thinking of Thatcherite Conservatism, in part guided by a return to the idea of the role of the 'Third Sector' set out by earlier Conservative thinkers such as James Douglas. However, where Big Society thinking differs from these earlier Conservative ideas of decentralisation is in the role it attributes to local neighbourhoods and communities, mutual organisations, and a national citizen service. On the face of it, support for these institutions seems designed to appeal across the political spectrum, but Ware suggests it is a fundamentally flawed strategy. Local neighbourhoods, in particular, look to be the vehicles of the Big Society, yet as Ware argues there is little reason to believe that they could be substantive sites of revived civic association. As territorial units, neighbourhoods have been weakened across the twentieth century by geographical mobility, the privatisation of lifestyles and more recent developments in social media that make 'virtual' communities as, if not more, important than local neighbourhoods. Thus for Ware, the Big Society 'comes no nearer than any of the earlier attempts to resolving the long-term difficulties of how to govern a large population that no longer inhabits the well defined territorial units through which traditional sources of power had been exercised earlier'.

The concerns expressed by Jennings and Ware regarding the social basis of the Big Society point to the difficulties and complexities involved in governing a society characterised by deep pluralism. The chapters by Jason Edwards, Richard Kelly and Robert Crowcroft, and Benjamin Williams explore in different ways the tension between the integrative social impulse of the Big Society and its seemingly centrifugal governmental commitments. Edwards argues that the problem stems from the manner in which the Big Society sees its institutions as 'free' only in the sense that they are free to pursue programmes of 'social action' that are oriented towards particular socio-economic goals, in particular the aim of restoring individual and social 'responsibility'. By drawing a contrast between the ideas of free institutions to be found in the work of Adam Smith and Edmund Burke—two figures who have been identified by Big Society thinkers such as Norman as key progenitors—Edwards claims that the Big Society is closer to a Burkean understanding of free institutions as the expression of a stratified organic social order. The Smithian view, in contrast, points towards the importance of the independence of free institutions—a freedom that is sustained under the invigilation of the state. At the same time, however, Smith's concerns about the corruption of public power lead to an intimation of republicanism in his thought in the view that free institutions must invigilate the invigilator. Edwards argues that this republican view of free institutions in political theory is overlooked by Big Society thought; the 'freedom' of its institutions is freedom only in managerial terms to pursue social goals set out by the state, not a freedom concerned with the autonomy of free institutions from the state and their political role in invigilating the public power.

Kelly and Crowcroft also turn to Edmund Burke's work, though to different ends. They see in Burke's work resources for a defence of 'conservative multiculturalism' as a vital supplement to the Big Society. Cameron's denunciation of multiculturalism in a speech in February 2011 is seen by Kelly and Crowcroft as a mistaken repudiation of an important part of the conservative tradition. Multiculturalism may be seen as having emerged organically, modern Britain being a society of 'little platoons' that are multi-cultural in character. The Conservative party, they suggest, would do well to recognise that its Tory values—'stressing tradition, authority, religious morality, established institutions and local paternalism'—chime well with those of many BME (Black, Minority, Ethnic) communities in contemporary Britain. Kelly and Crowcroft thus pose a challenge to the liberal and pluralist dimensions of the Big Society, highlighting one of the reasons why Tories have been uncomfortable with the Cameronian vision. Williams also addresses some of the problems Cameron has had in selling the Big Society to the Conservative party and the wider public. Part of this problem has involved the manner in which the 'broken society' has been constructed in Cameronism—a concept which has been taken by some Conservatives as an extreme exaggeration of the state of contemporary Britain. The prospects of the Big Society as a successful 'post-bureaucratic social policy' have been undermined by the extent of state intervention in social and economic life suggested by the notion of the broken society. In addition, as Williams and several other contributors suggest, the policy of austerity that the coalition has followed in its relentless pursuit of deficit reduction seems incompatible with the kind of social reconstruction that would be required to move towards the ideal of the Big Society.

The final three chapters turn to a detailed assessment of some of the key policies introduced by the coalition under the umbrella of the Big Society. Adam Leeder and Deborah Mabbett examine the Free Schools policy, which, by allowing schools to contract directly with central government, is designed to encourage parents in local communities to set up new schools for whose governance they will be (partly) responsible. Leeder and Mabbett argue that the governance arrangements put in place 'are liable to atrophy over time, leaving either teachers or for-profit education providers in charge'. Moreover, standards of education consistent with the public interest—standards the government is charged with preserving—are threatened by the fact that 'it requires that the public interest can be pursued just by aggregating numerous private interests'. The danger of the assumption that the public interest is just 'what parents want' is that it may lead to an education system that is 'even more divisive' than at present—something which in the long-run may be addressed by stronger state control over school governance.

Johnston Birchall addresses the devolution of public service provision to employee mutuals. Birchall points out that the coalition's commitment to mutualism is not as innovative as it might at first sight appear, with the 'new mutualism' of Labour in government having led to the promotion of foundation hospitals, and the various efforts of the Conservatives under Thatcher and Major to devolve public service provision to institutions such as grant maintained schools and Health Trusts. Nonetheless, the coalition's plans for the promotion of the role of employee-owned mutuals in public service provision go much further than anything seen before. Birchall's assessment of the policy to date is that its impact has been limited. There are a number of reasons for this: economic austerity discourages workers from wanting to take on risks associated with setting up mutuals; concerns over the capacity of relatively small organisations to fund pension schemes; and competition from large companies which tends to drive out small, local providers. In short, current conditions make mutualisation too risky for most employees.

Birchall points to a problem for the economics of Big Society thinking, which remains committed to the view that the character of the service provider is unimportant, be they private, public, mutual or cooperative organisations, as long as competition is encouraged and the provider gives best value for money. Yet it is evident that this commitment to neutrality concerning the internal constitution of the providing organisation is at odds with the notion of empowering self-governing civic institutions. Without extensive state involvement in crafting markets that work for particular kinds of market agents, existing markets will tend to favour and empower large private providers or simply fail to make provision for those with few or no resources to take to the market. In that scenario we are left with powerful private providers catering to resource-wealthy consumers, and the state or impoverished voluntary organisations providing for the less well-off.

Louise Bamfield makes a similar point in her exploration of the provision of 'early years' services for families and young children under the present government. The coalition has moved away from a universal system of early years provision, exemplified in the Sure Start programme, devolving responsibility for budgets to local authorities. This has lead to the scaling down and closure of Sure Start Children's Centres. Thus Bamfield argues that a seemingly decentralising act threatens to undermine Big Society aspirations for promoting personal agency and responsibility and encouraging civic engagement: 'Ironically, the shift away from universal provision will undermine both aims, since children's centres provide an ideal model of the independent, overlapping community, while also supporting particular individuals on a journey of personal empowerment.'

The volume opens with the transcript of a discussion between Maurice Glasman and Jesse Norman that took place at Birkbeck College in November 2011. As already noted, Norman is one of the leading intellectual exponents of the Big Society, as well as being a Member of Parliament and an important adviser to David Cameron. Maurice Glasman, ennobled by Labour leader Ed Miliband in 2011, is an academic and architect of 'Blue Labour'—a movement that has been of some influence in the interest shown by Labour under Miliband in the party's lost traditions of localism, mutualism and associationalism. The discussion between Glasman and Norman is salutary for two reasons. First, it shows that despite widespread cynicism about politics and politicians, high ideas still have an important role in public affairs. Only the most churlish critic of the Big Society would claim that is has had zero impact in promoting public debate on important issues about how we govern ourselves—a point, I hope, brought home by the publication of this volume. Second, it shows that whatever we might think about the character and prospects for the Big Society—and for some it is already looking like a decidedly exhausted project—it has contributed to an important shift in the language of politics in an age when new political solutions to a familiar crisis are desperately required. Clearly, the retrieval of a golden age of local community and civic activism is an unrealisable fantasy. However, the retrieval of ideas about how we might best govern ourselves democratically without subjection to the dictates of either the market or the state remains an immensely valuable project, towards which it is hoped this book makes a small contribution.

Note

1 http://www.cabinetoffice.gov.uk/sites/default/files/resources/coalition_
programme_for_government.pdf

The Big Society in Question

MAURICE GLASMAN and JESSE NORMAN

The following is the edited transcript of a discussion between Maurice Glasman and Jesse Norman that took place at Birkbeck College on 3 November 2011. The event was hosted by The Political Quarterly *and Birkbeck's Centre for the Study of British Politics and Public Life.*

Chair's question: What do you both understand by the 'Big Society'?

Jesse Norman At one level, the Big Society is a phrase and idea which is new in political debate in this country and in another sense is extremely old. In my answer, I would ask you to suspend any disbelief you might have about it arising from your own political inclinations and just try to take it in this context on the basis of the idea and on the basis of what I am going to say about its history.

When the idea was introduced in December 2009 in the Hugo Young Lecture by David Cameron, it was greeted with a mixture of reactions and those became crystallised when it was an important theme in the 2010 general election campaign. It has been described as either empty, or viciously full of content and a kind of cover for cuts. Actually I don't think it is either of those things. One way in which it differs from the Third Way, which I regard as a piece of pure triangulation with some political but no intellectual merit, is that there is this history, this coherent set of ideas sitting behind it and in many ways it is not a set of ideas uniquely identified with the right of the political spectrum. Quite to the contrary, the reason it has political purchase now is because in some respects it is picking up things that are very deeply embedded in the centre left.

So, what is it then? The way I tend to introduce it is by thinking about Hobbes and his idea of a social contract, which is designed to be an answer to the questions 'by what right does government exercise authority over us?' and 'what grounds the legitimacy of sovereign power of the state?'. Hobbes' answer is that the social contract is a rational reaction to the possibility of being in a state of nature that would otherwise exist and that this state of nature is one in which people are perennially in fear of violent death because there is nothing that prevents that happening. It is a Darwinian struggle, it is what he calls the war of all against all and in it life is, in his famous words, 'solitary, poor, nasty, brutish and short'. So what happens is that people get together, they give up a degree of their own self-sovereignty, their own autonomy; they repose that in a sovereign entity, they allow that sovereign entity through a process of consent or acknowledgement to exercise control

Published by Blackwell Publishing Ltd, 9600 Garsington Road, Oxford OX4 2DQ, UK and 350 Main Street, Malden, MA 02148, USA

over them and it does so by guaranteeing the external borders of the society and by guaranteeing its internal order. From that there arises all of the other things that make up a society. When you look at things this way, the Big Society can be seen as a kind of attempt to kick back on two of the implicit assumptions in that picture.

One is an assumption about institutions because in the Hobbesian picture, there are no institutions—there is only an individual or a set of individuals and the state. There is nothing else that fills this picture at all. It is, in effect, a piece of game theory. You start off with individual agents, you give them a utility function—in this case the desire to avoid violent death—you follow the logic and guess what? You end up with a theory of sovereign power and the state. It is rather like having a miniscule top hat and pulling out of it a rabbit the size of the Empire State Building. You start off with very small assumptions and you end up with marvellously fat conclusions. It misses out the idea of an independent or free institution. The other thing it misses out is the idea of a rich conception of human nature because these people are really just acting as what you might call economic automata, maximising their utility by trying to avoid death and other obstacles to self-gratification. So it has a very thin conception of human nature and that, by design, is part of the picture.

In contrast, the Big Society is about empowering free and independent institutions that lie between the individual and the state, and it is about empowering individuals on the basis of a rich conception of human nature.

Let me sum up with two points. The first is, if you read it like this, the Big Society actually is a rather deep intellectual attempt to correct some of the basic assumptions that sit behind our politics. The second thing is that it poses a challenge in each of these dimensions to conventional political thinking. So the emphasis on free and independent institutions points against a certain tendency to what you might call Fabianism, state-first thinking about society that has grown up in the country, across the political divide, mainly on the Labour side and at times on the Tory side: one thinks of Harold Macmillan and one thinks of the postwar period. It opposes positions sometimes regarded as on the 'right', what at times is called 'libertarianism', because if you have a rich conception of the individual, you don't have a view that people are just neoliberal walking automata. You are not just conservative, small 'c', about your politics, or Burkean about your politics as 'little platoons', you are also conservative about your economics and that is a rather interesting development because if there is one thing that we know from the financial crash and from Occupy Wall Street, the received understanding of economics is not working very well at the moment. It has challenges that face in both directions.

Finally, you will notice that neither of these ideas is enormously well picked up in our academic categories. We have well-functioning theories of the state through economics and politics; we have well-functioning theories of the individual through individual rationality, psychology and physiology. We don't really have well-functioning theories about all of the institutions that lie in between. Those institutions are what give point and purpose and meaning to our lives, whether it is Chelsea Football Club, the Women's Institute, the Church of England, the Jewish faith or Birkbeck College.

Maurice Glasman First of all it is important to say I agree with Jesse about the shared orientation that we have in terms of an essentially Aristotelian conception of politics, of politics that puts relationships and institutions in a very important place. But I think that the Big Society is almost like an abandoned child at the moment. It finds itself mired in the financial crisis, the lack of growth, the cuts agenda and all of that. It is in danger of looking superficial rather than deep.

In theoretical terms, I would say the position I develop, the 'good society', is quite conservative, and works with traditions focusing on reciprocity, but it is quite radical in its economics in contrast to the Big Society, whose weakness is that it cannot conceptually, as well as politically, confront money, power and capitalism as forms of exploitation. We are currently in a very exciting moment with the very strange story of protest against City.[1] When I went down there on the first day, the only question was 'are we going to abolish capitalism today?' (that was the radical view) and then the more moderate view was 'we are going to abolish capitalism tomorrow'. That was the sort of exchange that was going on and it has led to a profound discussion of the relationship between the great institutions of the realm: the Cathedral, the Church, what is the role of the Church in the polity; what is the role of the corporation of the City of London (which is one of the great institutions, the most ancient city democracy in our country and the only part of England that wasn't conquered by Normans in 1066). And these institutions have been entirely conquered by money and financial interests. Our most ancient democratic Big Society institution, the City of London, is now in fact a lobbyist for the financial sector and for the deregulation of everything, except, obviously, itself.

The reason I mention this is first to place this discussion in the very vivid contemporary moment in which we find ourselves, but also to point to the limits that the Big Society has. On the whole, its critique of the statism of New Labour is fundamentally correct: there was a humiliation and neglect of people, particularly poor people. They were not given any power. New Labour was excessively managerial in its conception of both the private and public sector. On a philosophical note, it was entirely driven by external goods: goods of equality, goods of eliminating obesity, eliminating sexual intercourse before the age of 21; accessibility, diversity, inclusivity, etc. The academics here will recognise this kinds of good under the label of 'aims and objectives', something we have to fill in for the Quality Assurance people when we write courses—that is, we are not interested in what you teach, rather the transferability of the skill that you teach and other external goods and external goals. The great thing about Jesse's work and the very important thing about the Big Society is that it tries to bring things back to the internal goods of practices and institutions of goodness, of knowledge, of skill, of excellence, of good practice. If there is a single rebuke to be made of the New Labour period it is that it had an absolute contempt for traditional practices and viewed them as blocking innovation, accessibility, modernisation in the public sector.

What is not present in and does not seem to be developing at all out of the Big Society agenda is a similar critique of managerialism applied to the market—the relentless concentration of power in the money markets in particular. In an Aristotelian sense, the great problem is that money power is the greatest form of external good because what it does is it transforms all of the different forms of internal goods into one external metric which then becomes an end in itself, but the end is the insatiable desire of people for more money.

In that sense, what you have is a very great timidity upon the Conservative side of the Big Society agenda in extending the critique of the state to a critique of the market and therefore looking at the type of institutions, vocational institutions, even—perish the thought—trade unions, that have a role of defending human dignity through democratic association and that gets to the nub of the issue. The issue is: what does Jesse mean by free institutions? Institutions like universities, the British Medical Association, the Law Society have powers over their members and a very important part of the good society agenda is to increase the autonomy of such institutions in order to promote the good within the economic sphere. Here there is a very strong stress on the authority of vocational institutions to interfere with managerial prerogatives where the short-term interests of capital conflict with the preservation of knowledge and the necessity of innovation within that sphere. Vocational institutions play a very important role. Knowledge institutions, like universities, are relentlessly pushed to be subordinate to external goods as laid out by the state, but what about the specificity and value of their traditions? Birkbeck used to be a sister institution of what was the original London Metropolitan University, the Workers Educational Association—indeed Birkbeck and the Workers Educational Association in East London used to work out of the same building. The point being that there is a very specific internal good relating to Birkbeck (and the WEA) about opening up knowledge and education to working people. That is what I would call its vocation, and it has the character of an internal good.

So just to summarise, in the good society approach there is great overlap with the Big Society in terms of its view of the state, but the proviso is that voluntary association in itself is insufficient; there has to be strong, democratic, autonomous institutions that uphold the good. In terms of state reform, the three 'Blue Labour' Rs would apply: relationships, reciprocity and responsibility. In respect of relationships, when Jesse talks about the opposition between the Hobbesian state and the individual, it is inconceivable from my perspective that you don't also talk about markets—so that there is the state and market in the context of a society, and what has been extremely attenuated is the relational culture that builds power for individuals to associate. This idea was present within a certain pre-1945 Labour tradition that resisted both the exploitation of the market and the oppression of the state. In regard to reciprocity, here we have roughly speaking three forms of power. There is market power, which has the form of the contract which is the exchange of goods between people through the exchange of equivalents overseen by contract. And then you have state power, which fundamentally manifests itself through forms of redistribution and coercion. And finally, there is relational power that is the form of a society. So the fundamental state power works through taxation and coercion, the fundamental market power works through exchange and contract, and then you have as the form of social power a democracy that works through the building up of associations in pursuit of the good. And it is through this democratic society that responsibility is engendered.

What has been neglected, I would say, is that we have swung relentlessly since the 1930s between state power and market power. What is absolutely necessary is a new politics that uses power as rooted in the associations and relationships people can generate with each other in pursuit of the common good. Just to pick up on a small hint given by Jesse, I think that would lead to a transformation of the role of faith communities in the pursuit of the good. Christianity in its Catholic form and in certain of its Protestant forms is very important and there is a growing body of Islamic thought that is concerned with pursuing good and forbidding wrong and I think that is a very interesting voice in this.

Roughly speaking, a democratic decentralised society built around human relationships is central, so as well as relationships, reciprocity and responsibility, I would just mention the three Vs, which are vocation, virtue (the internal goods that institutions uphold, standards of excellence and quality, and innovation around these standards) and value. Capital doesn't generate value, management doesn't generate value, the workforce generates innovation and value. And I am very committed to the re-establishment of vocational colleges, regional banks, representation of the workforce, and the governance and balance of power. Ultimately, the weakness with the Big Society is at the moment it doesn't have a radical and traditional view of the constitutional changes that we need at local levels, at local government levels and in the countryside to renew the power of people to associate in order to transform their lives, because it is still quite committed to a concept of volunteerism that cannot change the domination of capital.

Chair's question: What are the intellectual antecedents of the Big Society? To what extent is there in the history of British (and/or English) thought precedents for the Big Society?

MG Let's talk about this as a mutual tradition and something opposed to straightforward liberalism, which is by definition social contractual, abstract, individual. We can talk about it as an aspect of the national tradition. There are two points. The first is that alone in Europe, there developed in England a concept of the balance of power. This was transformative for England as a tradition. It was never accepted in England that there was the divine right of kings. It wasn't just challenged by the Levellers and the Diggers, it was absolutely challenged by Parliament, by the City of London and challenged on the basis of ancient liberties. The idea of the free-born Englishman was fundamental. When William the Conqueror came, there was a refusal of statute law, there was a refusal of the will of the king and it was done on the basis of ideas of liberty and democracy. This is the very interesting inheritance. It is not purely Anglo-Saxon, it is also in the Nordic tradition, in the Danish tradition and continuing the Roman tradition of citizenship and civic life, and this is certainly the case in the history of London as a city.

What we have therefore is very distinctive form of a British polity that is based on the idea there should never be domination of a single sovereign will and this took the form of the ancient constitution. One of the pillars of the ancient constitution is in a weird way being played right now at the footsteps of St Paul's [the Occupy movement]. The first and perhaps least relevant aspect was the monarchy. The monarchy in that time expressed leadership and political action; it was the executive, as well as the idea of family and tradition. Then there was Parliament, split into two, with the House of Commons representing the people on a territorial basis and the House of Lords traditionally more vocational: the Church and the universities were represented there as well as the land. The Church was an endowed landowner who consistently opposed the enclosure of land in favour of the common good until Archbishop Laud had his head chopped off, and it hasn't spoken about capitalism since. This is the terrible silence of Rowan Williams at the moment, who is sitting there, desperate to say 'we are with the protesters and we understand there has been a huge dominion of the rich for too long in our country'. But in the ancient constitution, the Church represented just that. Then there is the City of London which is the fourth pillar of the ancient constitution which is supposed to represent the democracy of the City.

The idea was of the balance of those institutions and that is extremely unique in the development of European thought. We swung between divine right monarchy and popular sovereignty. It has never been the case that the English tradition has been of unmediated popular sovereignty. The rule of the Commons, the rule of Parliament has always been mediated by other traditions and institutions that hold it in balance.

In terms of the Big Society, it is vitally important that we look at a very distinctive national tradition: one that is paradoxical and not rational, that is not committed to the priority of liberty or the priority of equality, but to both; that is committed to very strong democracy and individual liberty and doesn't see those two as conflicting; and committed to local institutions and that have the authority to pursue the common good. We never had the split between Church and State; we never had the split between the principle of democracy and monarchy; we never accepted the Norman Conquest as a *fait accompli*. The Norman Conquest was a blow, but now we are getting there! It is not just the Levellers in the south; it is also the pilgrimage of grace, the Catholic tradition in the north that did not accept the enclosures and the dissolution of the monasteries. I could go on, but that is a huge aspect of this neglected tradition that says we are not French and we are not American either, but we are distinctively English and the English tradition is both radical and traditional and does not accept that ranking priority of rationalism, but believes the virtues of the country lay in the tensions of the energy generated by conflicting systems of sovereignty held simultaneously.

JN I agree with a lot of what Maurice has said and it is no accident that it was the Stuart monarchy's desire to insist on the divine right of kings in the early seventeenth century that helped to precipitate the coming apart of these different parts of the estates of the realm and therefore the English Civil War, or the War of Three Kingdoms as it is sometimes known.

But I do think that there is a pervasive intellectual mistake which Maurice is making, that is worth just bringing out, and that is between the politics of the Big Society, the label as it is brought into politics, and the ideas that sit behind it. It is very important to say that because if you don't say that, it is very hard to understand that actually the ideas we are talking about contain within them a profound critique of financial capitalism. And not only do they contain a profound critique of financial capitalism, it is also the only really interesting critique that can be made because the Left, essentially, in its post-Fabian form, really lacks the ability to articulate the problem, which is that capitalism is not one thing. It is an enormous array of possible different ways of organising an economy and part of the problem is with the idea that somehow history ended in 1989 with the end of the opposition between capitalism and communism. Of course, history did not end; as Francis Fukuyama acknowledges, it only just began. It was at that point we had to start reflecting on what capitalism really meant and what variety we wanted. One of the things that unites Maurice and me is that we are perfectly clear we do not want the current variety of financial capitalism.

Originally, the basic source is Aristotle: the idea of habit, the idea of taking an individual as a person seriously in the way they actually live and by extension taking a nation seriously in its own actual cultural traditions and seeing what resources can be quarried out of that. In Aristotle, the idea of habit naturally generates the idea of a habit pursued well or a virtue or a habit shared, a practice or a practice taken as a habit shared, shared over a period of time or an institution. That is where the idea of an institution really comes from: it has an Aristotelian root.

What is fascinating is that the modern idea of the Big Society in my reading, certainly from a centre-right reading, and there is a parallel story to be told on the centre-left, goes back to the eighteenth century; it goes back to Adam Smith and it goes back to Burke. Smith's first book was *The Theory of the Moral*

Sentiments, and not *The Wealth of Nations*. *The Theory of the Moral Sentiments* has as its governing idea the notion that morality is fundamentally based on a notion of sympathy or mutual recognition. There is a radical egalitarianism and there is a radical Aristotelian attention to what an individual is actually like—to an individual's psychology—and it is that that is used to ground his morals. What comes out of that in Smith is a very nuanced and thoughtful understanding of the market, in which there is no time at all for this completely financially dominated notion of markets in which they are ends in themselves or are completely frictionless activities which must be allowed to flow as freely as possible. To Smith, a market is a cultural artefact. It is an embedded thing you find in society. It has a purpose and its purpose includes allocating certain goods and that is why markets are allowed to exist and that is why people grant them that degree of legitimacy.

Burke picks up this idea; Burke and Smith have very similar economics although Burke's aren't that well known, but actually, he is very, very Smithian in his economics, in some respects in a parallel way rather than derived (they knew each other quite well). Burke takes this understanding both as a philosopher and as a politician. It is a very radical conception because if you take that notion of fundamental equality for granted, as an assumption of your moral picture, and you regard these free institutions— 'little platoons' as he calls them—as being foundationally important to society that derives from them, then of course a threat to those little civil institutions, to that culture, to those traditions, will be any form of excessive power. In Burke, you see the attack on excessive power played out through a whole series of battles. One is his attack on the king through the holding of a so-called 'double cabinet' throughout the 1780s. A second one, most famously, is his attack on corporate power: the East India Company which he regards as looting and abusing its own status in India for personal good. So a radical critique of excess is embedded in this Big Society tradition.

The nineteenth century was a high point in liberalism. John Stuart Mill in his economic writings says you should only pay attention in economics to the human individual as a vehicle for gain or loss. That is the tap root of this notion of liberalism that Maurice and I are both fighting.

If you come into the twentieth century, you get Michael Oakeshott who sustains and elaborates the Burkean critique of rationalism—the idea that you can impose a plan on people, that you can take institutions and corral them on a Procrustian bed, cut off the bits that stick out at the end and stretch the bits that don't quite make it to the end of the bed. Oakeshott, of course, also makes a very important distinction between civil association and enterprise association. Civil association is construed under the category of practice, while enterprise association lies under the category of purpose. That gives him a critique of totalitarianism and that is what happens when a society is taken over for a governing purpose. That purpose might be religious purity, it might be racial purity as in Nazism, it might be a certain concept of productivity of industrial strength as happened with Stalinism.

The final person I want to mention in this whistle stop tour is the most misunderstood and most bandied-around name in this area, Hayek. Everyone thinks Hayek is a pure apostle of the free market. He is not. Hayek takes the view I take: he says it would not be too much to say that we as individuals are determined by our positions in society. He has a very heavily relational view of the individual and he also famously says no one can be an economist who is only an economist. He takes into the practice of economics itself the requirement that people are not just to be considered as little automata, but have to be granted a wider hinterland and be understood as culturally embedded. All that story fits very compatibly with the picture Maurice has so eloquently painted of the different estates of the realm.

Chair's question: But is it not the case that historically the state in England (and Britain) has always been much stronger than you both suggest? This is not a recent innovation: what we think of as the 'Common Law' was given form by the state after the Norman Conquest and was absolutely consistent with the King's law.

JN I think you misread the Common Law slightly. The Common Law is a set of decisions made by judges over six hundred years. It is the effect of that very gradual accumulation of decisions that sets the laws by implication, because of the precedent that they set. The reason why that is so important is because it is genuinely a law of the land—because those judges would have been sitting around the country making decisions on specific cases which are then brought together and codified in various ways—most famously, by Blackstone in the eighteenth century. It is precisely that Burkean process of linking to the land through these little institutions and building up a common social understanding that is so telling. And you are right, the state did grow up in a completely different way in this country from others for a variety of extraordinarily interesting reasons.

You can date the history of the state to somewhere between King Alfred and Thomas Cromwell depending on which part you think makes the difference. The settlement of 1689 when William III comes over and we create the King-in-Parliament as the sovereign power unleashed an extraordinary moment in British history because it was the first time that the monarchy had explicitly been, as it were, trapped by Parliament. The reason why that is so important is that the monarch then became trustworthy, because Parliament was essentially in control. And because the Crown became trustworthy, the national finances which were still located in the King became trustworthy and robust. Instead of forced loans and the sale of peerages and Crown lands to raise money, the King could credibly borrow, and because he could borrow, Britain's national debt went through the sky. The King brought with him various wonderful Dutch financial practices, which were instrumental in the creation of the Bank of England. All of that was good because it had a balance to it—the balance which has now been lost in our financial markets. It meant that in the eighteenth century, we were fighting a whole series of continental wars at interest rates that were 4 per cent below the continental superpower, France. That means that the Battle of Trafalgar was essentially won in 1689. It wasn't won in 1805.

It remained a settled policy of British naval power to have more ships than the rest of the world's navies combined until about the 1870s. The reason I mention this is the fact that we had a navy and were a seaborne nation profoundly contributed to our pluralism as a country. Broadly speaking, if you have an army, you can make them fight by pointing a gun at men and telling them they need to go and fight. It is very compatible with high levels of hierarchy and centralisation. If you run a navy, you are stuck if don't have the consent of the people involved, because every ship is a mini city in its own right. Every ship relies on a staggering array of artisans who make the ships themselves, the ropes, the sails. It is an amazing middle-class artisanal plurality that was the guarantor of this very diverse constitution that we ended up with. That is why Anglomania—a passion for England and for English values and openness and tolerance—swept across Europe in the eighteenth century, and was secured by the settlement of 1688 and by the navy. That is why Voltaire could look across the channel and weep with anger and rage that these values couldn't exist in highly centralised, rather autocratic, highly hierarchical, heavily church dominated France.

MG There are lots of interesting things there, Jesse. One important thing to mention is the British Empire and the distinction between the maritime economy, a commercial and commodified economy, where the was no state regulation and couldn't be any state regulation of contract, and the territorial economy which was a direct inheritance from Athens and in a way from Rome of the rulership of the seas. That was a crucial thing with the navy.

Back to your question. The City of London was the key to the debt that generated naval power. It is the reason why the Treasury has had such a large role in the formation of the British state. What was unique in its formation was this combination of the Royal Navy and the Treasury. We've lost the navy and unfortunately we still have the Treasury. One of my arguments for Labour when it next gets into power is to get Industry in at number 11 and break up the Treasury.

What was vital was not just that Britain was a seafaring nation, but the institutional nature of the state and its role. The state was very powerful in Britain in many different ways and it took many different forms and there was always this refusal of the City of London to accept the royal prerogative and to defend the principle of federalism, of local democracy, and the refusal to allow the king to appoint the mayor. So in London today, we are still not a united city, we still live in a shanty town structure. What is the Greater London Authority? It is an elected body, but are they advisers, are they some kind of parliament, are they a council, are they with the Mayor? It is all just managerial nonsense. Then you've got the Corporation of the City of London which has not been allowed to legislate from time immemorial. So what you have is a state that is powerful and has powerful institutions but is never entirely dominated by any single interest or a simple principle of its organisation. It is a silly argument that says we are basically America. That is a kind of liberal madness.

What is necessary is to have a different concept of what diversity means, of what pluralism means when thinking about the development of the state in terms of institutional balances of power. What happened over time, the global, the international, the maritime economy came to play an increasingly important role and so where we are today with this huge volatility and dependence on financial services is due to the incredible power that international capital and business always had in the British state, and it meant that industrial capital got beaten decisively in whatever form that took, whether it be Wilsonian industrial policy or Baldwinian national renewal.

JN But what about the Labour story, Maurice? What about Gordon Brown saying in the city of London: we will do for this country's economy what we have done for the City of London?

MG Yes, and it turned out to be a prophesy. But I want to get to Hayek as this is important theoretically and politically. In Hayek's anthropology, which I am inspired by and I think is brilliant, he talks about tradition as a mediating principle between instinct and rationality and how it is that in England in particular certain forms of tradition preserve promise-keeping, honesty and relationality, from the excessive demands of a rationality that tries to individualise us and tries to abstract us from all forms of embedded reason. On the other side, he refers to a certain form of instinct, what he would consider an atavism that is hostile to outsiders and development of what he calls a 'catallaxy—a system of cooperation between people where enemies are turned into friends. In his economics, however, he just talks about the state and the market. He doesn't theorise in any serious level what those traditional institutions would be that would preserve knowledge, honesty, trust, skill, within a rationalist economic system. There is a theoretical tension that we have got going and I am constantly trying to bring this into regulating market exchanges.

Chair's question: Going back to Jesse's account of Smith and Burke's importance for the Big Society, might we not perhaps see two different visions of the Big Society here? On the one hand, Smith's advocacy of markets and 'commercial exchange'—in its broadest sense of cultural and economic exchange between active citizens—is concerned with countering the corrupt uses of the state by the aristocracy, whereas Burke's organicist advocacy of the 'little platoons' is in many regards a defence of social hierarchy and exclusion, involving a role for natural aristocracy. Does this map onto a split in the contemporary conservative account of the Big Society between the kind of view of active citizenship in Jesse's work, and the more organicist view to be found in the work of someone such as Phillip Blond?

JN I don't think that Smith is an enormous advocate of what is understood now as *laissez-faire*. That wasn't his term. It was a term that was used by the physiocrats and I am also slightly nervous about reading the market as the supervisor of the state. The state wasn't really regarded as a problem in such a way as it is now in eighteenth-century Scotland. The monarchy is a different matter. There is a sense in which Smith targets the aristocracy and what you might call the producing interest—often represented by the same people as the aristocracy would progressively coopt the very rapidly industrialising new money. I don't divide it up the way you do. Equally I don't think that Burke holds quite the view that you describe. Burke is deeply small 'c' conservative. There is a notion of the social order which is the relationship between institutions. They have embedded wisdom; it is in the nature of that social order, which has historically evolved in Britain, that there is a group of people who have the burden and also the privilege of being the leading people in that social order. He defends the aristocracy of virtue rather than the aristocracy of privilege to which he is extremely hostile in many ways. He has this extraordinary tension and interplay between his views of society as an organic ordered whole and his very radical critique of revolution as that overturns this ordered whole.

We have just had the 221st anniversary of the publication of *Reflections on the Revolution in France* in which Burke does something remarkable. He was regarded as the man by many people in Britain who had been the great apologist for the American Revolution, and they thought he would support the French Revolution. This was quite wrong: what he really doesn't like is the abuse of power, and the Crown was abusing its power against the colonists and he thinks in contrast the revolutionaries in France were imposing their power on society. He says, forget all these highfalutin 'ideas'. The social order, the common law, the understanding of the land, this root in society is being swept away in France and the results can only be disorder, violence, terror and autocracy. And guess what, they then get disorder, violence, terror and autocracy. So he was absolutely right about that. I think there is extraordinary tension between that notion of social order and his own remarkably egalitarian views of individual virtue and capabilities. Burke gets into a problem: if you have a manifestly unbalanced society that is grossly out of whack as our society is now, I don't think Burke is going to say that is all hunky dory, but you need reform to correct the problem. What you must not be doing is leaping off the other end with some disastrous set of innovations or revolutionary change that will themselves do more harm than the good they seek to solve.

MG Jesse and I have never discussed Burke before! I wrote a piece on Burke saying that he was right about revolution, that it must lead to terror and it is completely conceptually impossible and that the idea there is going to be something radically new leads to a complete madness about who you are and what you are and a blindness to continuities through time and therefore a deep uselessness. That is true with the centralisation of the French state and is also true with all revolutions that they must lead to an unknown terror which wraps itself up in a superficial rationalist virtue.

But I maintain that Burke's view of the market and in some ways of the American Revolution prefigures the lack of development of a radical critique of the market we find in liberalism. This is also the dilemma with Smith. What Mandeville and Smith and the whole lot came up with was a wrong paradox. The paradox they put forward which we are now living in the ruins of, economically as well as politically, is essentially the statement that if you do bad, it will end up good. But the most good you can do is to be bad. That is the invisible hand. We've got to the point where we may as well try being good. Acting consciously and explicitly discussing what is the good and trying to achieve it, because the selfish motivations of individuals on the market haven't succeeded in producing public benefit. And as a massive signal that the invisible hand doesn't work that way, it leads to the storing up of trouble in two forms. The first is the depletion of the inheritance of moral resources because there is not necessarily an evolutionary view that we must be bad in order to be good. The second is the depletion of the institutions necessary to uphold the concepts of a person capable of choice, love and responsibility, capable of living in the world and being good. It is very important that this idea of good, the turn to the good, the politics of the common good is actually recognised. And there, I do think that there is a very wonderful, repressed Labour story to be told about ordinary people organising together, associating together to preserve their families, their areas from this domination by the rich manifesting in the state and the market, which is Burkean in so many ways but was not championed by Burke. There are other thinkers, and I think that Tawney is a very important thinker here, who we need to reconsider.

Note

1 Glasman is referring to the Occupy Movement in the United Kingdom, whose first action was to attempt to occupy the London Stock Exchange on Paternoster Square in October 2011. When this failed, the protestors set up a camp outside St Paul's Cathedral.

Red or Orange: The Big Society in the New Conservatism

PAUL KELLY

SHORTLY before the 2010 election, Phillip Blond, the director of ResPublica, published *Red Tory*[1] as an agenda for a new Conservatism that rejects the liberal ideas that have dominated British politics for much of the twentieth century. Blond is also great advocate of the 'Big Society'—one of the campaign themes of David Cameron, who has expressed interest in Blond's ideas about third-sector transformation of public policy delivery, civil society and the recovery of mutualism. *Red Tory* is seen as one of the founding texts of the Big Society. Blond's book is a complex mix of high theory, the history of ideas, policy advocacy and political positioning. Underlying the whole perspective is the claim that our current social and political malaise is the fault of liberal ideas and the liberal reforms from the 1960s onwards. Blond's radical critique of liberalism is familiar stuff and could have been derived from any number of philosophical communitarian critiques of Margaret Thatcher's social and economic reforms; indeed, it bears a striking similarity to the Alasdair MacIntyre's 1984 book *After Virtue*.[2] This should not be altogether surprising given the philosophical and theological sympathies of both authors. Although Blond draws on the ideas of new-Orthodox Anglican theologians such as John Millbank, Millbank himself draws much inspiration from Catholic thinkers such as Henri de Lubac. This Catholicism in its Anglican or Roman variant is key to understanding Blond's critique of liberalism just as it is for MacIntyre, but it also explains the 'red' element of Red Toryism in that it plays on an ambiguity between communitarian socialism and the 'redmeat' of the Tory tradition going back to Coleridge, Carlyle, John Henry Newman and Ruskin as well as anti-statists such as Hilaire Belloc. This older Tory tradition understood the nature of intermediate institutions, civil society and structural pluralism that allowed corporations such as churches, guilds and universities as well as mutual associations and cooperatives to exist alongside the state without being absorbed by it.

The book certainly presents an alternative vision of society which fits nicely with aspirations to liberate the civil society or the Big Society and it supports some of the rhetoric of 'Broken Britain' popularised by Iain Duncan Smith. Blond's eclectic blend of high theory coupled with his magpie-like approach to the history of ideas and political ideology has provided a challenging resource for scholars who are always keen to compartmentalise political ideas. But he has by no means provided the definitive account of the Big Society or the overarching narrative within which policy makers can explain and defend their mutualist or civil society solutions to the strategic retreat of

Published by Blackwell Publishing Ltd, 9600 Garsington Road, Oxford OX4 2DQ, UK and 350 Main Street, Malden, MA 02148, USA

the state in the face of the financial crisis. There is a continuing debate amongst conservative thinkers about the underpinnings of Big Society reforms and that debate reflects a deeper debate about the nature of conservatism in the twentieth century.

Another leading figure in this debate is Jesse Norman, MP for South Herefordshire, whose recent book *The Big Society*[3] has provided one of the most coherent attempts to explain what Big Society thinking is and how it fits within the conservative tradition. Like Blond, Norman's Big Society thinking is influenced by mutualism and civil society solutions to replace the institutions of the welfare state, but the intellectual framework for these ideas is very different from Red Toryism. Where Blond draws upon European philosophical and theological thought and nineteenth-century organic conservatism, Norman's conception of the Big Society draws on the ideas of an important British political thinker of the twentieth century: Michael Oakeshott. And where Blond sees the task of the Big Society as the remedy for the failures of liberalism, Norman's conception of the Big Society is a reconciliation between liberalism and conservatism. My concern in the rest of this chapter is to examine the Big Society debate as part of that reconciliation and to explore the consequent new Conservatism that emerges from it.

'Liberalism' and new Conservatism

With the permanent decline and fracturing of the Liberal party, liberal ideas and ideology in Britain have been in search of a new political vehicle for much of the twentieth century. The once dominant political force associated with Gladstone, Asquith and Lloyd George collapsed in the early 1920s and has never fully recovered, nor is it likely to. Yet the humbling of the Liberal party as a significant national electoral force has not been matched by a similar displacement of liberal ideas and ideology. Conventional wisdom and much progressive historical political commentary are focused on the amalgamation of liberal ideas with the Labour party. On this view, the history of the Labour party since the Second World War has been one of awkward attempts to graft a left-liberal ideological project onto the corporatist institutional culture of the British labour movement. This process had two main phases: first the implementation of Beveridge's welfare state as part of the radical Attlee government of 1945; and this was followed in the 1960s with the liberal social reforms of the often underrated Wilson government and the 'enlightened' social liberalism of Roy Jenkins.

This story has bewitched historians, commentators and not a few leading politicians to the extent that they have been unable to comprehend the recent coalition agreement between the Liberal Democrats and David Cameron's Conservative party. The coalition agreement is the betrayal of a common progressive project that unites the Labour party and the Liberal Democrats: Clegg's Liberal Democrats are betraying the cause by going over to the natural enemy, the Conservative party. This widely accepted idea that the

Liberals and Labour form common progressive cause is misleading for it obscures a deeper story about the complex relationship between liberalism and conservatism: a story that has been insufficiently noted by Conservative commentators as they have also tried to characterise liberalism as the junior partner of the Labour party or as an alien and dangerous philosophical opponent that is also at the heart of national decline.

Ideological conservatism from Margaret Thatcher to David Cameron has been influenced by the thought of the two intellectual giants of late twentieth-century British political theory: Michael Oakeshott and Friedrich Hayek. The former is a liberal who describes himself as a conservative, whereas the latter is clearly a conservative, but one who famously denies the fact, whilst at the same time claiming to be a liberal.[4] Both thinkers are concerned with the complex relation between conservative politics and policy, and liberal ideas and practice.

The Conservative–Liberal Democrat coalition illustrates this complex but sympathetic alignment between political conservatism and liberal ideas—one could almost characterise Cameron and Osborne's Conservatism as an Orange Book Conservatism, after the infamous Liberal text of 2004. The Orange Book liberals identify four phases of liberalism: personal, political, economic and social. The task for the liberal politician is to strike the right balance between these different dimensions, but also to recognise that some of them, such as the liberal political reforms of extending the franchise, have become the common currency of all parties. In the same way, economic liberalism has become a common strand of other ideological positions.[5] Although the characterisation of the four phases of liberalism is undeveloped in the *Orange Book*, it does provide a tool for analysing the differential impact of liberal ideas on public opinion and British political parties over the last century.

Even if one thinks that political ideas are merely epiphenomenal, it is undoubtedly the case that they have an important role in an adequate characterisation of current politics. One can conceive of politics as a struggle between great ideologies in which policy debates are merely microrepresentations of profound philosophical differences about who we are and what we are doing. Yet even if one takes the more cynical view that ideological debate is only about positioning, the struggle for ideas still matters. All new leaders, especially when they are trying to avoid setting out specific policy agendas, try to create an impression or mood for their agenda or government. Blair tried a number of different positions including communitarianism, 'the stake-holder society' (drawing on ideas from Will Hutton and popularised by the IPPR [Institute for Public Policy Research]) and of course the Third Way. It was, therefore, not a surprise that Cameron has also tried to re-present what he takes Conservatism to be. What is perhaps interesting about Cameron's positioning is the explicit attempt to court Liberal Democrats. In a speech in 2007 in Bath he claimed:

I am a liberal Conservative. Liberal, because I believe in the freedom of the individual to pursue their own happiness, with the minimum of interference from government. Sceptical of the state, trusting people to make the most of their lives, confident about the possibilities of the future—this is liberalism. And Conservative, because I believe that we're all in this together—that there is a historical understanding between past, present and future generations, and that we have a social responsibility to play an active part in the community we live in. Conservatives believe in continuity and belonging; we believe in the traditions of our country which are embedded in our institutions. Liberal and Conservative. Individual freedom and social responsibility.[6]

Given what happened in May 2010, this is a particularly interesting and prescient claim, but in terms of positioning it reveals something important about the possibilities of a New Conservatism in the early years of the twenty-first century. On one level it would be surprising if Cameron did not make an attempt to entice Liberals away from a possible centre-left coalition, and subsequent electoral strategy confirms that attempt to absorb part of the Lib-Dems—both voters and party members. Yet the choice of identification as a liberal Conservative is indicative of something more fundamental but perhaps less surprising than might seem. There are many ways in which British society has undoubtedly become more liberal in the last fifty years. Patterns of deference and the standing of once fundamental institutions such as the Church of England have largely evaporated. Toleration of difference and diversity are also widely practised as is shown by the British Election Study's long-term monitoring of British public opinion. The British people do not like others breaking the rules, but they seem far less troubled about what those rules should be. These are just illustrations of the wider hold that liberal ideas, particularly with respect to personal liberalism, have taken in British society.

Perhaps to Rawlsian liberal-egalitarians, Cameron's account of liberalism is pretty tame stuff, but not too many generations ago this would have been a very radical position indeed; it could have been penned (minus the reference to conservatism) by Beveridge and other giants of the liberal pantheon such as Mill or T. H. Green. Slowly but surely the ideas of political, social and ethical individualism with its scepticism about the powers of the state to enshrine an idea of the good have become the common currency of political debate. Just as some version of the market economy is—despite the current financial crisis— the only form of economy on the horizon, so the idea of a broadly neutral state is equally the only form of the state that can accommodate the fact of the pluralistic society that is modern Britain. As John Gray writes: 'The project of restoring an organic national community as currently advocated most perceptively by Roger Scruton, is a distraction from serious policy making in a society that is irretrievably pluralist.'[7] The political task facing politicians of all parties is accommodating to that fact rather than trying to recreate a more homogeneous and integrated organic society that has been desired by generations of traditionalist conservatives from Coleridge and Disraeli to Phillip Blond, Aristotelian communitarians such as Alastair MacIntyre, and more recently in the conservative leftism of Maurice Glasman's 'Blue Labour', but which probably never existed in the first place.

In practice the state may well be far more paternalist than this liberal self-understanding claims, but as New Labour found out when it tried to introduce policies such as Identity Cards as well as measures such as speed cameras, the lack of a convincing paternalist political language was illustrated by the ease with which opposition was able to coopt discourse about the over-weaning state and its threat to independence and initiative. Politics cannot simply be about what works even if that remains the central aspiration of effective government. Political practice needs a convincing legitimating narrative and in present circumstances that narrative must be broadly liberal. The abandonment of aspects of the liberal settlement of the 1960s is simply irrelevant as major policy platforms for parties that need to seek the broad support of the people. Whatever the views of evangelical or Roman Catholic MPs and voters, there is simply no widespread appetite to repeal the right to a legal abortion; similarly whatever the views of Margaret Thatcher, few people were inclined to mourn the repeal of Clause 28 of the Local Government Act or support any other civil disabilities on homosexuals, whatever individual backbenchers may think. Margaret Thatcher's attempt to marry economic liberalism with traditional morality was tested to destruction in the years between 1979 and 1997, and attempts to revive it under the ill-fated leadership of Iain Duncan Smith resulted in an internal coup and his replacement as leader.

Given these fundamental shifts in British social attitudes, Cameron's claims about Conservatism in the speech cited become far less paradoxical when juxtaposed with liberalism. If the traditions and social practices of society become more liberal as a result of wider social forces, then that which is to be 'conserved', or the community and traditions we should identify with, are also those that have been liberalised by time and experience. In fact, one could argue that Conservatives ought to be liberal as anything more substantial, nostalgic or anti-liberal is likely to be a rationalist abridgement of our political traditions and practices: this is Gray's argument against the nostalgic conservatism of Roger Scruton. Scruton's conservatism would be a radical, even revolutionary, challenge to most people's lives and self-understandings as opposed to the Aristotelian middle-way between two extremes that characterises the working ideology of practical conservatism. The attempt to recreate a nostalgic version of Britain in the 1950s would be precisely the kind of rationalist social engineering that conservatives reject. It is precisely this adaptation to the times which explains how the Conservative party became such a successful electoral force for much of the twentieth century, and it was the abandonment of that strategy for a more purely ideological politics that confined them to the margins of politics for a decade and half from 1997.

The Big Society as Orange Book Conservatism

The liberalising of Conservatism can be seen as merely clever or necessary positioning on the part of Cameron as he recalibrates the claims of Conservatism to the mood of the British public, and one does not have to look to hard to find individual conservatives who hold illiberal and reactionary views on many issues. But the identification of a liberal Conservatism as the model for a new Conservatism also draws attention to a debate within liberal political thought itself, particularly that variant of British liberalism associated with Berlin, Hart, Hayek and Oakeshott. This liberal discourse is high-minded theory or philosophy and therefore conducted at considerable remove from the policy debates of most political parties, but it has not been irrelevant as Jesse Norman's own brand of the Big Society as a version of liberal Conservatism attests. Hayek and Oakeshott mark out different positions on the liberal terrain of politics on which the main British political parties position themselves. Indeed, two important liberal thinkers—Hayek and Oakeshott—have been coopted into, or identified with, the project of a liberal Conservatism.

Hayek is famously associated with the new-Right conservatism of Margaret Thatcher. It is said that Sir Keith Joseph gave Margaret Thatcher a copy of Hayek's seminal work *The Constitution of Liberty* and this is supposed to have shaped her politics during her radical government. This is a nice story, but almost certainly apocryphal, and she certainly did not pursue a policy agenda on the basis of a large book on political philosophy written in America in the 1950s by an émigré Austrian. Yet Hayek's critique of welfare or social liberalism, economic planning and the welfare state certainly provided ammunition for conservative politicians and commentators seeking to reject the Labour–Conservative corporatist consensus of the 1960s and 1970s and an armoury of arguments for positions they already accepted on the basis of intuition.

Hayek's critique of the welfare state had been around a long time and some of it is to be found in *The Road to Serfdom* published in 1944 as the threat of the fully mobilised democracies of the successful allied powers sought to turn the recently vindicated powers of the state towards the provision of welfare and social justice—the fulfilment of the social liberal promise of New Liberals. Hayek's concern was that the rational liberalism of the social liberals would result in the sort of state direction that would inevitably lead to totalitarianism. This slippery-slope argument had little purchase in Britain in the 1940s and 1950s, but by the late 1960s and 1970s the argument that the expansion of the state led to greater freedom and opportunity seemed to be refuted by economic stagnation and dreariness of public life.

Hayek's *Constitution of Liberty* is in part a celebration of inequality as a condition of the material progress he saw in the consumer society of the United States. Furthermore, it is a defence of an Anglophone or anti-rationalist tradition of freedom associated with Hume, Smith, Tucker, Burke and Paley, and ending only with J. S. Mill's apostasy. This, he contrasts with the French version of rationalist freedom associated with Rousseau, the Physiocrats and Condorcet which, according to J. L. Talmon, leads to totalitarianism. More importantly, Hayek's argument rehabilitates a liberal individualism that celebrates free markets and the spontaneous order that emerges from the exercise of individual freedom and choice. His call for a robust individualism and free markets appealed to the desire to privatise nationalised industries and open up the economy to the power of individual initiative and entrepreneurialism. Yet as John Gray has noted, Hayek's argument did not merely provide ideological support for privatisations and deregulation. It was a peculiarly sympathetic strand of liberalism for conservatives because of Hayek's emphasis on the institutional and cultural conditions of free markets and open societies. The rule of law, private or several property and the freedom of contract, as well as the settled practices of morality which have similarly grown up spontaneously, rather than being imposed by some external rationalist legislator, are all crucial to the conduct and success of market or free societies. Conventional morality is of a piece with market freedom, so much so that Hayek saw the conservative tendencies of his own argument and tried to distance himself from them—at least by characterising conservatism in an implausibly reactionary form. The kind of conservatism that Hayek describes in 'Why I am not a Conservative', published as the postscript to *The Constitution of Liberty*,[8] is one that draws a clear distinction between an anglophone classical liberalism and a European reactionary conservatism that, in its rejection of the legacy of the French Revolution, adopts the political theology espoused by thinkers such as Carl Schmitt and rejects methodological individualism in favour of authoritarian collectivism and the primacy of political authority.

For many critics of Hayek, as well as many conservatives themselves, the important role of tradition and convention has been overlooked, with attention being focused on his defence of free markets and economic deregulation. On the philosophical level, Hayek's epistemological individualism and critique of central planning has overshadowed the evolutionary social conservatism upon which he bases his account of a liberal economic order. He has been transformed into a crude libertarian defender of capitalism. For those on the left, the libertarian defence of capitalism has meant that Hayek has not been accorded serious attention. Yet Hayek's importance is his challenge to the social and ethical liberalism of Isaiah Berlin and H. L. A. Hart. Although Hayek's grand theory covers epistemological, ethical and political issues, his major contribution to liberalism and conservatism is tied up with an implication of his rejection of, or challenge to, the welfare state and nationalisation rather than his moral conventionalism. This contrasts clearly with the liberalism of Berlin or Hart.

Berlin is often criticised as a small 'c' conservative liberal by those on the left, and his championing of negative liberty in his famous lecture 'Two Concepts of Liberty' is seen as part of a tradition of 'Cold War Liberalism' that includes Hayek, Karl Popper and Michael Oakeshott in Britain, and Raymond Aron in France. Yet the championing of negative over positive liberty and his defence of value pluralism in a number of essays and lectures distinguishes his work from the likes of Hayek and Oakeshott and has shifted the attention of liberal political theorists and many liberals in centre-left politics from a preoccupation with the role and function of the state to questions about moralism within policy making and legislation. For Berlin and for his colleague and friend Herbert Hart, the tasks of political philosophy are primarily ethical and they have little or nothing to say about the extent and structure of the state as long as it does not impose a controversial morality on those subject to its power. Berlin is quite explicit about this, claiming that 'political philosophy, . . . is but ethics applied to society'. One could claim that for Berlin the great debates about the nature and scope of the state have been settled by history in favour of some version of the mixed economy defended by Labour and the Conservatives in the 1950s and 1960s.

Questions about state involvement in the economy are primarily technical questions which fall outside the remit of political philosophy and theory and on which there seems to be an academic consensus that excluded Hayek's Austrian School economics. Given this fact, liberals of a Berlinian cast of mind could and were as at home in the Labour party as in a party of their own. Hart was supportive of the Labour party, whereas Berlin's politics are more ambiguous. But if the nature and scope of the state and economy fail to be the main dividing line between liberals and conservatives, the attitude of Berlinian or Hartean liberals to conventional morality did indeed set up a clear positioning of liberalism towards the political left. Hart's famous attack on legal moralism and his debate with Patrick Devlin over the Wolfenden Committee's recommendations on sexual offences and the decriminalisation of homosexuality clearly set this strand of liberalism against the supposed moral conservatism of British society and the arguments for the value of conventional morality that underpinned the spontaneous order of liberty that Hayek defended in *The Constitution of Liberty*.

Although much debated at the time, and a staple for undergraduate courses in political thought up until the 1980s, much of the debate between Hart and Devlin now seems quaint by contemporary standards. Nobody could seriously claim that advocating the removal of civil disabilities against homosexuals is akin to treason. Yet the contrast between the Hayekian and Berlin/ Hart versions of liberalism are very clear. The transformation of the Conservative party from the mid-1970s to the mid-1990s was clearly marked by a resurgence of Hayekian liberalism as the dominant conservative discourse, with its economic liberalism and superficial anti-welfarism coupled with a tough minded social moralism that could justify Clause 28, amongst other things. Yet as the world has changed considerably since the 1960s in terms of economic globalisation and interdependence, the clear opposition between the ethical liberalism of Berlin and Hart and the classical liberalism of Hayek has become less easy to sustain. Hayek's variant of liberalism moved from the margins to the mainstream and became one of the dominant strands of conservative thinking as 'freeing-up' the economy became the most important political issue. The ethical liberalism of Berlin and Hart, whilst still important came to be seen as lacking a plausible political theory of the state, and as many liberals within the Labour party moved to the Social Democrats and then into either the new Liberal Democrats or back to New Labour, the political task for liberals was transformed into combining the Berlin/Hart assault on liberal moralism with some recognition of Hayek's challenge to the scope and extent of the welfare state—that is, combining economic liberalism with personal liberalism.

At one level this is precisely the synthesis that is found at the heart of the famous *The Orange Book* edited by David Laws and Paul Marshall in 2004, which contains contributions from many prominent Liberal members of the current coalition government. For Hart and Berlin, much of conventional morality—particularly legal moralism—is an outmoded legacy of a world we have lost; it is both undesirable and irretrievable. Hayek's central claim was that the spontaneous order of freedom and an open market society required the conventional morality and legal moralism that ethical liberals dismissed. We cannot simply abandon the conventional moralism of a spontaneous order and graft social liberalism onto the classical economic liberalism that Hayek also defends. In other words, we cannot simply humanise and modernise Hayek with a large dose of Berlin as the New Labour project appeared to hope in its earliest manifestations with Tony Blair's acknowledgement of his intellectual indebtedness to Berlin. This explains the successful adoption of Hayek's philosophy of spontaneous order as new discourse for conservatism during the 1980s and 1990s. Hayekian free-market social conservatives retain a powerful voice amongst the Conservative back benches, but they have not been without their critics on the political right.

John Gray was a sometime defender of Hayekian liberalism in the 1980s, but by the mid-1990s had come to be an important critic. He argued that Hayek's position was untenable as the main threat to the settled patterns of convention on which a free spontaneous order depended is actually the unfettered market that has been unleashed by Hayekian inspired conservatives or what are sometimes described as 'neoconservatives' in the United States and 'neoliberals' in Europe. In Gray's view, we can only lament the inevitable self-destruction of free societies as Hayekian conservatism devours itself and as reactionary Toryism is impotent to do anything about it.

Hayek is not the only major contributor to British philosophical conservatism. Of equal importance in the development of conservative thought is Michael Oakeshott—a central figure in Jesse Norman's *Big Society*. Like Hayek, Oakeshott was associated with the London School of Economics, and through his teaching helped shape a generation of scholars and students who would contribute to the recovery of conservative thought and practice following the seeming triumph of the welfare state. Oakeshott's philosophy is subtle and difficult to capture in a few simple propositions. Although he wrote major philosophical texts, his preferred style was the essay where he could examine and reflect on an issue or problem from a variety of angles without necessarily settling on a simple moral or lesson. In general, Oakeshott favoured the idea of political theory and the practice of politics as a conversation as opposed to an argument.

A number of these essays are brought together in his most famous book *Rationalism in Politics*. Through a combination of political scepticism and communitarianism, Oakeshott distinguished himself as a conservative and provided the basis for the recovery of a conservative voice in political theory. Whilst Hayek shied away from the title of 'conservative', Oakeshott was more comfortable with the name, especially in the essay 'On being Conservative' where he identifies it as a disposition or character of mind as opposed to a theory or set of practical principles and values. Through his influence, the conservative voice in political philosophy is preserved into the early twenty-first century, yet that conservative voice remains distinctive. Despite being invited to the Conservative Philosophy Group in the 1970s and his thought being associated with the renewal of political conservatism under Margaret Thatcher, Oakeshott's conservatism remained a philosophical disposition rather than an ideological commitment. He rejected an ideological approach to politics, even including the ideology of anti-ideology that was espoused by Hayek. Consequently, he can be associated, in only the most loose and general sense, with the development of the 'new-right' in the late 1970s. It was this rejection of ideological commitment that is at the heart of Oakeshott's conservative disposition and it is precisely this which allows him to combine liberalism and conservatism in the most interesting way. Although Oakeshott made a point of defending the conservative disposition at precisely the time when everyone was a liberal, his contrarianism should not mask the extent to which he too is a major liberal thinker and it is this that opens the way for Cameron's liberal Conservatism and its connection with the Big Society as new conservatism's big idea.

Oakeshott did not like Berlin and Berlin was happy to reciprocate the dislike, but Oakeshott did admire Hart and took his work on law very seriously. He claimed not to have much interest in liberalism remarking: 'What may now be meant but the word "liberal" is anyone's guess.' Yet this remark is also instructive as it is not quite the dismissal of liberalism that it seems. Oakeshott is actually endorsing the claim that at the most general and abstract level liberalism had exhausted its specific meaning and become the terrain of political discourse so that all are, to some extent, either liberals or politically marginal. On this view, conservatism is an approach or attitude towards that terrain of political experience. In modern British politics it is not possible to be anything other than a liberal without being inauthentic or theatrical. The only interesting and non-theatrical issue is how one might respond to that mode of practical experience. The useful contrast is, therefore, not between liberal and conservative, but between rationalist and conservative.

In analysing this contrast in his book *Rationalism in Politics*, Oakeshott echoes themes and ideas that are prevalent in the work of Berlin, Hayek and even Karl Popper. Rationalism is the flaw of all enthusiastic reformers who try and reduce the complex manifold of human experience to a simple system or set of rules and principles. The threat of rationalism is that it desiccates political and moral experience with dangerous consequences. He writes:

Moral ideals are a sediment; they have significance only so long as they are suspended in a religious or social tradition, so long as they belong to a religious or a social way of life. The predicament of our times is that the Rationalists have been at work so long on their project of drawing off the liquid in which our moral ideals were suspended (and pouring it away as worthless) that we are left only with the dry and gritty residue which chokes us as we try to take it down.[9]

In this passage there is timely warning to those who wish to reform social traditions on the basis of technical knowledge and expertise, but also to liberals such as Hart, that the legal transformation of conventional morality comes at a price. As such this is a familiar conservative position and one that combines the two perspectives of Cameron's liberal Conservatism. If we read this alongside Oakeshott's 'The Political Economy of Freedom' we can see a strong affinity with Hayek's amalgamation of economic liberty and social conventionalism. Yet it would be a mistake to see Oakeshott simply as another anti-foundationalist Hayekian.

His conservatism and liberalism is more subtly restated in his latter book *On Human Conduct*.[10] In the second of the three essays that comprise this book he develops his model of civil association. His point is to characterise the life of the *cives* as one shaped by participation in a system of non-purposive or 'adverbial' rules that constitute the opportunities and identities of that person in a world alongside others. The point about this mode of political association is that it is immanent within the tradition of European and British politics and it is in a constant tension with another important mode of political being—namely the enterprise association, where life, identity and rule is directed towards some external end or substantive goal. These two categories of association provide the key to understanding the nature and role of the modern state as a form of political association. No actual state is ever either a pure civil association and possibly only extreme totalitarian states approximate to a pure enterprise association, but each helps us to situate our practice and our self-understandings. What is interesting about this model is that it partly replicates the distinction between the conservative disposition and that of the rationalist, but more importantly it also marks a distinctively liberal model of the state as impartial or neutral between conceptions of the good life or the end of politics. It is as if Oakeshott has deliberately translated the Rawlsian idea of the neutralist state into a more conservative idiom without committing himself to the normative conditions of social justice.

One can make two observations about this account of the state as a civil association. First, the idea of a purely civil association can still contain within itself a form of normativity as philosophers from Cicero and Kant, to Rawls and Dworkin have pointed out. This is not a night-watchman libertarian state, and Oakeshott is studiously silent on whether the terms of civil association can be undermined by gross inequalities of power and status. Such feasibility constraints are irrelevant to the categorical distinction he is making. However, as the category is supposed to be one that applies to human conduct and especially that made possible by adverbial rules, the question of what the conditions of maintaining a system of adverbial rules are is not something to which he can be wholly indifferent. It would not be impossible to find some room for an Oakeshottian conception of justice along the lines of Rawls's definition of social justice as 'a fair scheme of social cooperation between individuals who disagree about fundamental ends' as long as one avoids the further Rawlsian attempt to give content to that abstract definition.

Second and more important, the idea of civil association and the related idea of law as *lex* or constitutive rules as commands leave open the contingent content of those rules and that form of political life. The task of government for a *cives* within a civil association is to tend to the maintenance of that form of life. This is certainly a conservative attitude and one consistent with his earlier essay 'On Being Conservative', but it says absolutely nothing about what should be conserved other than the way of doing things, and this is certainly a liberal view. Whatever else Oakeshott is interested in doing in this complex essay, he is not interested in recovering or returning to a set of institutions and practices that no longer have the purchase they once did on our lives. Although conservative and interested in history, he was not a reactionary, and whilst fascinated by religion, he was not religious—in fact, in his personal life he was notably bohemian.

In many ways Oakeshott's liberal conservatism has been liberated by events from its possible association with Hayekian conservatism and many Oakeshott scholars are inclined to interpret and defend him as a liberal—albeit one who differs markedly from the prevailing liberal-egalitarianism of Rawls or Dworkin. He does not confront the challenges and social changes of the 1960s with suspicion and hostility, nor is he a reactionary trying to re-impose a lost moral order. However, unlike the liberalism of Hart or Berlin he does not have the suspicion of religion or other sources of tradition as optional modes for living in a modern pluralist world. In many respects his liberal pluralism is far more pluralist than Berlin or Hart as there is no implicit assumption that a genuinely liberal social order will naturally tend towards a uniform society of liberals. It is for this reason that one can find echoes of Oakeshott in curious places—Bhikhu Parekh's multiculturalism is a good example. His conservative liberalism aspires to be genuinely pluralistic and at home in the world as it is.

This is, at least superficially, how a Big Society conservative such as Norman is trying to position himself in constructing a new Conservatism that develops beyond the Hayekian neoliberal variant that dominated during the 1980s and 1990s. The Big Society is not merely an attempt to downsize the state and replace centralised provision with mutualism and localism. These are merely tactical means for facilitating a free society that does not dominate. Of particular interest is the conception of freedom that underlies the Big Society and that, according to Norman, is provided by Oakeshott rather than Hayek as the Oakeshottian understanding provides a response to the traditionalist conventionalism of Hayek whilst also responding to Gray's claim that liberal rationalism is self-undermining. This powerful reorientation of conservative liberalism may not be the official doctrine of the Conservative party, but it does throw some light on Cameron's attempt to recover a liberal strand of conservatism and entice Orange Book Liberals into a longer term intellectual coalition with the Conservative party. The philosophical stand of the Big Society espoused by Norman might therefore be seen as an attempt to construct an 'Orange Book Conservatism'.

Notes

1 P. Blond, *Red Tory*, London, Faber & Faber, 2010.
2 A. MacIntrye, *After Virtue*, London, Duckworth, 1984.
3 J. Norman, *The Big Society*, Buckingham, University of Buckingham Press, 2010.
4 M. Oakeshott, *Rationalism in Politics*, London, Methuen, 1968; F. A. Hayek, *Constitution of Liberty*, London, Routledge & Kegan Paul, 1962.
5 P. Marshall and D. Laws, eds, *The Orange Book*, London, Profile, 2004, pp. 18–42.
6 D. Cameron, 'A Liberal Conservative Consensus to Restore Trust in Politics'. Speech delivered in Bath, 22 March 2007. Quoted in M. Beech, 'Cameron and Conservative ideology', in S. Lee and M. Beech, *The Conservatives under David Cameron*, Basingstoke, Palgrave Macmillan, 2009, p. 26.
7 J. Gray, 'A Conservative disposition', in *Gray's Anatomy*, London, Allen Lane, 2009, p. 139.
8 F. A. Hayek, 'Why I am not a Conservative', in *Constitution of Liberty*, London, Routledge, 1962, pp. 397–414.
9 Oakeshott, *Rationalism in Politics*, p. 36.
10 M. Oakeshott, *On Human Conduct*, Oxford, Oxford University Press, 1974.

Cameron, Culture and the Creative Class: The Big Society and the Post-Bureaucratic Age

ALAN FINLAYSON

Introduction

THE THEME of David Cameron's 2011 speech to the Conservative party conference was 'leadership'. Leadership was what the coalition government was exercising in sticking to its austerity programme. It was what the country was doing through the military in Afghanistan and Libya, and by initiating aid programmes for child vaccination in Nigeria. It was also something that 'the British people' could, would and should do. 'The argument I want to make today is simple: leadership works,' said Cameron. In tough times the spirit and genius of the British people would come to the fore and they would take the lead:

That's why so much of my leadership is about unleashing your leadership. Giving everyone who wants to seize it the opportunity, the support and above all the freedom to get things done. Giving everyone who wants to believe it the confidence that working hard and taking responsibility will be rewarded not punished.

Classical Thatcherism (self-reliance unhindered by either a socialist state or socialist scroungers) allied to a kind of libertarian egalitarianism (in which everyone should be an entrepreneur) here issues in the seemingly un-conservative thought that everyone is 'a leader'. What might this tell us about the general ideology of 'Cameronism'?

A clue to the sources and implications of this very particular ideological cocktail was provided by the music that accompanied the close of the speech and Cameron's exit from the hall: 'You Get What You Give', by The New Radicals. Not long ago the Conservative party would have sung collectively 'Land of Hope and Glory' or 'Rule Britannia'. In 2011 they listened to an American, up-tempo, 'alternative' dance-rock song, the lyrics of which appear to recommend 'the dreamer's disease' and the vandalising of Mercedes-Benz cars, and to complain about 'health-insurance-rip-off-lying-FDA-big-bankers-buying'. The previous day, the Home Secretary, Theresa May, had been played out to the sound of The Dandy Warhols' 'Bohemian Like You': 'I really love your hairdo, yeah/I'm glad you like mine too/See we're looking pretty cool/Getcha!' On finding out that his song had been used in this way, The Dandy Warhols' front-man Mr Courtney Taylor-Taylor asked: 'Why don't these assholes have right-wing bands make them some

Published by Blackwell Publishing Ltd, 9600 Garsington Road, Oxford OX4 2DQ, UK and 350 Main Street, Malden, MA 02148, USA

right-wing music for their right-wing jerkoff politics?' He answered himself: 'Oh, because right-wing people aren't creative, visionary or any fun to be around.' Adding that the political left also lacked creativity, he then expressed dislike for 'ANY people who take sides in politics' and advocated charitable donations 'to people who get on a plane themselves and go to Haiti or Africa and help other people'.[1]

With these not uncommon sentiments the American rock singer was closer to the world view of the British Conservatives than he knew. The ideal form of Cameronite politician is the sort of person who has close ties to the rock music industry and 'probably' took drugs, partied at university, swears and makes dirty jokes in public and, forgoing suit and tie, wanders the office shoeless. He or she is part of what journalist Ann McElvoy perceptively identified as the 'The Jam Generation' (a reference to Cameron's expression of affection for 'Eton Rifles' by New Wave group The Jam); someone whose Desert Island discs are impeccably 'graduate alternative': Bob Dylan, Pink Floyd, The Smiths, Radiohead, REM.[2]

Post-Thatcherite and postpunk politicians unmoved by the ideological enthusiasms of the 1980s, convinced that the benevolent state is a myth and social conservatism eccentric, the Cameronites think themselves creative and are excited by a do-it-yourself mentality and aesthetic which they understand as 'entrepreneurial'; 'you get what you give' is the closest they get to a definition of justice and they want to be 'bohemian like you'. In Cameronism, the bourgeois values of individuated liberty and accumulation join hands and sing in harmony with the bohemian ethic of aesthetic individualism and desire for work that is creative and meaningful as well as remunerative. It is, said Cameron in 2005, important to care about the 'quality of life as well as the quantity of money' and he has since forced Thatcherism to leapfrog over the Blairite knowledge-economy driven modernisation of Britain, introducing it to the Cyberpunk DIY generation: everyone is first and foremost a creative being; everyone is an entrepreneur in waiting; the state is stifling and everyone is a leader.

I introduce Cameronism in this way—in terms of its cultural orientations, its affective tone—in order to indicate that 'the Big Society' and related concepts cannot be understood without an appreciation of the extent to which they are embedded within, and expressive of, what Raymond Williams called a 'structure of feeling'—that is, something both more and less than an ideology; a way of experiencing the world, a mood and sensibility shared by a group of people but which, a product of social and historical context, is not merely accidental or subjective. A number of trends (in work, in popular ethics, in social expectations as well as ideologies), extending from the 1960s to the present, have cohered in a class of people who experience themselves and each other as part of an 'anti-establishment' culture of self-possessing creative and innovative individuals who are capable, and desirous, of being both economically and socially responsible for themselves and for the world as they see it. What I want to explore in this chapter is the congruence of ideas about the Big Society with this cultural outlook, and in particular the way in which it contributes to a distinct concept of 'post-bureaucratic' government.

I begin by describing the 'structure of feeling' that shapes Cameronism through characterising its ideal typical expression in the form of Bono, the rock star philanthropist. I show how the Bono-ist *mentalité* is manifested in Cameronism—in hostility to the state and belief in the power of individual social action—and in a theory of government for the 'post-bureaucratic age'. I then show how this view, far from being marginalised by the economic crisis, is in fact a central element of the Conservative attempt to reimagine capitalism. Here I focus on 'Hilton-ism'—the outlook of Cameron's Director of Strategy Steve Hilton, which is primarily concerned with conceiving of governance in terms of consumer decisions and corporate responsibility.

Bono-ism

'My name is Bono and I'm a rock star' was how Paul Hewson introduced himself to the Labour party conference in 2004. He then apologised for being nervous, explaining that he was not used to being in front of crowds smaller than 80,000—that is, he reminded the Labour party who was lending status and authority to whom. Bono is a more powerful and far more significant political thinker and actor than all but a handful of the members of the Labour party. A popular creative artist, he is also a successful businessman, managing a brand, maximising returns and minimising his tax bill. This has enabled him to exercise a form of intellectual and cultural leadership, providing him with a platform from which to address world leaders and to advocate charitable and debt relief for developing countries. He is an example of how, today, a combination of financial and cultural capital enables individuals to accrue political and intellectual capacity independently of political parties or even nation-states. But Bono is also an example of a particular 'structure of feeling': an individualised aestheticised perspective on the world combined with a philanthropic attitude and scepticism about the formalities of political processes.

His foreword to *The End of Poverty* by the economist Jeffrey Sachs (whom Bono refers to as 'Jeff' and 'my professor') exemplifies this attitude. It emphasises the personal 'journey' of the two men, the 'affront' of poverty and the attitude required to end it: Jeff has passion and presence as well as logic; he can see the real world behind the statistics and he is angry. Because we are all bound together, Bono argues, the fate of others should concern us for pragmatic as well as ethical reasons and this constitutes a challenge, a 'mission', for 'a generation'. The rock star and the architect of economic shock therapy for postcommunist Europe come together, agreeing, as Bono puts it, that both markets and placards go together, while '[i]n Jeff's hands, the millstone of opportunity around our necks becomes an adventure. . .'; we can shirk our responsibility or live up to it and 'shift the paradigm'.[3]

This conception of life as an individual adventure, of social or economic problems as opportunities to demonstrate one's importance in the world, is an aspect of a more general worldview which we will here christen 'Bonoism'. The Bonoist is a particular sort of individualist. He (and it is almost always 'he') believes that the individual should be the starting point of thinking about life, the universe and politics, but does not believe that the individual is first and foremost a bearer of interests. Rather he emphasises individual powers of creativity, originality and innovation. Thus the Bonoist is neither selfish nor simplistically utilitarian. He wants his life and actions to have a positive impact on other people (partly because this is evidence of his individual affective capacity).

It follows that there is such a thing as society, although the Bonoist is just as sure that it is not the same thing as the state. The Bonoist is not likely to succumb to the cultic appeal of Ayn Rand since, although he shares with her a belief in the power of individual genius, he does not believe that social action will reduce or harm him. His good and the social good are the same because by acting individually to bring about social goods, he realises himself and is recognised by others. Thus, for the Bonoist, tackling poverty, for instance, is a social responsibility; one achieved by rolling forward 'the frontiers of society',[4] enabling professional, personal, corporate and civic responsibility.

The Bonoist inherits from both hippies and punks a measured dislike of 'the system'. He does not like conformity and does not like to think that his behaviour is driven by rules he did not make. He won't necessarily wear a suit and tie to work or take off his sunglasses to meet the Pope. For the same reason, he is unhappy with the moral obligations of socialism—partly because they come from without, but also because they presume that he does not know what is the best way to make the world a better place. He wants to help the poor, but he wants to do it by setting up his own charity. If worried about the quality of education, the Bonoist will open up his own school. Here again the exercise of his own creative genius is in harmony with the social good precisely because he was free to take the ennobling responsibility upon himself. The Bonoist contrasts asking what government can do with asking what people can do; passing laws to make people good with 'realising that we are all in this together'; 'waiting for the state to do it all' with 'taking responsibility'. He thinks that 'Labour's outdated state responsibility has failed' and wants people to say 'loudly and proudly' that 'this is my country, this is my community: I will play my part'.[5]

Importantly, the Bonoist's concern is not only, and perhaps not mainly, with what 'the system' does to the weakest. It is with what 'the system' does to him. It saps his creative powers. The Bonoist is not lazy. He believes in hard work, but also believes that hard work can and should be fulfilling. Indeed, it must be since work enables him to manifest his creativity in the world and thus prove his existence and powers. He does not want to be alienated from his labour, but thinks that alienation is a state of mind rather than anything to do with the sociology of property relations. For the Bonoist, the challenge is to make work good so that through it people can 'actualise' themselves and find spiritual gratification.

And just as work should be humanised and creative, so should the state. The Bonoist thinks that the Fabian state imposes standardised prescriptions upon complex problems and the 'rigor mortis' of contemporary economic theory has reduced us to utilitarian calculating machines (the phrase is Jesse Norman's). Both have caused us to forgot 'the things which make society flourish: people, institutions, culture'. Rationalism, the Bonoist argues, reduces subtle activities to a mere set of rules or instructions and undermines human associations by tying them to particular goals. He would prefer 'a new kind of association, one based on affection rather than procedure or purpose', a 'philic' association which understands that 'what motivates human beings needs not merely to be a matter of stick and the carrot, complying with rules or achieving some collective goal'. The Bonoist wants a 'connected society'.

Here, the Bonoist's concerns with politics and social decline and decay are as much aesthetic as moral. Confronted by hopelessness or despair, he is likely to find it obscene before finding it unjust (and, importantly, for the Bonoist, these two words mean the same thing). Like Edmund Burke, he wants aesthetic values to be central to politics. But unlike Burke, the Bonoist does not believe in a sublimity that exceeds human understanding; the creative force is not ultimately divine and everyone shares in it equally. The human being is 'fundamentally a bundle of capabilities . . . striving for self-expression'. The capacity to do something such as make music is not dependent on genius—'in fact the truth is that almost everyone has musical ability, but that hard work and focused practice are what really matter' and we should make it 'a social and economic, as well as cultural, priority'.[6]

Because of this absolute faith in the equal creative potential of all people, their capacity for innovation and entrepreneurialism, the Bonoist finds it hard to envisage contradictions between social position and individual action. The Marxists are unfair to think that people in positions of power or in command of great wealth must act against the common interests (just as they are elitist to think that without power people are lacking in something). Indeed, the Bonoist is generally not keen on sociology. Concepts such as 'social structure' locate the sources of conflict in something other than the will and set limits on the power of the individual. The Bonoist prefers the sciences of psychology (which today include marketing, behavioural economics and neurology). These teach the ways in which unhealthy dispositions in the self and others may be transformed. One reason the Bonoist wants to encourage music is because it has social, cognitive, emotional and therapeutic benefit; it even has neurological effects which encourage creative thinking and problem solving. For the Bonoist, change is a state of mind.

While he believes in a social good, the Bonoist does not believe in subordinating himself to a common good that is external. The Bonoist is a kind of Romantic, believing himself to be a creative and unique person who must be guided by his own inner drives—that is, what matters is the quality of the individual will and it is important that one cultivates and demonstrates one's good will. In this sense, his Rousseauian impulses are refracted through Kantianism. However, the Bonoist's God is no Protestant God. The Bonoist is certainly faith-friendly, but in a nondenominational way which emphasises upbeat faith and communitarian activity over belief or theology. He probably does believe in 'a' God and practises what we might call 'recreational' spirituality: worship as a hobby or outlet rather than a calling. As such, the Bonoist's faith enhances him. His God does not smite, humble or judge; He (sometimes She) lends us His (occasionally Her) powers of creativity, innovation and origination. For the Bonoist, the starry skies are within and fidelity to our own awesomeness is the sum of the moral law.

It follows that the Bonoist is no Puritan. As well as being relaxed about personal morality, he also likes to consume. What matters is that the good will consumes in harmony with the body and with nature. Thus the Bonoist is reconciled with consumer capitalism. Acquisitiveness is ethical if the one acquiring also takes responsibility for their choices and buys from those that also donate to charity. Consumers should see purchasing as akin to voting, and should take their responsibility seriously. They should 'ask questions, visit websites, take an interest' in what they buy.[7] For Bono-ism, the solution to corrosive capitalistic consumption is more capitalism of a kind that is not red in tooth and claw, but in Red™ sunglasses bought with a Red™ credit card.

This structure of feeling—a mélange of moral, political and aesthetic sensibilities bound together by a conception of the expressive, creative and consuming (mostly male) individual—is the philosophical expression of a class formation: those whose labour is not directly productive, but is also not wholly intellectual and whose income is derived from the production, manipulation and circulation of symbolic forms. These are the people Richard Florida has celebrated as the 'Creative Class' who create 'meaningful new forms'. That includes, of course, those working in arts, design and media. But far more numerous are those working in marketing and public relations and at the front end of scientific and technological invention. It also includes, importantly, those who manipulate the symbols and equations of financial transactions. For this class, the defining characteristic of human beings is not what the Marxists thought—their capacity to materially transform the world—nor what the traditional Conservatives thought—our natural arrangement in a divinely and hierarchically ordered moral universe. Nor is it the capacity for utilitarian calculation promoted by economic Liberalism. What is definitive of the human is the capacity for creation, for innovation in thinking and communicating. In this way the creative class generalises its own experience and aptitudes and at various talks organised by TeD (Technology, Entertainment and Design) or the RSA (Royal Society for the Encouragement of Arts, Manufactures and Commerce) is gratified to discover that this is not only the spiritual but also the biological essence of humanity, 'hard-wired' in our neural structure, embedded in evolutionary imperatives.

One of the things that Blairism was, was the attempt to incorporate the Bonoist worldview of the creative class with the ideology of Social Democracy. For New Labour the creative economy promised a utopia of non-alienated Labour in harmony with the human spirit, and in which the liberty of the one enhanced the competitive edge of the many.[8] The challenge for Blairism was to overcome the Labourist celebration of manual labour and help everyone to be a Bonoist, ready to 'unleash their potential'. The Big Society is the attempt to join the Bonoist creative class to Conservatism. Where New Labour engaged the state in the micromanagement of the production of recruits to the creative class, Cameronism conceives of the task as the recruitment of Lieutenants for the 'little platoons' whom it charges with the social responsibility to innovate, connect and build institutions: everyone can be a leader.

Cameronism

In Cameronism, the Bonoist perspective manifests itself first and foremost as an anti-state ideology. Under the banner of 'Direct Democracy', writing in 2006, a group of insurgent Tories (Michael Gove among them) declared that where Thatcherism had had to deal with the command economy, the problem today was 'the command state'. They acknowledged the growth of a corrosive individualism and lack of social conscience, but blamed these on state intrusion into personal, family and community life. As Cameron put it in 2009, with sentiments at odds with traditional conservatism, the expansion of the state had suppressed natural '[h]uman kindness, generosity and imagination'. The solution proposed by Direct Democracy, and partly implemented by Cameron in office, was to weaken and reduce that state by decentralising and localising: free schools, elected police chiefs, the socially interventionist state supplanted by the socially interventionist community, 'state welfare' with 'social welfare'. Strikingly, this vision is more Thomas Jefferson than Samuel Smiles, based on the belief that people are socially minded and will naturally assume responsibility for themselves and their local community.

This perspective, freed from conservative anxieties about 'personal' morality (marriage, homosexuality, 'alternative' lifestyles') enabled Cameronism to separate the critique of the state from the critique of '1960s' individualism, and to embrace libertarian themes of self-government and local autonomy. The critique of the state and the embrace of 'social responsibility' could then be articulated with celebration of a particular kind of post-1960s individualism. In calling for the rolling back of the state, and the creation of 'avenues through which responsibility and opportunity can develop . . . actively helping to create the big society; directly agitating for, catalysing and galvanising social renewal' Conservatism claims the legacy of 'the 1960s revolution'.

However, although opposition to the state is a definitive component of Cameronism, unlike either traditional Conservatives or full-throttle Libertarians, Cameronists want to use the state to change society. As Cameron has put it (in one of his most Maoist moments): '[I]n the fight against poverty, inequality, social breakdown and injustice I do want to move from state action to social action. But I see a powerful role for government in helping to engineer that shift. Let me put it more plainly: we must use the state to remake society.' This enables the translation of the Big Society into a theory and practice of government in 'the post-bureaucratic age'. According to Michael Gove, this term describes 'precisely' a 'new world being shaped by the economic, cultural, social and technological forces of our time'. In the past, 'authority in society was exercised on the basis of clan, family and local loyalties. The county gentry administered the law, individual noble houses marshalled men for conflict, news was exchanged at the parish pump or village inn, commerce was carried on at the market town and status was overwhelmingly a matter of birth'. But all this was swept away by modern communications and transport bringing us to 'the bureaucratic age' in which nation-states took over responsibility for the military, for welfare, and thus also for taxation, creating extensive and powerful bureaucracies. But now social and technological change has destroyed the concentration of resources that made social democratic bureaucracy possible. Thanks to Tivo and the iPlayer, there has been a 'transference of power from the centralised bureaucracy to the empowered individual' and for Gove what has happened in broadcasting 'is a metaphor for what is happening across the economy, and across society', in medicine, politics and markets. We live in a post-bureaucratic age shaped by transparency and easy access to information about performance and costs, empowering individuals to form 'open source' networks while living off their intellectual capital.[9]

The idea of the PBO (post-bureaucratic organisation) comes directly from the world of organisation and management studies. Here it was a way of describing changes to workplace organisation and was closely related to the ideas that fed early New Labour: postfordism, the network, the primacy of knowledge and so on. Bureaucracies, it is argued, confine people within their official roles, making them responsible only for their own activity and not for that of others. As a result, organisations become sluggish, wasteful of intelligence and slow to respond to change. In contrast, the emerging PBO is open to change, development and participation. It is decentralised and competitive, fuelled by influence rather than power. Porous and open-ended, the PBO enables entrepreneurial behaviour and is open to partnership with other organisations.

In such firms, lacking a mass of employees in a stable division of labour, and in which work tasks are too flexible and developmental to be overseen by a rigid bureaucracy, the question arises of how people might be managed. Where Rousseau had once sought to resolve the paradox of how one could submit to civil law yet remain self-governing, contemporary personnel managers must work out how to manage a formally free workforce. The answer given by theorists of the PBO is that they can do so by helping employees to become self-governing (forcing them to be free, as it were). This requires transparency, such that each employee knows what everyone else is doing, and assessment by results rather than by fidelity to procedure. Such properly incentivised liberty spurs novel forms of cooperation, entrepreneurial innovation and creativity, contained within a self-regulating work culture.

Cameronism generalises this to the management of public services (by enhancing transparency and increasing competition while promoting professional values) and to the management of society as a whole. Here, because it does not want to proliferate formal rules and regulations, or explicit rights, and because it is interested in governing through cultural disposition, the Cameron government emphasises the power of social pressure and of social norms. This is the thinking behind 'behavioural change' or 'nudge' policy which first came to prominence under Blairism (and the architects of Blairite behaviour change policy have returned to government under Cameron). As Steve Hilton puts it: 'One of the core values of progressive Conservatism is designing policy that goes with the grain of human nature.' In other words, one does not try to transform people directly but instead creates an environment in which they naturally do the right thing. In a speech to launch the Network for a Post-bureaucratic Age (PBA), in 2010, Cameron argued that:

[This age] is just as much about behavioural economics as data transparency, about social pressure as internet protocols. . . . It's about understanding that you can make doing the right thing more appealing through incentives like money . . . you can apply gentle social pressure by making it clear to people that others—their friends and neighbours—are already doing the right thing. This simple understanding of what makes people tick—distilled into the right policies—is going to have a massive impact on what government does and how it does it.

As a mode of governance, the PBA is about integrating people at the level of values and employing forms of control rooted in norms and the observation of compliance with them. Like Wikileaks, the coalition thinks that the harsh light of day will prevent the accumulation of corrupting forces: it has furthered the publication of spending decisions (so that citizens can keep track of things) and invited people to access government data (at data.gov or police.uk) and create their own visualisations and 'Apps'. These go along with various devices such as elected mayors, police commissioners and e-petitions, as well as means of promoting and rewarding values-driven behaviour such as the revival of the Empire Medal, National Citizens Service and Big Society Awards.

Hiltonism

Numerous commentators have suggested that such ideas, while important for Cameron at the start of his leadership of the Conservative party, lost relevance as the fiscal crisis of the British state intensified. However, the coalition's understanding of the causes of the crash, and of its remedies, has been profoundly shaped by the ideology of the Big Society. Indeed, because it sees the crash as a symptom of the bureaucratic age, the coalition advocates post-bureaucratic thinking more rather than less. To understand how and why we have to dig deeper into 'Hiltonism'.

Steve Hilton, Cameron's chief adviser (at the time of writing on 'sabbatical' at Stanford University), is a quintessentially Bono-ist individual. His work experience is entirely concerned with the manufacture and manipulation of symbolic forms. He has worked in advertising, social marketing and public relations consultancy and, by marriage, is closely associated with Google, to whom Cameron explained, in 2007, that Conservatives have

always preferred to place our trust in the ingenuity of human beings, collaborating in messy and unplanned interaction, to deliver the best outcomes. You might call it the wisdom of crowds. Or as Edmund Burke put it more than two hundred years ago, 'the reciprocal struggle of discordant powers will draw out the harmony of the universe'.

Hilton believes passionately in those powers although he understands them as the cultural, moral and aesthetic power of capitalism.

In his 2002 book *Good Business* (co-authored with Giles Gibbons) Hilton argues that where governments have been failures at tackling social problems business has the power and the public trust to solve them; after all, it knows how to change consumer behaviour. The goal of Hilton and Gibbons, then, is to encourage capitalists to use 'their unique and powerful position in the public consciousness for social as well as commercial ends'. They acknowledge that anti-capitalist activists have a point, that 'there are real issues of social and environmental performance, ethics, accountability and justice' but insist that pro-social causes and capitalist business are not antithetical. The two must learn how to work together—'placards plus markets', as Bono put it—and people 'don't have to make a choice between making money and making the world a better place'.

The key concept of *Good Business* is Corporate Social Responsibility (CSR). New communication systems will aid the spread of information about firms' activities, enabling rapid and effective criticism to which they will have to respond. Impressively, the book envisions a 'new technology—smart bar codes that consumers can scan to find out about a product's origins and its producers' corporate record'. There is indeed now an App for this. But, they stress, business people really do care about social issues and 'a new generation of senior executives, many of them with socially liberal values established during their formative years in the 1960s, and crucially many of them women, is starting to change the conventions of doing business'. Companies should welcome the kind of transparency and openness which could have prevented corporate disasters such as Enron and see CSR as a wise form of risk management, reducing legal threats and image problems while rendering formal regulation redundant.

Importantly, Hilton and Gibbons go further than this. Corporations should not only respond passively to social concerns, they say, but actively lead them. 'You need to demonstrate social leadership outside your business,' they urge. 'It's not enough to change your company. You should use your company to change the world' developing mass engagement, transforming brand status while engaging with people emotionally and so winning 'hearts and minds—and wallets'. That means not only complying with environmental or social standards and sponsoring a few upmarket events, but taking on projects with a social purpose such as school bus services, kerbside recycling and so on; not merely marketing how great a firm is, but directly engaging in social leadership activities.[10]

Hilton and Gibbons thus demand something not only from critics of corporations, but from the corporations themselves. In Bono-ist terms, they invite them to be part of the 'challenge' and the 'adventure'. In so doing, they recognise and applaud the extent to which the activities of the large corporation have exceeded the boundaries of the market, going beyond mere 'externality recognition',[11] and have become part of the polity. And this is the other side of the Big Society. The use of the state to 'galvanise' individuals to take responsibility from the state is accompanied by the attempt to reconstitute capitalist firms as kinds of political actor, to demand that they be responsible and to then give them civic duties (founding or partnering social enterprises, volunteering their workforce and so on). Thus, Cameron has recently asserted the venerability of the Conservative principle of social responsibility 'recognising that people are not just atomised individuals and that companies have obligations'. The challenge of the economic crisis is to make sure markets are informed by and inform such responsibility by, of course, managing entrepreneurs through transparency not regulation, promoting the 'insurgent economy where we support the new, the innovative and the bold'—that is, an economy built on the Bonoist characteristics of 'intelligence, ingenuity, energy, guts'.[12]

Conclusion: beyond the Big Society

In formulating concepts, politicians, their advisers and supporters draw on the resources bequeathed them by ideological tradition and history and which they adapt to make sense of the world as they have experienced it. The Big Society is a political theory made out of well-established Conservative arguments about the cause of our present discontents (an over-extended, inefficient and corrupting state), allied to a more general sociocultural 'structure of feeling' (Bono-ism), which expresses a general vision (Cameronism) connected to a theory of governmental and social organisation in the 'post-bureaucratic age' (Hiltonism). In this way, a particular social group, a class, at a particular point in its development, has generalised its experience into a philosophy of society and a mode of government.

However, as we have seen, far from freeing culture and individuals from the state, allowing aesthetic or affective communities to form and reform as they might, Cameronism is in fact about the yet more refined use of the state to govern them. Indeed, far from breaking with the Blairite approach,

Cameron has taken it further, increasing the use of behavioural change strategies and governance through culture and norms. Such continuity is indicative not of how far Cameron has moved Conservatives to the mythical centre ground, but rather of the breadth of the 'creative class' which shares in the Bonoist structure of feeling. Fundamentally, that class thinks of our common culture as something produced *for* the commons not *by* it. And although some of its intellectuals, such as Jesse Norman, talk in Oakeshottian terms of 'civic association', it is clear that they do not really appreciate the ambiguity and paradox of historic, culturally complex, intersubjective and intergenerational civic life which is tied to the complex rhythms of history and not amenable to trite periodisation. They conceive of society as a managerial problem, something that needs to be attuned to a theory such as that of 'post-bureaucracy' and, being most skilled in the manipulation of symbolic forms, think that what is required is a better will, more sophisticated marketing and some creative can-do spirit. As such, their outlook appears very much in tune with the times but is, of course, a product of the times and not an account of them. Cameronism and Hiltonism can see clearly the contemporary creative entrepreneur, but they cannot see the conditions that made him or her possible. The 'reciprocal struggle of discordant powers' may yet rattle the post-bureaucratic age and reveal that the universe is in harmony with a tune not even Bono can hum.

Notes

1 C. Taylor-Taylor, 'About this political rally in the UK playing "Boho"', 5 October 2011, http://www.dandywarhols.com/news/about-this-political-rally-in-the-u-kplaying-boho/

2 See V. King, 'Tory MP Louise Mensch "probably" took drugs in club', *BBC News*, 30 July 2011, http://www.bbc.co.uk/news/uk-politics-14342674; J. Delingpole, 'Cameron, Osborne and the Bullingdon Set', *Daily Telegraph*, 28 March 2011; C. Moodie, 'George Osborne jeered off stage after making foul-mouthed joke at GQ Awards', *Daily Mirror*, 8 September 2011; M. Kite, 'Eyebrows raised over "shoeless" adviser standing in for David Cameron', *Daily Telegraph*, 26 March 2011; A. McElvoy, 'Britain just got Weller: meet the Jam generation', *Spectator*, 13 February 2008; BBC Radio 4, *Desert Island Discs*, 2006, http://www.bbc.co.uk/radio4/features/desert-islanddiscs/castaway/8d5bcfbc

3 Bono, 'Foreword', in J. Sachs, *The End of Poverty: Economic Possibilities for Our Time*, London, Allen Lane, 2005, pp. vii, viii.

4 See D. Cameron, 'Tackling Poverty is a Social Responsibility', Scarman Lecture, 24 November 2006.

5 D. Cameron, 'We Stand for Social Responsibility', speech at the Conservative party conference, 12 October 2007.

6 J. Norman, *The Big Society*, Buckingham, Buckingham University Press, 2010, quotes on pp. 101, 103, 211, 209.

7 S. Hilton and G. Gibbons, *Good Business: Your World Needs You*, New York, Texere, 2002, p. 234.

8 A. Finlayson, *Making Sense of New Labour*, London, Lawrence & Wishart, 2003.

9 M. Gove, 'The Democratic Intellect: What Do We Need to Succeed in the 21st Century?', Sir John Cass's Foundation Lecture, 2009; see also D. Cameron, Speech to Google Zeitgeist Conference, 12 October 2007.

10 Hilton and Gibbons, *Good Business*, quotes on pp. xiv, 51, 122, 90–1, 207.

11 See C. Crouch, *The Strange Non-death of Neo-liberalism*, Cambridge, Polity Press, 2011, p. 138.

12 D. Cameron, Speech on Moral Capitalism, New Zealand House, London, 19 January 2012.

Big Societies, Little Platoons and the Problems with Pluralism

RODNEY BARKER

ONE OF David Cameron's more surprising contributions to the Conservative party's election rhetoric was the 'Big Society'. In government, the phrase has been revived as a commendation not of one big society, but of lots of smaller ones. It is not the only murmur on the right in favour of groups, associations, institutions and communities outside the state. Phillip Blond has argued for a 'Red Toryism' involving the decentralised group life associated with G. K. Chesterton and the distributism of Hilaire Belloc. Conservatism is dipping its toe in the waters of pluralism.

What kind of water is it, and aren't there already quite a few far outside the Conservative party and the right who have for long been a lot more than toe deep? On the left there has been some aggrieved sense of clothes being stolen. Pluralism in one form or another—trade unionism, guild socialism, the cooperative movement, municipal socialism, workers' control—is part of the left's democratic heritage. Left-wing and liberal pluralists inherit a rich, vigorous and varied tradition. Yet they should not be lulled into assuming that because the principal contributions to pluralism have been on the left, all pluralisms are progressive or benign. The left should assert its contribution to the pluralist tradition, but be wary about with whom it shares the credit. At the same time, it should recognise that on the left, pluralist arguments have frequently provided an antidote or a provocation to over-authoritarian approaches to social progress and unimaginative orthodoxy in concepts of human well-being and flourishing.

Pluralism is not a monopoly of the left, and because it is so rich and diverse, it is always necessary before anything else to ask exactly what kind of pluralism is being proposed, who benefits, who is in control and who is being controlled. The word 'pluralism' is a numerator, not a denominator; it tells us that there are many different collections of people, but not what kind of collections they are. The word indicates a range of related arguments, a family perhaps, but a very extended one and one not derived from a single intellectual ancestor. Burke's 'little platoon'—a phrase the right is now bandying about—is a capacious and empty term, which can cover a fox hunt or a hedge fund just as easily as it can cover a parents' group or an allotment association.

The possibilities and uncertainties of abstract pluralism, and the need to ask very specific questions about who, what and where, are neatly illustrated in Charles Crichton's 1953 Ealing comedy, *The Titfield Thunderbolt*. Central government, in the form of a nationalised railway service, announce the

Published by Blackwell Publishing Ltd, 9600 Garsington Road, Oxford OX4 2DQ, UK and 350 Main Street, Malden, MA 02148, USA

closure of a branch line. A group of local residents cooperate to take over and run the line themselves. Yet in order to do so, they need to obtain the assistance and capital of a local retired businessman, and to overcome the opposition of the local bus operator. So local initiative triumphs over London bureaucracy, but it only does so because it has the support of local privilege and local wealth that is accepted by a small town which is socially homogeneous save when divided by the bribes and machinations of capitalism. At the same time, public service triumphs over private profit. Change any one of those elements, and the character of the outcome is changed. That is the character of pluralism once it moves from rhetoric to application—a character that can as easily enhance as challenge governmental, social or economic privilege. To be described as pluralist, an arrangement must possess diversity; to be described as progressive, left or liberal, it must promote equality in some feature of its life. There are many arrangements which easily fulfil the first criterion, but promote the opposite of the second.

The antagonistic varieties of pluralism

Pluralism can be an acceptance of existing and unequal powers and privileges just as readily as it can be an insistence on equality of responsibility and status. There is nothing inherently egalitarian or radical in pluralism; everything depends on what kind of pluralism is being spelled out. The 'Big Society', like any other member of this broad family, is an initially empty concept, given substance by the groups and institutions chosen, the powers accorded to them and the functions they perform. Pluralism is a hold-all category covering a range of positions from individual choices at one end of the scale to comprehensive communities or ways of life at the other. There is a similar range in the governmental response to diversity, from acknowledging it and working with it, to assimilating it in the creation of a single social identity, will or purpose. The radical left contributions have been made around the middle of the scale, after unqualified individualism has been left behind, but before the community has arrived as a monolith swallowing up individual character, at a midpoint where solidarity avoids both unsociable self-interest, on the one hand, and communitarian orthodoxy, on the other.

The scale of pluralism from individual to community or way of life is shaped by the size of the forum within which plurality is possible. The smaller the forum, the greater the individual liberty, so that at one end of the scale the smallest forum is the individual. At the other end of the scale, groups are subordinate to an overall national community identity and so groups, rather than individuals, are the principal actors. At the individual choice end of the scale lays the argument, put forward by Isaiah Berlin, that there is a plurality of goods which do not sit in a single hierarchy, and may therefore present individuals with choices between incompatible actions. It is not possible to be at a football match in Manchester and a concert in London at the same time. Such an argument has no necessary political dimension, though it does have subversive implications for any appeal to a common national culture or community.

Acknowledging the importance of groups can still leave the individual, rather than the group, at the centre of the argument. In this species of pluralism, any individual is a member of or associated with a variety of groups or associations, no one of which adequately expresses the individual's identity, but each of which contributes to an identity that can be unique in its combination of characteristics: agnostic saxophonist vet; Hindu plumber; trade unionist long distance runner. Early twentieth-century British pluralists such as J. N. Figgis, who argued for state recognition of groups and associations such as the church as political persons, at the same time saw such groups and associations as providing the elements from which the individuality of persons was formed. People 'will grow to maturity and be moulded in their prejudices, their tastes, their capacities, and their moral ideals not merely by the great main stream of national life, but also, and perhaps more deeply, by their own family connections, their local communal life in village or town, their educational society (for it is of the essence of education to be in a society), and countless other collective organisms'.

The next move along the scale from individual to central state is to place the principal emphasis not on the individual for whom groups are a source of unique combinations of features of identity, but on groups as having a social identity of their own. Whilst there is something of each position in the arguments of pluralists such as Figgis, the move is a crucial one since it takes the argument from an emphasis which is liberal and individualist, to one which is, or is potentially, communitarian or at least social. An individual may, in such an account, still belong to many groups, but an important part of the expression of that individual and of the representation and promotion and defence of his or her identity, is through and by a group or groups.

The next stage, portmanteau pluralism, can describe whole patterns of goods, so that what are being compared, but not placed in an ordinal scale, are ways of life or communities, not simply the various choices of the individuals which might make up such ways of life. This next version of the argument sees the most important type of group as a community with a more or less comprehensive pattern of values that can provide, not perhaps the whole of an individual identity, but the principal components of such an identity. A community of this kind is far more influential than a simple group or association, and has moved beyond the pluralism of individual choices. An individual chooses a comprehensive package, rather than constructing an identity from whatever social elements he or she chooses.

In the even more authoritarian version, the community chooses the individual, rather than vice versa. It is 'her tradition' or 'his heritage'. Both the soft and the harsh versions are a move from pick-and-mix or *à la carte*, to fixed menu. The boundary between solidarity and orthodoxy has been crossed. This is the position adopted in the multicultural arguments of writers such as Bhikhu Parekh, or the communitarian arguments of writers such as John Gray for a *modus vivendi* between 'different cultural traditions, ways of life and peoples'. If the communitarianism with which New Labour toyed under Tony Blair means anything, it means a social life that leaves less room for individual variety because it sees communities as comprehensive off-the-peg cultural packages.

Each of these points on the scale is an ideal type, and the case made at any one time is likely to be a mixture of elements from various points under the pluralist umbrella. The pluralists favoured by 'Red Tories' are an instance of this. Belloc and Chesterton argued for a redistribution of wealth to assist households as the starting point of public life, but at the same time envisaged this redistribution taking place within an homogeneous national cultural and religious community. Similarly, in the argument of Isaiah Berlin, these two possibilities, of individual choices and collective ways of life, are each found when he calls for 'more room for the attainment of their personal ends by individuals and by minorities'. Minorities, however few their members, are immediately less fluid than individuals, and the collective values, patterns of behaviour, conventions of social relations and forms of expression which characterise them, however much they may arise from individual preferences, also constrain each member in a manner that the varied preferences of an individual alone, do not.

Governmental responses to pluralist diversity

The next move along the scale is from arguing that groups, associations and communities have a real identity, that they are real social actors, to arguing that they are or should be important political actors. This can be further strengthened by arguing, as did the legal theorist F. W. Maitland, that they are not only social persons, but legal ones, thus further solidifying their identity.

An acknowledgement by government of pluralist diversity does not necessarily involve governmental pluralism. The first choice is between local and central government as the principal actors. If the former, and if local power is to be real and not merely a matter of presentation, there is a possibility of different policies and different priorities in different parts of the country. The second choice is between seeing diversity as components contributing to a consequent national consensus, or responding to different components with different policies. That choice can be made both nationally and locally, adding a further complexity.

Whilst a pluralist state may be the last point on a scale, it is not necessarily a political resting point. It is not even a single form. On the one hand is a representative pluralism that, within the framework of a single system of law and practice, incorporates or attempts to incorporate the diversity of its citizens. There have been moments when pluralists such as Cole have seen variety—in this case, the addition to the formation of public policy by a greater role for trade unions, not as a necessary, natural and permanent feature of human life, but, at least potentially, as a way of moving ever closer to a single, fuller conception of the general will. This is a pluralism of representation that sees ultimate harmony achieved by the fullest possible expression of partial varieties.

On the other hand is a governmental pluralism that devolves its powers to or shares them with various communities, frequently religious communities, functional groups, regions and associations. So John Gray argues for juridical, or as he calls it 'legal', pluralism, with a polity composed of, or if not composed of, then containing, distinct communities with their own laws. Earlier pluralists drew back from this proposal, arguing that government should respect the self-management of groups and associations, rather than that it should devolve its own powers to them. A state characterised by constitutional, governmental or judicial pluralism would have precedent in the parallel jurisdictions, secular and ecclesiastical, of Medieval Europe—a division that advocates of the rule of law sought to replace, both actually and theoretically. However, it contains permanent possibilities of intellectual incoherence, and real and continually present possibilities of practical incompatibilities of a disabling kind.

Such governmental or constitutional pluralism must have limits. There may be various practices of marriage within the territory of a state, but not different practices regulating on which side of the road vehicles drive. If the pluralist state is segmented according to collective identities that are spread evenly or randomly across its territory, as might be the case with, for instance, religious belief, then its structure does not necessarily presage further arguments for its own dissolution. If, on the other hand, its segmentation arises from geographically located differences in collective identity, as with a state composed of several geographically concentrated nations or ethnic groups, then the very existence of its constitutional pluralism may provide the grounds for its own dissolution.

Ambivalences in left-wing pluralism

Pluralism on the left re-emerged in the twentieth century's closing decades in response to a changing significance of class and a growing significance, in addition, of other dimensions of identity: ethnicity, gender, sexuality, religion. However, growing social complexity and the ideological vacuum that followed the collapse of Russian and East European communist regimes and the end of the Cold War made the difficulties and tensions within pluralism even harder to negotiate.

The left egalitarian use of pluralism marked a slow move away from a simple class analysis of politics, and a class prescription for political action. The 'rainbow' pluralism of the 1980s illustrated the divergence, but also the practical intermingling, of these two paths. Socialist pluralists at the close of the twentieth century argued, despite a recognition of varieties in the expression of interests, for 'the priority of class in socialist politics'. In

Hilary Wainwright's argument for a revision of Hayek to make associations of citizens and producers a source of policy information there was an imaginative dissolution of earlier ideological boundaries. Paul Hirst's advocacy of associationism as a means of transforming decision making at all levels with pluralist democracy went beyond guild socialism and workers' control to envisage democratic dispersal in every aspect of public life. Wainwright and Mike Rustin tried at one and the same time to assert the diverse identities of gender, ethnicity and sexuality, and to incorporate them all into the overall unity of a working-class socialist movement.

There are incoherencies in left-wing pluralism as with other varieties, at the level both of ideology and policy. The Blair government's first forays into localism with elected mayors, and nationalism with Scottish and Welsh parliaments and assemblies, was confounded by an assumption that local and regional government would nonetheless be a smooth cog in the workings of United Kingdom government. Yet left-wing pluralism has always been a way of giving responsibility to the less powerful and redistributing power downwards. It has never been a matter of either shifting burdens away from the fortunate, or removing restraints on privilege. At the point at which an individual's control over their own life is reduced or restrained, or the burdens on them increased, pluralism crosses to another part of the ideological spectrum.

Pluralism and the 'Big Society'

Rhetoric is never just rhetoric, and 'the Big Society' should not be dismissed as meaningless phrase mongering. There are many versions of pluralism, however, and some of them are on the right. The election rhetoric gave some clues: 'we're all in this together'; 'over to you'; 'join the government of Great Britain'. Whatever dumping of public babies on other people's doorsteps there is, central government is still going to set the rules and control the budgets. 'Free schools' will only be free of local control by dealing instead with central government. Each instance of pluralism can be judged on the extent to which it promotes greater equalities of status, power and human flourishing. That means both a sceptical approach to rhetoric, but also a judgement of any particular proposal not in terms of who has made it, but in terms of its character and likely consequences. A proposal cannot be accepted simply because it is pluralist, nor rejected simply because it is advocated by the right rather than by the left. Under New Labour, 'communitarianism' was accepted, by those who accepted it, with too little critical scrutiny, whilst egalitarian pluralism was too readily dismissed as standing in the way of reform.

If the social collectives from which the life of any individual is derived are varied, then groups and institutions are a resource for the citizen, not a defining community. That choice is just as relevant in responding to the rhetoric of the 'Big Society' as it has been in subordinating the individual to the church, the family or the ethnic group. Until the character of each small platoon is clear, scepticism is the first part of any response to it. The village can be as oppressive as the metropolis, and organisations outside the central state can be as exploitative, oppressive and destructive as any central government. Not every group, organisation, association or institution which is not part of government is automatically, necessarily or inherently virtuous or benign, anymore than the opposite is true. Putting your trust in the tenant's association or the union is not the same as putting your education or your health in the hands of United Outsourcing plc.; going to a church or a mosque or a synagogue is radically different from handing your identity over to a community or a culture, and running your own cooperative is a million miles away from 'joining the government of Great Britain'. Praising the 'little platoon' can sound enticing, but it is vital to find out first what the platoon does, who can join and who cannot, who the platoon commander is, and whether he or she has sealed orders.

called 'society' (other than as the sum of the individual 'men, women and families' of whom it was composed). Indeed, though she herself may have been unaware of the fact, her remarks echoed an understanding of the nature of 'society' that had been recurrent among political commentators, lawyers and users of ordinary language over many earlier centuries. In the Roman law tradition that was revived in much of Europe in the late-mediaeval period, a 'societas' was a contractual or 'partnership' arrangement between private individuals, which they could enter or exit at will, with little reference to wider public life. In its origins, this view of 'society' had been closely linked to the idea of 'property'. It meant that people who owned property (initially in land, but later extending to professional skills and other services) could enter into contracts, whereas those who had nothing to 'sell' could not (so that serfs, bondsmen and most women, who owned no 'property', could not be full participants in 'society').

A second very different tradition that had evolved over many centuries in much of Europe after the earlier withdrawal of Roman rule was that of a person's entitlement to support in time of need in his or her parish of 'settlement'. Whether such a claim constituted a form of 'right' was to be a matter of contention among lawyers over many centuries, but, from a very early date and in many contexts, it was recognised that the 'common people' in times of need had customary claims to support from levies on private property. This was a principle publicly recognised in both the 'charitable' and the 'poor law' provisions of the Elizabethan Poor Law Act of 1601.

A third tradition, largely forgotten until the fifteenth-century revival of knowledge about the ancient world, was the classical Athenian view that the 'civic' and 'social' spheres were one and the same. This semi-mythical ideal had of course applied only to a tiny slave-owning minority, and over many centuries had been largely transmitted not in the form of public laws and institutions, but by imaginative writers and theorists in the Utopian tradition. However, it was to be a recurrent theme in dissident writing about 'society' down to the present day. And the fact that its transmitters have included such disparate figures as Plato, Thomas More, Philip Sidney, William Morris, H.G. Wells and John Rawls makes their vision of 'society' as coterminous with independent 'citizenship', even of 'humanity', not necessarily coherent, but difficult to ignore.

Over long periods and in many languages, these three ways of imagining a 'society' often overlapped in everyday thought and speech. But from the mid-seventeenth century, the Roman law idea that a 'society' (both as a form of ownership and as a political unit) was made up of freely contracting individuals was to become increasingly pervasive in England, both in political thought and in the common law. It was central to the thinking of Hobbes and Locke, to whom membership of a 'civil society' meant the (assumed) contractual assent of property-owning individuals to be the subjects of a particular polity or state. A century later, the political economy of Adam Smith conjured up a vision of what he called 'a Great Society' (a term that was

Servile State or Discredited State? Some Historical Antecedents of Current 'Big Society' Debates

JOSE HARRIS

I think the things of which England may be proud are not her wealth, but her trade unions, her Friendly Societies, her co-operative societies, and her Charity Organisation Societies.

(Alfred Marshall, evidence to the Royal Commission on the Aged Poor, 1893).[1]

The adjective 'social' is harmless as describing relationships of all sorts between man and man. But its derivative 'Society' should be banished in the interests of clear thinking.

(J. D. Mabbott, *The State and the Citizen*, 1948).[2]

BRITISH political history is riddled with examples of parties, pressure groups and individual politicians unexpectedly taking up ideas and policies more commonly associated with their 'honourable opponents'. But few such transitions have been as dramatic as the shift from Margaret Thatcher's claim in 1987 that there was 'no such thing as society' to the proclamation by her successor David Cameron that a 'Big Society' was at the very 'core' of 'modern Conservatism'. 'We want the state to act as an instrument for helping to create a strong society,' Cameron declared in his Hugo Young lecture of November 2009. 'We understand that the big society is not just going to spring to life on its own: we need strong and concerted government action to make it happen. We need to use the state to remake society.'

This chapter will consider the historical antecedents of this bouleversement from various perspectives. I shall look first at the longstanding ambiguities surrounding the very concept of 'society' as understood in earlier periods of British history. I shall then explore ways in which rival visions of the role of 'society' have clashed in specific historic contexts (and particularly in the 'servile state' versus 'social security' debates of the early twentieth century). And finally I shall consider the relevance (if any) of those earlier contested understandings of 'society' to controversies that surround the interpretation of a 'Big Society' at the present time.

The evolution of 'society'

Margaret Thatcher was by no means unique among English-speaking commentators in expressing doubt about the very existence of something to have powerful long-term resonances in both 'liberal' and 'state-interventionist' thought down to the present day). In coining this term, Smith was referring to the rise of a worldwide economy of contractual exchange of goods and services in place of the communal production, regulated local markets and ties to a native birthplace that still prevailed in Scotland, England and much of Europe, even in his own time. But Smith was also putting forward the astonishing view that, for the first time in human history, 'all mankind', even the very poorest, were potential members of a 'Great Society' since any individual ('even the beggar') was now capable of engaging in 'free exchange'. Smith never disparaged the virtues of personal charity; nor, more surprisingly, did he wholly dismiss the possibility that a 'Great Society' *might* be run on state-directed lines. He portrayed reliance on communal benevolence as increasingly dysfunctional and outmoded in a world of universal free trading; while his brief discussion of a *dirigiste* model of a 'Great Society' suggested that he saw the latter, at least in a British context, as practically unthinkable.[3]

A generation later, Jeremy Bentham envisaged a much larger role than Smith had done for state intervention in such spheres as poor relief, education, public health and the management of charity. The differences between them, however, were perhaps less than was often supposed since the underlying aims of the Benthamite reforms were not to foster communal provision as a good in itself, but to induce individuals to provide for themselves by private contract wherever possible (a view embedded in the thinking behind the famous Poor Law Amendment Act of 1834). Living in a much more urbanised society than Smith, Jeremy Bentham and his followers had a larger conception that certain services, such as sewerage, drainage and public health, were intrinsically collective and public. But the very word 'society' was, in Bentham's eyes, at best a convenient shorthand or useful 'fiction'. What it emphatically did *not* mean was that 'society' meant some kind of undying metaphysical entity or organic community.

Everyday language of the eighteenth and early nineteenth centuries did not endorse Bentham's view that 'society' was a mere 'fiction', but instead used it to characterise an infinite variety of private voluntary arrangements. This in no way precluded the possibility that voluntary 'societies' might play an important role in public life, or cooperate closely with departments of local and central government, but (except in very unusual cases), they were not themselves part of such bodies. Over the course of the period, the term 'society' came to be used to embrace commercial partnerships and private companies; religious, cultural and scientific institutions; friendly societies, charities and trade unions; and the wider world of pleasure and 'sociability' ranging from 'High Society' and 'County Society' through to working-men's clubs and mere neighbourly social intercourse. Jane Austen's Mr Darcy, it may be remembered, belonged to 'society' when in London, but complained that there was 'no society' in Hertfordshire (referring in both cases simply to the company of individuals who thought and behaved like himself). And the term might also refer to personal relations of the most intimate kind, as in the 'mutual society' that 'the one ought to have of the other' prescribed for married couples in the Book of Common Prayer. Insofar as such diverse uses had anything in common, it was that 'societies' were created, managed and (in most cases) dissolvable by the will of their members. Some, like the Royal Society and the Society for Promoting Christian Knowledge, might be seen as playing an important role in the wider life of the nation. But many more were simply informal partnerships that ran their own private affairs, or lobbied for wider (though still largely local) legislative change, subject only to observance of the common law. Trade unions in particular—famous for their *internal* communitarian solidarity—nonetheless strongly resisted pressure to be treated *legally* as unitary or corporate entities. Indeed, down to the twentieth century they commonly referred to themselves as *'trade societies'*, thereby emphasising their immunity from any corporate liability for torts, crimes and breaches of contract committed by individual members.

This widely pervasive voluntarist and self-regulatory understanding of 'society' persisted in England for much of the nineteenth century, and came to be seen by many foreign observers as uniquely characteristic of English (or British) national culture. Indeed, the notorious 1834 Poor Law reform actively contributed to this culture since, by aiming to withdraw public relief from all but the wholly destitute, it gradually generated a new generation of philanthropy among the upper and middle classes, together with an explosion of charitable, friendly society and self-help schemes among the poor themselves. This shift of emphasis was fraught with privation for large numbers of poor people living in Britain, but by the 1870s it had generated what appeared to many observers to be a wholly new kind of 'modern' industrial society. Continental visitors as diverse as Hippolyte Taine, Martin Nadaud, Arwen Emminghaus and Paul de Rousiers, all commented on the high level of wages and savings among the English working classes, the wide-ranging 'social solidarity' and 'mutuality' of organised working-class movements, and the light-handedness or non-existence of public regulation of such bodies (particularly by comparison with France and Germany, where voluntary associations were legally compelled to be formally registered with local government or the police).[4] However, several of these observers also noted the relative weakness or absence of any more comprehensive sense of 'society' as expressing the wider life of the nation, greater than the sum of its parts. Nor did English writers on social questions appear have any understanding of 'society' as a supra-political vision of the whole life of mankind, of a kind which some continental theorists (e.g., Durkheim, Tonnies, Simmel) saw as evolving in Western Europe over the course of the later nineteenth century.

Some 'new views of society'

Nonetheless, certain more comprehensive and 'collective' conceptions of 'society' tentatively emerged in Britain in the wake of the French Revolution and Napoleonic Wars. Tom Paine in *The Rights of Man* in 1791, had put forward what was seen as the revolutionary claim that 'society', far from being an 'artificial' creation of human actors, was the 'natural', spontaneous and 'primordial' condition of mankind, whose proper role in human lives had been violently usurped by endless generations of 'aristocratic government'. In Paine's view, virtually everything habitually done by governments in his own and earlier times could far better have been 'performed by the common sense of society, without government'. This was a principle that he perceived as being acted out in the infant United States of America, where government itself, so he maintained, was 'nothing more than a national association acting on the principles of society'.[5]

Twenty years later, Robert Owen's *A New View of Society* propounded what seemed to be the opposite view: that 'society has hitherto been ignorant of the true means by which the most useful and valuable character may be formed'. This ignorance had led to 'filling the world with folly and inconsistency, and making society . . . a scene of insincerity and counteraction'. The solution, in Owen's view, lay not initially in 'society' per se, but in compulsory *state-enforcement* of universal schooling, the basing of wages on a 'labour theory of value' and universal technical training to transform the skills and characters of individual citizens. Human beings, Owen believed, were 'without exception universally plastic', and 'the character, conduct, and enjoyment' of children trained 'under the new system' would 'speedily become living examples of (its) vast superiority'. Only thus would be attained what Owen called a 'New View of Society'—that is, of universal skilled employment in self-governing public workshops at craftsmen's wages; the 'great object of which', he explained, was for the people 'to obtain wealth, and to enjoy it'. When this had been achieved, then 'society'—meaning the 'great mass of the people' organised in small cooperative groups—would be able to revert to its proper and 'natural' role of 'governing itself'.[6]

Tom Paine's and Robert Owen's distinctive programmes—the one invoking the virtues of 'society' to correct the perceived evils of the state, the other invoking transitional intervention *by* the state to correct the current *failures* of society—were to be widely influential in the rise of cooperative, labour and socialist movements in nineteenth-century Britain. Both authors used the term 'society' in a much more 'inclusive' sense than was common in the conventions of their day; and Owen in particular was unusual amongst English theorists of the early nineteenth century in explicitly conceiving of national 'society' as a composite social whole. In these respects (if not in their shared passion for 'equality'), their vision of 'society' closely resembled that of several major 'Tory' theorists of the early and mid-Victorian generations— among them such figures as R. B. Seeley, James Froude, Thomas Carlyle and John Ruskin. All these writers viewed 'society' not just as an aggregate of small groups, but as the corporate expression of national moral identity and interclass rights and duties; while Ruskin in particular focused on 'the state' rather than 'society' as the proper medium through which to promote such goals as public health, technical education, full-employment, national culture and well-functioning family life.[7]

Such ideas found some echo within the established and nonconformist churches, where eminent Victorians ranging from Lord Shaftesbury to Benjamin Waugh campaigned for new forms of partnership between voluntary philanthropy and the state to fill the gaps in social provision left by the Poor Law reforms of 1834. One of the most ambitious of these partnerships was the 'Civic Society' programme pioneered in the established Church of Scotland by Dr Thomas Chalmers, who aimed to collaborate with city authorities in providing family support, child care, job-training and 'friendly visiting' schemes for every poor household (a scheme that, in its underlying aims if not in precise details, seemed to anticipate certain aspects of 'Big Society' visions of the present day).[8]

Nonetheless, not all movements of thought about the *civic* importance of 'society' ran in the same direction. The mid-nineteenth century also saw the emergence of significant religious movements and groups who came to favour the *disengagement* of 'societies' from the state, and the assertion of their *separate* identities as essential to personal and group freedom. These counter-movements were provoked by attempts on the part of 'utilitarian' reformers in Parliament to redistribute church property rights and to impose public control over clerical appointments within the English and Scottish established churches. Such policies stemmed partly from anti-clericalism per se, but partly from attempts by socially pragmatic Christians to make churches more responsive to changing social needs. However, they provoked a powerful reaction among many churchmen, who revived the ancient claim that churches—far from being simply 'groups' within wider 'society'—were themselves divinely ordained 'societies', whose internal affairs could not rightfully be interfered with by any external secular power. These controversies provoked the conversion of significant numbers of Victorian Anglicans to the Church of Rome, the rise of 'Christian socialism' among many who remained, and the secession of a powerful majority of Scots Presbyterians under the leadership of Dr Chalmers (hitherto a bastion of church 'establishment') to form an independent Free Church of Scotland. Such disputes also had implications that went far beyond their immediate ecclesiastical contexts. They asserted the claim that 'societies' of all kinds, whatever their philosophical antecedents, had certain intrinsic identities that could not be overridden by larger ones, even by the secular state.

Although initially focused on church matters, these arguments were to be gradually appropriated over the following half century by many secular groups. As movements for 'state intervention' and 'social legislation' came to be seen as increasingly assertive in English public life, such diverse groups as libertarians, pluralists, syndicalists, cooperatists, guild socialists and Anglo-Catholics (sometimes overlapping with each other) came increasingly to favour a return to the autonomy of small self-governing groups, subject only to a framework of English common law.

A much more comprehensive, activist and regulatory vision of 'society', however, was simultaneously percolating into British public life from some quite different quarters, stimulated by the ever-growing pace and dislocation of industrial change. Between the 1830s and 1850s, the model that Adam Smith had rejected—of a 'Great Society' explicitly run on *state-interventionist* lines—was to be taken up and propagated, not by Smith's disciples in Britain, but by the school of French 'positivist' philosophers, headed by Henri Saint-Simon and August Comte. Both Saint-Simon and Comte were warm enthusiasts for Smith's vision of an unlimited global economy, but they and their disciples claimed that this model could best be attained, not by free competition and unregulated markets, but through increased regulation of business enterprise and official promotion of technical expertise, social policy, public education and public charities—all to be organised (or incorporated from the private sector) into specialist agencies of a centralised 'administrative state'. This model of a 'Great Society', based on planning, technocracy, personal 'altruism' and applied social science (all of which Comte subsumed under the label 'positivism') was to become an important strand in the doctrines and policies of the French Second Empire and later of the Third Republic.

Many aspects of this new 'positivist' understanding of a 'Great Society' were to be gradually inseminated into English thought over the middle and later decades of the nineteenth century, extending far beyond thinkers who specifically identified themselves as 'Positivists'. Among the earliest English advocates of positivism was John Stuart Mill, who for a time was strongly attracted to Comte's ideas because they seemed to hold out the promise of a wholly new kind of 'science of society'. Mill eventually lost faith in Comte, but British disciples or admirers of 'Positivism' were increasingly to be found among literary intellectuals like George Eliot and Harriet Martineau, radical business men like Charles Booth and William Rathbone, 'new liberals' such as Frederic Harrison and J. A. Hobson, and leading professors at Cambridge and the new metropolitan and provincial universities. Perhaps most influentially, 'Positivists' were to be found among prominent members of the early Fabian Society, such as Graham Wallas, William Pember Reeves, and Sidney and Beatrice Webb. Even members of the Charity Organisation movement (often seen as a bastion of late-Victorian *anti*-statism) were inspired by the success of the French Positivist movement in promoting cooperation between voluntary societies, the state and even the Catholic Church, particularly in such fields as family support and child welfare. Others influenced by such ideas included figures like Alfred Marshall, William Beveridge and the young Winston Churchill, who were not 'Positivists' in any formal or institutional sense, but who nonetheless shared the view that the long-term equilibrium of state, economy and society in Britain had become fundamentally out of balance. Like the continental visitors mentioned above, all were impressed by the vast range of English working-class friendly societies, savings clubs and voluntary self-help organisations. But they also drew attention to the persistence of a substantial minority at the bottom of English society (amounting perhaps to one-third of the working classes), for whom 'self-help' seemed to be largely out of reach, except through very haphazard and often grossly expensive channels.

Society and public policy

This longstanding history of debate and conjecture about the very nature of 'society' formed an important backcloth to what has come to be seen as the initial phase of the British welfare state as it emerged in the early years of the twentieth century. Such ideas might have had very limited impact, however, had it not been for the wide-ranging structural changes occurring in Britain and the wider global economy during the same period. Many of these changes were not fully understood at the time, but they nonetheless presented a major challenge to the delicate balance between a strong but strictly limited central government, global free trade, and the mass culture of voluntarism, localism, self-help and mutual aid that had evolved over the previous century. From the 1880s the prolonged depression in British agriculture, mass migration of the poorest classes to the great cities, the rise of large-scale unemployment, adoption of protective tariffs by other industrial nations and (at the turn-of-the-century) a cripplingly expensive imperial war all threatened to undermine Britain's long history of industrial and commercial predominance, steadily rising prosperity, and relative social and industrial peace. These problems were to be mirrored in a series of prolonged ideological debates about free trade versus protectionism, the distribution of wealth and income, 'voluntarism' versus 'state control', large-scale versus small-scale ownership of land, and the deeply embattled question of what were the functions of the ancient communitarian Poor Laws in a modern industrial and 'democratic' state.

Such debates, with all their complexities, cannot be reviewed in detail here, but one aspect of those controversies, relevant to the theme of this chapter, was the degree to which many of the issues involved appeared to foreshadow certain 'Big Society' dilemmas of the present day (including both the role of voluntary action, and new forms of partnership between society and the state). Since the 1880s and even earlier, many of the disputes that had arisen over 'individualism' versus 'state control' had increasingly been focused, not on the role of government per se, but on which of Britain's innumerable voluntary, charitable and private agencies should be brought into administrative and financial partnership with statutory public authorities. Professor Alfred Marshall's evidence to the Royal Commission on the Aged Poor in 1893 (cited above) precisely demonstrated the growth of the 'progressive' idea that a modest measure of 'redistribution' might be channelled by the state through reliable voluntary organisations (though Marshall also warned against the danger of charitable busybodies trying to dictate and take over the public role). Even the hostility to 'state intervention' often associated with the Charity Organisation Society largely stemmed, not from anti-statism per se (on the contrary, the COS was more than willing to act as the state's intermediary), but from the increasing readiness of public authorities to co-opt the services of other more populist and free-spending charities like Dr Barnardo's and the Salvation Army, of whom the COS deeply disapproved.[9] Such a perspective could also be seen in the many clashes between rival Christian denominations, and between secularists and Christians in general, over the role of religious bodies in the provision of state education. Here again, the underlying problem had ceased to be opposition to the very principle of state enforcement of compulsory schooling. Instead, it was about how far 'voluntary' and 'denominational schools' (including those run by the Established Churches) should receive public funding and work in cooperation with public education authorities, while at the same time retaining private control over curricula, the selection of pupils and freedom to teach their own confessional beliefs.

The long-drawn-out decline of British agriculture in this period and the rise of 'unemployment' as a serious industrial problem meant that such perspectives increasingly spilt over into the economic and industrial spheres. From the 1880s, both Poor Law guardians and ordinary local authorities were increasingly encouraged by central government to collaborate with charities, local businessmen and other private agencies in providing job information and actual employment through local development schemes, 'labour colonies' and rate-funded 'public works'. The rise of local authority housing schemes, pursued with no conscious reference to economic theory, likewise became an important medium both of public-private partnerships and of counter-cyclical public investment in years of trade depression. The Conservative government Irish Land Act of 1903 devoted an unprecedented share of British peacetime public expenditure to creating a new landed peasantry in Ireland, on lines that anticipated the social model to be eulogised a decade later in Hilaire Belloc's *The Servile State*—a work often cited with approval by advocates of a 'Big Society' in the present. Land reform in Edwardian England, Wales and Scotland was markedly more limited in scope than in Edwardian Ireland, but, nonetheless, Liberal legislation passed in 1908 set up a national Small Holdings Commission, and endowed English and Scottish county councils with powers of compulsory purchase of land in order to create agricultural smallholdings and local farmers' cooperatives. The latter worked in close alliance with the consumer cooperative movement, which enjoyed a period of extraordinary growth in both wholesale and retail activity throughout the decade-and-a-half leading up to the First World War.[10]

Similar partnerships between government and society were also envisaged in the policies for the relief of poverty, most closely associated with the 'New Liberal' programme of Asquith, Lloyd George and Churchill after 1908. The Old Age Pensions Act of 1908 introduced 'citizen' pensions for the 'aged poor', financed out of central government taxation and paid through the national network of the Post Office, but managed and monitored at local level by panels of charitable volunteers. And on a much more ambitious scale, the 1911 National Insurance Act introduced schemes of public-private partnership in social insurance provision, of a kind and on a scale unprecedented in earlier British history. Under this Act, a system of contributory social insurance against the risks of unemployment, sickness and long-term disability was applied for the first time to all industrial and commercial employees, female as well as male, who earned less than the prevailing income tax threshold of £160. Moreover, though the scheme was to be supervised by a National Insurance Commission, the Act also provided for voluntary and private sector involvement at several different levels. Thus, the day-to-day management of 'unemployment insurance' was to include advisory panels of workers and trade unionists, working in conjunction with labour exchange managers, while the 'national health' scheme was to be run by self-governing 'approved societies' (the latter to include friendly societies, collecting societies and 'not-for-profit' schemes set up by private insurance companies). Moreover, both schemes envisaged that—far from doing away with private saving—the extensive involvement of voluntary agencies would actively *reinforce* the national culture of thrift and mutual aid, not just among more prosperous workers, but among the very poorest of the industrial working class. It would thus make possible the gradual dismantling and eventual abolition of the means-tested English Poor Laws, which were increasingly seen in many progressive quarters as an archaic and semi-servile anachronism in a modern industrial age.

'Servile state' or 'discredited state'?

What was the exact nature of this pre-1914 programme of British social legislation, and what relation if any did it bear to current debates about a 'Big Society'? The latter is not an entirely anachronistic question, since several current enthusiasts for a 'Big Society' have looked back on the social reforms of the Edwardian era as providing either a ghastly prototype for the 'road to serfdom', or a positive template for experiments in social action and public–private partnerships at the present day. It is, however, a path fraught with pitfalls for anyone who hopes to make political capital out of Edwardian successes and failures in 'party political' terms. This is partly because many of the policies closely associated with Edwardian 'new liberalism' were subsequently to be adopted and extended by later Conservative and Labour regimes, and partly because some of the key figures in Edwardian liberalism themselves switched to other parties later in their careers. Moreover, even at the time, many critics and observers who identified themselves as 'Liberals' nonetheless deeply disagreed about both the political significance of the recent legislation and the wider relation of 'society' to the state.

Of no one was this more true than the Liberal author, satirist and critic, Hilaire Belloc, whose ideas, as mentioned above, have been identified as anticipating certain key aspects of present-day perceptions of a 'Big Society'.

Thus, far from portraying the recent social legislation as a triumph for popular democracy, Belloc's *The Servile State* denounced the whole 'new Liberal programme', and particularly the National Insurance Act of 1911, as the fruit of a sinister conspiracy between capitalists, bureaucrats and trade unions to demolish small-scale property rights and to reduce the British population to the mass slavery of imperial Rome. In Belloc's view there could be no freedom without universal rights to ownership of small-scale landed property, together with control over one's own workplace (as demonstrated, so he claimed, in early twentieth-century France, where recent attempts to introduce compulsory national insurance had 'broken down in the face of an universal and a virile contempt').

Although widely dismissed as utopian, Belloc's approach received some unexpected endorsement from the work of another unusual Liberal—the social investigator Seebohm Rowntree, who was an intimate friend and advisor of the Liberal Chancellor of the Exchequer, Lloyd George. Rowntree's revelations of the continuing extent of mass poverty in Edwardian Britain had been a major inspiration behind the New Liberal social insurance and old age pensions programmes. But Rowntree's study of the economy of Belgium, written at the very moment when he was advising the Chancellor on national insurance reforms, had unexpectedly concluded that the quality of life in Belgium's small-scale cooperative peasant communities was in many respects greatly superior to that of Britain's industrial working classes, even though average real incomes among the latter were much higher.[11]

A third unorthodox Liberal of the period, the political theorist Ernest Barker, also struck a dissentient note (though of a more positive and optimistic kind). Writing in the early summer of 1914, with no apparent foreboding of the imminence of war, Barker suggested that the political keynote of the previous decade had been not the 'Servile State', but the 'Discredited State'—by which he meant, not that the state had fallen into disrepute, but that under recent legislation the powers and functions of government had been continually hived off into the hands of specialist, self-governing, occupational and voluntary organisations within wider 'society'. Barker, who was a convinced 'pluralist', certainly did not disapprove of this trend towards the delegation and decentralisation of powers away from the state and into the hands of 'society'. But he nonetheless warned that voluntary 'associations' of all kinds (be they businesses, trade unions, denominations, charities or neighbourhood groups) might abuse or exceed their powers and themselves come to exercise tyranny over others. In that case it was the state's definitive function to intervene and reassert itself— a warning that echoed very similar remarks that had been made by Alfred Marshall about the over-intrusive ambitions of the Charity Organisation Society a generation before. [12]

Conclusion

How far do these controversies from earlier historical periods have any bearing upon apparently similar or parallel debates about the respective roles of state and society at the present day? At one level, the correct answer is 'none at all', since, as suggested above, both the roles of the institutions concerned and contemporary understanding of the words that described them have so often shifted unpredictably between different contexts and generations. The idea of the 'state' in the minimal sense of a public body able to impose its will by law or by force has attained some degree of common understanding over the course of the modern era. But the term 'society', even today, has attained no such minimal degree of consensus. Between Mr Darcy, Emile Durkheim and Margaret Thatcher (all of them key figures in expressing aspects of the modern social imagination) there seems no possibility of any shared ground. By the early twentieth century, and particularly among English theorists of the 'idealist' school, the term 'society' was being used in a much more 'public' sense than had been common a century before, with 'society' and the 'state' in some contexts coming to be used interchangeably. There was little sign in English usage of that period, of a perception increasingly found among continental theorists, that 'society' was a synonym for the whole of global reality, far more 'universal' than the state itself. Moreover, trends in British political philosophy throughout the interwar period, and indeed until much later, were to be deeply hostile to thinking about 'society' as anything more than the accumulated acts of individuals (the more holistic conception being seen as, at best, muddle, at worst, implicitly totalitarian). Such perceptions have changed radically since the 1960s, but, for the alert citizen, 'society' in all its many guises and sizes still needs to be defined and explained.

Notes

1 *Official Papers by Alfred Marshall* (ed. J. M. Keynes), London, Macmillan, 1926, p. 262.
2 J. D. Mabbott, *The State and the Citizen: An Introduction to Political Philosophy*, London, Hutchinson, 1948. Mabbott's book, based on lectures given in Oxford in the mid-1940s, was to be the main introductory textbook on political thought used in British universities until the late-1960s.
3 A. Smith, *The Theory of Moral Sentiments* (1759, Indianapolis, 1959 edn), pp. 85–6, 234–5.
4 M. Nadaud, *Histoire des Classes Ouvrières en Angleterre* (Paris, 1872); A. Emminghaus, *Das Armenwesen und die Armengesetzgebung in Europaische Staaten* (Berlin, 1870); P. de Rousiers, *The Labour Question in Britain* (Macmillan, 1896); E. Dueckershoff, *How the English Workman Lives* (P.S. King, 1899). Nadaud in particular was astonished at the density of self-governing associational life that he observed among the English lower classes, and the almost total absence of continental-style 'police regulation'.

5 T. Paine, *The Rights of Man, 1791* (ed. G. Claeys), Cambridge, Cambridge University Press, 1992.

6 R. Owen, *A New View of Society* (ed. J. Saville), London, Macmillan, 1991.

7 On Ruskin's largely negative views of 'society', see J. Ruskin, *Works* (eds E. T. Cook and A. Wedderburn), London, George Allen, 1905 and 1907, esp. volumes 17 and 29.

8 T. Chalmers, *The Christian and Civic Economy of Large Towns* (ed. David Gladstone), London, Thoemies, 1995.

9 G. Wagner, *Barnado*, London, Weidenfeld, 1979.

10 British Parliamentary Papers, *Annual Report of the Industrial and Agricultural Co-operative Societies in the United Kingdom* (Cmd 6045, 1912); *Annual Returns of the Co-operative movement in Great Britain* (Cmd 6946, 1912-13; Cmd 7283, 1914).

11 B. Seebohm Rowntree, *Land and Labour: Lessons from Belgium*, London, Macmillan, 1910, pp. 525–47.

12 E. Barker, 'The discredited state: thoughts on politics before the war', *The Political Quarterly*, o.s., 1915, pp. 120–1; *Official Papers of Alfred Marshall*, London, Royal Economic Society and Macmillan, 1926, pp. 211–2.

Tocqueville and the Big Society

JEREMY JENNINGS

EVERY Tocqueville scholar knows that America was not the only country to secure his interest. Throughout his life Tocqueville always turned towards England and (like his fellow French liberals) he did so because he saw that England, like America, might avoid the perils of a mass democracy. For Tocqueville, England at its best was an aristocratic society characterised by 'self-government'. Yet, during his first visit to England in the early 1830s and following the passing of the first Reform Bill, he sensed that these aspects of English society might soon be swept away. Although Tocqueville's admiration for English society remained (this is, for example, an important sub-theme contained within *The Ancient Regime and the French Revolution*), his doubts about the potential longevity of the English system of aristocratic and local self-government were only to increase over time. Nor were Tocqueville's concerns without foundation. The administrative calamities of the Crimean War (commented upon by many French liberals) forced the British government to begin a process of administrative reform that, over time, was to turn Britain (in the words of the late W. H. Greenleaf) into a 'much governed nation'. As Herbert Spencer noted in his comments on the 'coming slavery', this process was well under way by the end of the nineteenth century and was only further extended during the twentieth century with the creation of the welfare state—a process supported by Liberal, Conservative and Labour governments alike. It is no surprise that when Friedrich von Hayek wrote *The Road to Serfdom* the country he had most clearly in mind was England.

The worm began to turn in the 1970s when Britain reached a point of near economic and political collapse. It was at this point that Margaret Thatcher emerged, campaigning, in no uncertain terms, to 'roll back the frontiers of the state'. Whether it is true that Mrs Thatcher held up a copy of Friedrich von Hayek's *The Constitution of Liberty* and proclaimed 'this is what we believe' is uncertain, but there can be no doubt that the Conservative government under her leadership implemented many reforms which had an authentic Hayekian ring. It is not my intention to discuss the question of the character of these reforms. Rather, my point is that Mrs Thatcher's programme also sowed the seeds of a civic conservatism which can be regarded as the first of what has proven to be a series of attempts to secure an elusive reinvigoration of what we now know as 'civil society'. The next attempt came with Tony Blair and the 'Third Way' rhetoric of social solidarity and partnership. Reduced to a single-minded obsession with target-setting, this proved something of a failure, with the years after Mr Blair's departure being characterised by massive increases in government expenditure and taxation under Gordon

Published by Blackwell Publishing Ltd, 9600 Garsington Road, Oxford OX4 2DQ, UK and 350 Main Street, Malden, MA 02148, USA

Brown, with disastrous economic and social consequences. However, the aspiration to shift the balance away from the state towards society quickly re-emerged in the guise of Prime Minister David Cameron's calls for what he and his government continue to refer to (although now less frequently) as the 'Big Society'.

On first hearing, this had something of an instinctive appeal and, with Edmund Burke and his 'little platoons' in mind, I found myself vaguely enthused by what looked like an attempt to steer a course between the Scylla of Thatcherite individualism and the Charybdis of Big Government social-ism.[1] Since then I have not only struggled to understand what the Big Society might amount to, but have also begun to wonder whether it will work. Indeed, I have increasingly found myself wondering whether I want it to work.

In search of guidance I turned to the government's key document on the subject entitled (rather promisingly) *Big Society, Not Big Government*. The basic premise is that Britain has a broken society whilst the core idea, as outlined by David Cameron, is that of a different kind of society 'where the leading force of progress is social responsibility, not state control'. This, Mr Cameron goes on to specify, means 'breaking state monopolies, allowing charities, social enterprises and companies to provide public services, devolving power to neighbourhoods, making government more accountable'.[2] Underpinning this is Mr Cameron's suggestion that politics should not be reduced entirely to economics. Taken as a whole, therefore, the Big Society appears to be a mixture of voluntarism, local democracy, civic-mindedness and community spirit. As a programme for change this looks to be both morally and politically admirable.

Doubts start to creep in, however, when we look at the policy details. I will pass over the enthusiastic endorsement of Saul Alinsky's Industrial Areas Foundation and its 'generations of community organisers, including Barack Obama', and mention the creation of a Big Society Bank, a National Citizens' Service designed to ensure that all sixteen year-olds 'serve the community', the transformation of the Civil Service into a 'National Civic Service' involv-ing 'regular community service', and, most remarkable of all, an annual 'Big Society Day' when the government would use 'all the levers at its disposal to ensure that [this] becomes a mass-participation event'. Not to put too fine a point on it, the latter sounds remarkably Orwellian. Dig a little deeper and we see that the project of making localism a 'part of every day life' panders to two of the greatest obsessions of the British middle classes: the desire to reduce the cost of local government and to prevent the building of new houses in their neighbourhood. Eighteen months into the life of the government, the recent proposals to relax planning regulations leave little even of the latter in place and arguably the only evidence that the Big Society vision is being realised is to be found in Michael Gove's academies and free schools programme.

What initial conclusions can be drawn from this? First, in the words of *Daily Telegraph* columnist Mary Riddell, the Big Society agenda has looked both 'unworkable and vacuous'. Whatever enthusiasm it first elicited seems now to have evaporated. Second, the Big Society reads very much like top-down, government-led reform rather than an attempt to facilitate a bottom-up resurgence of associational life built upon active and responsible citizenship. Indeed, it is not clear that the ambition is to secure that end, as little attention has been paid to the institutional framework this would require. Third, if the Big Society idea is as important to the government's ambitions as David Cameron has claimed, it could quickly find itself losing any sense of direction. As Charles Moore observed at the end of July 2011, 'the Big Society notion floats rather aimlessly in the air'.[3]

How might political theory cast light on these issues and problems? Jesse Norman has usefully suggested that the intellectual origins of the Big Society lie in a rejection of the prevailing Hobbesian view of the dual (and exclusive) relationship existing between the state and the individual.[4] Given his political sympathies, Norman not surprisingly turns to Edmund Burke as a counter-blast to Thomas Hobbes, but there are many other writers who might be cited as positing an alternate description of a triangular relationship existing between state, intermediate or corporate group, and the individual. From this country, F. W. Maitland, John Neville Figgis, Sir Henry Maine and the young Harold Laski readily come to mind. From France one might turn to the rich strand of *ultramontane* Catholic thought; to Pierre-Joseph Proudhon, Georges Sorel and other writers associated with the syndicalist tradition; and to republican writers such as Alfred Fouillée and Emile Durkheim associated with the doctrine of solidarism. From America one might look at the works of Gabriel Almond and Sidney Verba on civic culture and, more recently, of Robert D. Putnam and others theorists of social capital.

However, as the introductory remarks to this chapter suggest, a critical appraisal of the associational and participatory dimensions of the Big Society idea can also be gleaned by looking at the writings of Alexis de Tocqueville and the broader tradition of liberalism in France. A recent book by Annelien de Dijn accurately summarises the origin of this tradition of thinking.[5] After the publication of Montesquieu's *The Spirit of the Laws* in 1748, she contends, there emerged a form of 'aristocratic liberalism'. If these liberals believed that liberty was to be protected through the checking and balancing of power rather than through the self-government of the people, their 'ideal', she argues, was 'that of a pluralist . . . society, in which "intermediary bodies" (often envisioned as an aristocracy, but not necessarily so) existed between the government and the people'. In their view, a levelled and atomistic society of the kind created by the absolutist French monarchy offered little or no protection against despotism. This conviction was only strengthened further in the postrevolutionary period but was now deployed as an alternative to revolutionary republicanism and Bonapartism. Both, as the writings of Benjamin Constant illustrate, were held to impose a deadening uniformity upon a subject people and both countenanced the extension of central government beyond its legitimate boundaries. In this new political climate, however, French liberals for the most part recognised that there was no possibility of restoring the aristocracy to its former, pre-1789 position in French society. In these circumstances, the challenge facing them was that of finding barriers against excessive administrative centralisation and of reinvigorating communal life in what was increasingly seen as being (irreversibly) a society of equals. Only if this were done could the moral, intellectual and political impoverishment of the country be halted. As early as 1821, for example, Prosper de Barante argued that the 'free and regular management of local affairs' gave citizens strength and wisdom, destroyed their sense of 'isolation' and 'apathy', taught them to know and love public order and, as importantly, not 'to tremble docilely' before men of power.[6]

Despite his position (in the words of Robert Putnam) as 'the patron saint of modern social capitalists', Tocqueville was therefore not the first to diagnose the problems arising from a situation where a strong State faced isolated individuals and weak communities. Rather, his originality was to provide a new response to these issues by transposing them onto the New World. As Tocqueville pointed out in his introduction to *Democracy in America*,[7] 'a great democratic revolution' was taking place in the United States. His whole book, Tocqueville confided, was written 'under the impression of a sort of religious terror' produced 'by the sight of this irresistible revolution that has marched for so many centuries over all obstacles'. 'A new political science,' Tocqueville concluded, 'is needed for a world entirely new.'

When Alexis de Tocqueville arrived in America in early May 1831 he quickly realised that he was visiting 'the most singular country in the world'.[8] Writing to Ernest de Chabrol from New York, scarcely a month later on 9 June 1831, he asked his friend to imagine 'a society formed of all the nations of the world . . . in a word, a society lacking roots, memories, prejudices, habits, common ideas, a national character'. Without a common language, beliefs and opinions, it was, Tocqueville went on, a society held together only by individual self-interest and by the fact that its physical situation was so fortunate that private interest never acted contrary to the general interest. There was no public power and, given the absence of enemies, no need of one. Consequently there was no army, no taxation and no central government to speak of. Executive authority was 'only the transient executor of the will of elected bodies', possessing neither money nor influence.

America was additionally a land where 'the restlessness of the human spirit' did not mobilise political passions. If change seemed 'man's natural state', everyone left the State alone. Also evident to Tocqueville was America's 'mercantile spirit'. 'Nothing,' he wrote, 'is easier than enriching oneself in America' and the Americans as a people 'put one in mind of merchants who have convened as a nation just to do business'. The Americans therefore were not 'a virtuous nation in the strict sense of the word'. The ancient European traditions of family pride, honour and virtue did not exist. But Americans were disciplined and their morals were pure. They had none of the vices arising from idle wealth.

Some three weeks later, having travelled as far as Yonkers, twenty miles from New York, these first impressions were supplemented by further insights into the character of the American people and the nature of American society. To Louis de Kergorlay, he announced that he was struck by 'the broad communality of certain opinions'. 'I have yet to hear anyone,' he wrote, 'whatever his social rank, publicly express misgivings about the republic being the best of all possible governments or challenge the proposition that a nation has the right to live under a government of its own choosing.' The vast majority in America, Tocqueville observed, understood republicanism 'in the most democratic sense'. Second, all Americans shared a faith in man's good sense and wisdom and embraced the doctrine of human perfectibility. 'While everyone acknowledges,' Tocqueville wrote, 'that the majority may err on rare occasions, no one questions the necessary rightness of its decisions in the long run, or disputes the fact that it is not only the sole legal judge of its interests but also the surest and most infallible.' From this flowed the conviction that enlightenment could not be spread broadly enough. By way of summary, Tocqueville concluded that Americans 'sincerely believe in the excellence of their government; they believe in the wisdom of the masses, assuming the latter are well-informed, and appear to be unclouded by suspicions that the populace may never share in a special kind of knowledge indispensable for governing a state'.

The same letter—now being written from Colwells, 25 miles further from New York—highlighted other aspects of American society. One was the unusual place occupied by religion. 'I was struck upon arriving here,' Tocqueville told Kergorlay, 'by the precise practical measures associated with religious worship.' The Sabbath was strictly observed and public opinion, as much as the law, obliged people to abstain from all forms of entertainment. Yet these external forms, in Tocqueville's opinion, concealed 'a reservoir of doubt and indifference'. For all that, Tocqueville also believed that the 'Christian religion has stronger underpinnings here than in any other country'. 'I'm sure,' he continued, 'that it influences every political adminis-tration.'

Another aspect of American society derived from the impact of laws governing inheritance. With the abolition of primogeniture, Tocqueville commented, the aristocratic bias of the early republic had been 'replaced by a democratic thrust of irresistible force'. The effects were visible everywhere: '[A] perpetual instability in men and laws, an external equality pushed to a limit, a uniform style of comportment and way of conceiving ideas.' The populace, Tocqueville wrote, 'favours those who flatter its passions and descend to its level'. This was not a process that could be reversed. Hence-forth, Tocqueville concluded, democracy 'will be a fact that a government may pretend to regulate but not to halt'.

Reflecting upon what this meant for France, Tocqueville believed that the utmost had to be done 'to endow democracy with incentives for order and stability'. No time should be lost in reforming the institutions of the state so as to associate citizens with their own affairs and to give them a 'vested interest in local concerns'. As for America, already at this early stage in his visit Tocqueville identified two things that might militate against the consequences of an unrestricted democracy. The first was an 'extreme respect for the law'. The second was 'the facility with which people dispense with government'.

It would be unnecessarily unkind to suggest that these first impressions were hardly modified by what Tocqueville saw during the rest of his nine-month stay in the New World, but they did contain strong intimations of what would in due course form the content of the most famous (and, some would say, best) book ever written about the United States. In particular, Tocqueville had seen that the people were in a very real sense the ones who governed and that there were no significant obstacles preventing them from making their wishes felt in all aspects of daily life. This observation was to be at the heart of *Democracy in America* and it presented Tocqueville with the central question he was there to address: how could liberty be preserved in a democratic social state characterised by the equality of conditions?

It was, Tocqueville argued, of the very essence of democratic government that the 'dominion of the majority be absolute'. If this had the beneficial consequence that laws were almost always designed to benefit the interests of the greatest number, it also had the potential to unleash a new kind of tyranny in the form of the tyranny of the majority. This, Tocqueville observed, took various forms. The majority insisted that its desires be indulged 'rapidly and irresistibly' in the form of law. Second, it encouraged the arbitrary actions of public officials because the majority regarded them as 'its passive agents and willingly relies upon them to take care of serving its designs'. Even more significantly, the tyranny of the majority existed as a 'moral force' exercised over the expression of opinion. 'I know of no country,' Tocqueville wrote, 'where, in general, there reigns less independence of mind and true freedom of discussion as in America.' This was a form of tyranny that left the body alone but enslaved the soul. It was, moreover, a form of tyranny that no despotism of the past had been able to exercise.

The fact of the matter was, however, that America had to date managed to avoid the most deleterious consequences of this tyranny. It was in his reflections on how and why this was the case that Tocqueville most directly addressed issues of relevance to current debates about the Big Society. In what was originally intended to be the last chapter of his first volume, published in 1835, Tocqueville highlighted three causal factors which, in his opinion, explained the survival of a democratic republic in the United States. These were laws, mores and 'the particular and accidental situation in which Providence has placed the Americans'. After much hesitation and uncertainty, Tocqueville concluded that laws and mores were more important than circumstances and it was to these, rather than to physical causes beyond human influence, that the 'Anglo-Americans' owed their 'grandeur'.

Tocqueville's comments on what he saw as the influence of the laws can be summarised briefly. Three institutions, he argued, contributed more than all the others to maintain democracy in America. The first was the federal constitution and its related system of decentralised administration. 'Situated close to the governed', the government of each individual state, was 'alerted daily to needs that make themselves felt'. New projects and plans excited 'universal interest and the zeal of the citizens'. The 'public spirit' of the Union, Tocqueville wrote, was 'only a summary of provincial patriotism'. The second were the institutions of the township, witnessed first-hand by Tocqueville in New England. 'Town institutions,' Tocqueville wrote, 'are to liberty what primary schools are to knowledge; they put it within grasp of the people; they give them a taste for its peaceful practice and accustom them to its use.' Passions which might otherwise have disturbed society were transformed by being expressed 'at the centre of the ordinary relations of life'. Tocqueville saw, however, that those who governed often saw 'strong and independent' local institutions as 'exposing the state to anarchy'. The third institution highlighted by Tocqueville was the judiciary. This is of less relevance to our present inquiry, but it is nevertheless important to Tocqueville's argument that an independent judiciary and, in particular, the practice of judicial review (unknown in Tocqueville's France), played a key role in constraining the extension of the activities of the state. 'The power granted to the American courts to rule on the unconstitutionality of laws,' Tocqueville wrote, 'still forms one of the most powerful barriers that has ever been raised against the tyranny of political assemblies.'

When Tocqueville spoke of mores, what he had in mind was 'the whole moral and intellectual state of a people'. While he admitted to an admiration for the 'practical experience' of Americans, for their respect for the law and for the strength of the American family, he paid particular attention to the influence of religious beliefs, arguing specifically that, among Americans, religion 'must be considered as the first of their political institutions'.[9] It was religion, Tocqueville insisted, that 'best teaches the Americans the art of being free'. There were several aspects to this argument. Religion, in Tocqueville's view, acted to elevate the aspirations of the majority, whilst at the same time diminishing the element of caprice in their actions. It made people more aware of the importance of human liberty. For Tocqueville, then, the spirit of religion and the spirit of liberty were not antithetical. Clearly this is an argument that many of today's militant secularists would not find congenial, but for Tocqueville it drew heavily upon his observations of the way in which the Roman Catholic Church was flourishing in the democratic environment of American society. He therefore endorsed the separation of Church and State. It also drew upon his recognition that in America religion was not overly concerned with dogma or liturgy. If in America there were innumerable sects all praying to God in their own way, they all agreed on the duties men owed to each other and they all preached the same morality. Not unimportantly, Tocqueville also noted that all these sects existed 'within the great Christian unity'.

These were the conclusions reached in the first volume of *Democracy in America*. Such was Tocqueville's optimism that he believed that similar democratic institutions, if introduced prudently, 'would be able to subsist elsewhere than in America'. The Americans, he concluded, 'have shown that we must not despair of regulating democracy with the help of laws and mores'. In particular, they had demonstrated how we might avoid the twin perils of despotism and anarchy. The tone of the second volume was however much less hopeful.

Published in 1840, the focus here was less upon institutions and more upon the sentiments and opinions produced by the equality of conditions. Three 'passions' in particular, each taken by Tocqueville to be typical of democratic society, were identified, and each posed a threat to liberty. The three passions were: a love of equality, a taste for material well-being, and individualism. Of the first, Tocqueville commented that democratic peoples preferred 'equality in liberty' and, if they could not obtain this, 'they still want equality in slavery'. They will suffer 'poverty, enslavement, barbarism', he continued, before they would 'suffer aristocracy'. As for the taste for material well-being, if Tocqueville was aware that, when linked to industriousness, it might produce positive outcomes, he also saw that it could entirely absorb the preoccupations and activities of democratic man, leading him to forego his rights and freedoms in the name of order and stability. It was, however, individualism that, in Tocqueville's opinion, posed by far the greater threat to liberty. The word was new, first appearing in French in the early 1820s, but in Tocqueville's usage it was defined as 'a considered and peaceful sentiment that disposes each citizen to isolate himself from the mass of his fellows and to withdraw to the side with his family and his friends'. It arose, Tocqueville believed, from the social and geographical mobility typical of democratic societies. As a consequence, not only were the bonds of human affection weakened, but the members of society acted 'like strangers to each other'. Democratic man, in short, was primarily concerned with himself, living 'entirely within the solitude of his own heart'.

What Tocqueville was describing, therefore, was an individualistic and atomistic society where individuals had come to expect nothing from others and where they had become accustomed to consider themselves in isolation. These individuals, Tocqueville wrote, 'readily imagine that their entire destiny is in their own hands'. For the moment I will pass over the question of whether this resembles the society in which we ourselves now live and limit myself to the observation that, in Tocqueville's opinion, it was precisely such conditions that facilitated the extensive growth of the state. As individuals withdrew from public life, government filled the vacuum.

However, at this point in the development of his argument, Tocqueville did not conclude that all was lost. This was so because he identified two countervailing forces which might yet combat the damaging consequences of social isolation. The first was what he described as 'the doctrine of interest well-understood'. We might more easily make sense of this as enlightened self-interest. Americans, Tocqueville noted, willingly gave up a portion of their time and wealth to help others. In itself, this did not make them virtuous but it taught them, by dint of small gestures every day, how to combine their own well-being with that of their fellow citizens. Such actions, Tocqueville wrote, formed 'a multitude of steady, temperate, moderate, far-sighted citizens who have self-control'. If Tocqueville attributed these habits and practices to the teachings of unspecified 'American moralists', he again drew attention to the role played by religion in facilitating and encouraging such behaviour. American preachers, he noted, gave as much attention to how we lived in this world as they did to how we secured eternal felicity in the next.

In America, then, indifference towards others had not been raised to the status of a public virtue. Not only this but, as Tocqueville observed, 'Americans of all ages, of all conditions, of all minds, constantly unite'. They formed associations 'to celebrate holidays, establish seminaries, build inns, erect churches, distribute books, send missionaries to the Antipodes; in this way they create hospitals, prisons, schools'. Everywhere one saw government in France, in America one saw an association. It is hard to overstate the importance that Tocqueville attached to this aspect of American society, for he saw that it was through the administration of small things, rather than through involvement in the general affairs of a country, that citizens were brought close together and that they became interested in the public good. It was in this way that they came to understand the need they had for one another. 'In democratic societies,' he affirmed, 'the science of association is the mother science: the progress of all the others depends on the progress of the former.'

For Tocqueville the stakes here were very high. If the citizens of a democratic society did not acquire the practice of associating together and of producing things in common, 'civilization itself would be in danger'. There would, he argued, soon be a return to 'barbarism'. It is at this point that Tocqueville's focus started to turn to the dangers ahead and where he began to describe what we might see as the major challenges faced by any strategy built upon a notion of a Big Society. As Tocqueville observes: 'Unfortunately, the same social state that makes associations so necessary to democratic peoples makes these more difficult for them than for all other peoples.' In other words, given that in democratic societies all individuals were independent from one another and therefore individually weak, there was the permanent risk that government would everywhere come to take the place of associations.

It was thus at this late stage of his argument—in the final chapters of the second volume of *Democracy in America*—that Tocqueville identified a second form of despotism and one that was largely, if not entirely, unfamiliar to his French liberal forbears. As Tocqueville wrote: 'The thing is new, so I must try to define it, since I cannot name it.' Despotism in the past, Tocqueville argued, 'was violent but its extent was limited'. Even under the greatest power of the Roman Caesars the details of individual life and social existence largely escaped their control. The thrust of Tocqueville's argument was that the modern state—as exemplified in Napoleon Bonaparte's First Empire—pos-

© 2012 The Author. The Political Quarterly © 2012 The Political Quarterly Publishing Co. Ltd

sessed previously unknown instruments of administrative control and that these were being deployed in a society where virtually all secondary or intermediate bodies had been destroyed. Speaking now of Europe, he argued that 'it is the state that has undertaken almost alone to give bread to those who are hungry, relief and a refuge to the sick, work to those without it: it has made itself the almost unique repairer of all miseries'. By way of illustration, he observed that the state 'often takes the child from the arms of its mother in order to entrust it to its agents'. Religion too had become an arm of the state. This then was a form of 'soft' despotism. If it was milder and preserved the external forms of freedom, 'it hinders, it represses, it enervates, it extinguishes, it stupefies, and finally it reduces each nation to being nothing more than a flock of timid and industrious animals of which the government is the shepherd'. Our leaders would not be seen as tyrants but rather as schoolmasters and we would console ourselves with the thought that we had at least chosen them ourselves.

Yet, for Tocqueville, this was not the whole picture. 'There is among the modern nations of Europe,' Tocqueville now observed, 'one great cause that . . . contributes constantly to expand the action of the sovereign power or to augment its prerogatives. . . . This cause is the development of industry.' By bringing a multitude of people together in the same place new relations were created among them, and, Tocqueville argued, 'it is natural that the attributions of the government grow with it'. To that extent, in Tocqueville's words, the 'industrial class . . . carries despotism within it and that despotism expands naturally as it develops'. More than this, as nations industrialised they felt the need for roads, canals, ports and 'other works of a semi-public nature'. In such circumstances, not only was government the 'greatest industrialist', but it tended also to become the master of all the others. Thus, governments came to appropriate the greater part of the produce of industry and state control became ever more intrusive and detailed, all initiative being taken away from the private individual and handed over to a government that constantly extended its reach.

This was Tocqueville's chilling description of the new features of despotism.

I see an innumerable crowd of similar and equal men who spin around endlessly, in order to gain small and vulgar pleasures with which they fill their souls. Each one of them, withdrawn apart, is like a stranger to the destiny of all the others, his children and his particular friends form for him the entire human species. . . . Above those men arises an immense tutelary power that alone takes charge of assuring their enjoyment and looking after their fate. . . . It works willingly for their happiness; but it wants to be the unique agent for it and the sole arbiter; it attends to their security, provides for their needs, facilitates their pleasures, conducts their principal affairs, directs their industry, settles their estates, divides their inheritances.

Little by little, in Tocqueville's opinion, such despotism enervated the soul and extinguished the faculty for independent thought and action, every citizen 'falling gradually below the level of humanity'. It could be argued that this has proved to be the most pervasive despotism of the modern age, and so much so that we have largely ceased to see it as a form of despotism. It also helps to explain why the attempt to forge a Big Society might not work: over time the state not only destroys the sense of community spirit and individual initiative, but also destroys the very possibility of their revival.

Let me conclude this part of the chapter with two thoughts from Tocqueville. The first is his comment that, for all the faults of the system of soft despotism, it was still 'infinitely preferable to one that, after concentrating all powers, would put them in the hands of one unaccountable man or body'. What we have now, in other words, might be better than the alternative. Second, if centralisation was the 'natural' form of government in democratic societies, it followed that 'individual independence and local liberties will always be a product of art'. The condition of social and economic equality will always favour uniform and strong government.

Finally, let me turn to the question of why, irrespective of the difficulties of its practical application, the very idea of a Big Society might not be appealing. If Tocqueville was realistic enough to appreciate that there was no possibility of reconstructing the aristocratic society of the past, this did not prevent him from using the aristocratic past to criticise the democratic present. This was evident throughout *Democracy in America*. Not evident here—although clearly apparent in Tocqueville's letters written from America and in his Notebooks—was that he did nevertheless find something resembling such a society in North America: in Quebec.[10]

A visit to French-speaking Lower Canada had not been part of Tocqueville's original itinerary but he and his travelling companion Gustave de Beaumont ultimately found a visit to the land of their abandoned countrymen to be irresistible. There—to their surprise and perhaps out of wishful thinking—they found 'the old France', a country not only where, as he told his mother, 'the French nation of Louis XIV's day survives unspoiled in its mores and language', but also where 'the people in general are more moral, more hospitable, and more religious than in France'. Nor were the French Canadians touched by the mercantile spirit of their neighbours. 'They make fine warriors,' Tocqueville wrote, 'and are fonder of action than of money.' Their villages, with 'a church topped by a cock and a cross with the *fleur-de-lys*', resembled those of France, the people being both happy and prosperous. 'Four times a day,' Tocqueville wrote, 'the family, consisting of vigorous parents and plump, joyful, children, gathers around a round table. After supper they sing old French songs. . . . On Sundays they play and sing after services. The priest himself shares in the communal gaiety.' What else did Tocqueville describe as part of this idyll? 'Public opinion,' he noted, 'has incredible power in these villages. The people would never turn a thief over to the authorities, but the minute suspicions are raised against a man, he is forced to leave town. Nothing is rarer than a girl who has been seduced.' Moreover, the distinctiveness of this society, with its separate language and customs, was preserved through the strict separation of what Tocqueville regarded as the French and English 'races'. It was to be feared that, with the passage of time, a fusion between the two races would occur but 'fortunately', Tocqueville observed, religion stood as 'an obstacle' to intermarriage. The Quebecois, he concluded, were religious on principle but also 'by dint of political passion'.

There is something deeply troubling about this description. Even in Tocqueville's day it smacked of a misplaced nostalgia for an imaginary and lost golden age, but when viewed from the perspective of a large and complex society characterised by religious, ethnic and cultural diversity, this vision of families and communities bound together in a homogeneous social structure looks positively oppressive. It reads almost like an invitation to return to the 1950s, with Mum, Dad and the children sitting by the radio, the first immigrant from the West Indies not yet off the boat, and any poor girl who had the misfortune to find herself pregnant ostracised and hidden from view. This is probably unfair as a description of what the Big Society might look like, but it does capture something of the flavour of the policies now being put forward to repair a supposedly broken Britain.

To conclude, if the reaction to the idea of the Big Society has largely been that of either incomprehension or scepticism, what I have tried to explore is the sense, if any, we can make of the Big Society when approached from a Tocquevillian perspective. As we have seen, for Tocqueville a rich associational life of the kind he witnessed in America was able to flourish because there was respect for the law, no widespread reliance upon government and an accepted place in society for the spirit of religion. It was, he believed, 'the manners and customs of the people' that kept the quest for material well-being and the pursuit of individual self-interest in check. Accordingly, individual liberty and the practices of association were preserved, despite the fact that the social condition of America was one of equality and one where the tyranny of the majority—especially with regard to the expression of opinion—was an ever-present threat. From this perspective, Britain at a minimum lacks the two most important things which, in Tocqueville's opinion, prevent the dominance of the centralised state: the spirit of religion and the mores of liberty. What possible purchase, it might therefore be asked, could the idea of a Big Society have in a mobile, atomistic, secular and urbanised society like our own? Where Tocqueville saw religiously inspired philanthropy, we see bonus-inspired bankers guiltlessly making themselves rich. The lawlessness and wanton consumerism of the summer riots of 2011 should alone give us pause for thought. In a society where we have increasingly closed ourselves off from one another it is virtually impossible to define anything beyond a very narrow conception of the common good— unless it should be the building of ever-bigger shopping malls. In brief, it could be argued that we have become precisely what an increasingly pessimistic Tocqueville feared we would become: individuals who are indifferent to the plight of others and whose only concern is our own material well-being.

© 2012 The Author. The Political Quarterly © 2012 The Political Quarterly Publishing Co. Ltd

If that is so, we run the risk of basing policy upon misplaced nostalgia. As Adam Nicolson has recently commented,[11] in David Cameron's hands the idea of a Big Society looks rather like a 'sentimentalised' version of the traditional ideals of the English gentry. As members of the government continue to tell us, we are all in this together. As Nicholson points out, this 'gentry vision . . . doesn't grasp the fact, or perhaps even want to admit the fact, that competition, unkindness, rivalry and dominance always lay behind the beautiful sense of community which the gentry world embodied'. Seen thus, the Big Society looks disturbingly like a Downton Abbey version of politics and the world.

Not only this but, as Tocqueville feared, the long march to create the Welfare State has effectively destroyed the customs and practices of associational life in modern British society and there must be a real doubt about the very possibilities of bringing about their resurgence. Dependency upon the state is a fact of life for large sections of the British population. The hope of Mr Cameron and his colleagues is that if the state ceases to fulfil a function, this function will be taken up by individual citizens, neighbourhoods, charities and local organisations. The suspicion (witness the relatively trivial example of local libraries) is that such functions, however useful they might be, will simply cease to be performed and that the most vulnerable members of our society will suffer as a consequence and that the burden will fall largely upon women as carers. This, it might be argued, is a price worth paying if, as a consequence, it reduces government expenditure and serves to redefine what are taken to be the proper functions of the state, but it also suggests that David Cameron's ambitions for a Big Society—like the similar ambitions of Lady Thatcher and Tony Blair before him—will come to very little.

Notes

1 See R. Harris, *The Conservatives: A History*, London, Bantam Press, 2011, pp. 516–18.

2 D. Cameron, 'Our "Big Society" Plan', 31 March 2010, http://www.conservatives.com/News/Speeches/2010/03/David_Cameron_Our_Big_Society_plan.aspx.

3 'Our governments have lost faith in the powers of their people', *Daily Telegraph*, 30 July 2011.

4 J. Norman, *The Big Society: The Anatomy of the New Politics*, Buckingham, University of Buckingham Press, 2010, pp. 92–6.

5 A. de Dijn, *French Political Thought from Montesquieu to Tocqueville: Liberty in a Levelled Society?*, Cambridge, Cambridge University Press, 2008; see also J. Jennings, 'Constitutional liberalism in France: from Benjamin Constant to Alexis de Tocqueville', in G. Stedman Jones and G. Claeys, eds, *The Cambridge History of Nineteenth-century Political Thought*, Cambridge, Cambridge University Press, 2011, pp. 349–73.

6 See J. Jennings, *Revolution and the Republic: A History of Political Thought in France since the Eighteenth Century*, Oxford, Oxford University Press, 2011, pp. 180–2.

7 A. de Tocqueville, *Democracy in America*, Indianapolis, IN, Liberty Fund, 2010.

8 F. Brown, ed., *Alexis de Tocqueville: Letters from America*, New Haven, CT, Yale

University Press, 2010, p. 71. The best account of the visit to America made by Tocqueville and Gustave de Beaumont remains that of G. W. Pierson, *Tocqueville in America*, Baltimore, MD, Johns Hopkins University Press, 1996. For a more recent account, see L. Damrosch, *Tocqueville's Discovery of America*, New York, Farrar, Strauss & Giroux, 2010.

9 For a contemporary discussion of this issue that largely confirms Tocqueville's conclusions, see R. D. Putnam and D. C. Campbell, *American Grace: How Religion Divides and Unites Us*, New York, Simon & Schuster, 2010.

10 See Brown, *Alexis de Tocqueville*, pp. 76, 170–9; O. Zunz, ed., *Alexis de Tocqueville and Gustave de Beaumont: Their Friendship and their Travels*, Charlottesville, VA, University of Virginia Press, 2010, pp. 118–26, 314–23.

11 A. Nicolson, *The Gentry: Stories of the English*, London, Harper Press, 2011, pp. 416–18.

The Big Society and Conservative Politics: Back to the Future or Forward to the Past?

ALAN WARE

James Douglas and the Big Society

FOR DECADES centre-right politicians have been searching for alternatives to the central state as the supplier of various types of public goods. Usually the 1980s are associated with an emphasis on such provision being via the market, as far as that was possible in Britain. Of course, the steam was to slowly escape from the New Right 'engine' during the 1990s, but it is important to recognise that alternative approaches had been discussed even at the height of enthusiasm for profit-based enterprise. In 1983, the former Director of the Conservative party's Research Department, James Douglas, published a book, *Why Charity?*, that focused on a rather different approach to social provision.[1] Nor was this contribution by an unorthodox, though loyal, Conservative light on ideas; rather it was a theoretically informed monograph drafted while the author spent two years at Yale University's Program on Non-profit Organizations, and in which he acknowledged the advice of such 'heavyweight' academics as Bruce Ackerman, Robert Dahl, James Fishkin and Charles Lindblom.

Douglas argued that there was a Third Sector in society, paralleling the state and the market. However, it was a sector that combined two different kinds of organisations. On the one side there were those concerned with 'social objectives' of which he says:

It is not merely physically but logically impossible for government to pursue the full range and diversity of social goals that its citizens seek. The range of diverse goals that the society as a whole can pursue is increased by voluntary social action that supplements the social action government can demand of all citizens and will be increased still further by tolerating social action for which government take no responsibility itself.

However, the alleged Third Sector also includes:

organizations—such as mutual associations, trade unions, professional associations, and clubs—that are not necessarily concerned with objectives of social value. In these organizations, the benefits may be quite as internalised as in a commercial undertaking. There is no particular difficulty in explaining why governments will normally be inappropriate to take on the roles they perform in society, since they are established to provide benefits for themselves rather than for the generality of citizens.

Published by Blackwell Publishing Ltd, 9600 Garsington Road, Oxford OX4 2DQ, UK and 350 Main Street, Malden, MA 02148, USA

It should be clear from these statements that, although there are some differences, the territory that has more recently been marked out by the Conservative party for its Big Society programme is not a million miles away from Douglas's Third Sector.

Before turning to those differences it is worth stating, in his own words, one of the main conclusions of Douglas's analysis. On the role of voluntary organisations as mediating structures, he noted:

> [T]hey are more than merely supplements to the activities of the public sector; they are, like the public sector itself, part of the means by which, in conjunction and in harmony with the public sector, society expresses and acts out its social purposes. . . . [W]e can expect that, in the last quarter of the twentieth century the structure of the welfare state will subtly change. The components of public finance and professional service will diminish, at least relatively, and the components of private funding and volunteer services will tend to increase and the two become closely allied.

Now it should be obvious that one aspect of Douglas's prognosis for the future was absolutely correct, but part of it was also wrong—and it was wrong because his characterisation of the 'Third Sector' was misleading.

Douglas was right in arguing that the structure of the welfare state would change. Indeed, the delivery of many services funded by government was to alter quite significantly subsequently. The traditional British model of public administration that publicly funded activities should usually be supplied by government (at one level or another), rather than by other kinds of agencies, gave way to a more pluralist regime. Across the political spectrum there developed over a thirty-year period much greater acceptance of the idea that the delivery of services could be left to nongovernmental agencies, even while they were paid for from public coffers. Of course, much still remained that divided left from right. Which services should be retained for exclusively public delivery, the terms on which non-public agencies could be permitted to be suppliers, the regulatory regimes that had to be in place to ensure value for money, fair access for everyone to services, and so on—all remained potentially controversial. Yet the presumption that the state itself would always be the deliverer, unless there was good reason why it could not be, had far fewer adherents at the beginning of this century than it had had in 1983. In many ways, the British model of service delivery had given way to the American model in which supply of government-funded services was undertaken by third parties—a model to which the term 'third party government' was applied in the 1980s, although the phrase never really caught on.

However, the notion that the role of 'volunteer services' would increase was always implausible unless an expanded meaning was given to the word 'volunteer'. Excluding the mutual organisations from Douglas's supposed 'Third Sector', only a relatively small proportion of the income of organisations in that 'sector' could be regarded as self-generated. The year after *Why Charity?* appeared, John Posnett published data showing that a mere

9 per cent of the total income of non-religious charities came from donations, while a further 8 per cent came from rent and investments.[2] The major share of their income came from either fees for services that they provided, whether paid for privately or by government agencies, or from government grants. The widespread popular perception that charities received much of their money from donations was wide of the mark, partly because such donations were a small proportion of British domestic expenditures. In the mid-1980s the median donor in virtually every income group in Britain was contributing no more than between 0.3 per cent and 0.4 of his or her income to charities.[3] Nor was the situation much different if the supply of labour in the 'volunteer services' was considered; for many, volunteers were a relative small proportion of that labour, with paid employees being used to deliver services.

Of course, there were important subareas of Douglas's 'sector' where donations or volunteers, or both, were of far greater importance than in the typical charity, and the former did correspond quite closely to the popular idea of what a charity was. Yet, overall, the 'Third Sector' was a category more akin to 'other' or 'none of the above' than anything else; it was an aggregation of very different kinds of organisation, of which only some were 'voluntary' in the sense of largely depending on donations and volunteerism. Between them, that group was never going to provide a basis for the important mediating structures Douglas seemed to envisage in the future. This is not to deny their value, but it is to say that the scope for them transforming welfare provision on Douglasian lines was always limited.

Ultimately what restricted Douglas's influence in the 1980s was not so much that he exaggerated the potential for his 'Third Sector', but that it fitted ill with the dominant ideas in the Conservative governments of that time. Theirs was to be a world of individuals and families who, in exercising their choice in free markets, would be the agents of change in British society. Having tried to reduce the power of a whole range of intermediate organisations—trade unions, local governments, the professions, universities and the rest—the last innovation that governments led by Margaret Thatcher wanted was to bring in a whole series of other intermediaries between citizen-consumers and the central state. While voluntarism itself was compatible with the government's aims, the larger organisations inhabiting Douglas's universe might end up undermining the prospects for that project.

The demise of the project was to come with massive electoral defeats in 1997 and 2001. By then it was increasingly clear that an electoral appeal based heavily on the individual living in a low-tax regime was insufficient for garnering more than about one third of the electorate's votes. The comments in 2002 of then party chair, Theresa May, at the Conservatives' Annual Conference, that the party was perceived as the 'nasty party', symbolically marks the beginning of a search for a supplement to its New Right thinking. By the 2010 election, with a manifesto advocating something called the 'Big Society', the Conservative party might appear to have moved back to the kind of ideas Douglas was outlining more than a quarter of a century earlier.[4]

There is much in that manifesto that meshes with the Douglas arguments, such as the claim that:

Our public service reform programme will enable social enterprises, charities and voluntary groups to play a leading role in delivering public services and tackling deep-rooted social problems.

There is also evidence that, in part, the programme is merely a further extension of developments in the preceding decades that had been foreseen by Douglas, with a mixed delivery of services rather than the state being the default deliverer:

We will introduce a fair deal on grants to give voluntary sector organisations more stability and allow them to earn a competitive return for providing public services. We will work with local authorities to promote the delivery of public services by social enterprises, charities and the voluntary sector.

Nevertheless, there are also clear differences between the Douglas case for a Third Sector and the Big Society, of which three are especially important.

The politics of the Big Society

The emphasis on neighbourhoods and communities

Douglas said nothing specifically about the level of society to which the Third Sector would be directed, whereas the Manifesto is far more focused, stating that: 'Our reform agenda is designed to empower communities to come together to address local issues.' Douglas was essentially pre-Thatcher in his orientation; he did not concern himself with the possibility that the institutions in the Third Sector might come to exercise undue power over the public policy process through a combination of their size and their centrality in providing certain kinds of social policy in the future. Whatever else it was going to do, the Conservative party of the twenty-first century was not going to reverse the Thatcher administrations' assaults on the power of intermediary organisations in the British state. By focusing on small, neighbourhood-based groups that, between them, were never likely to be a source of countervailing power in the state, the contemporary Conservative party has avoided any possibility of undoing those aspects of the Thatcher Revolution.

A role for mutual organisations

Douglas had analysed why there were mutual associations in society as part of his overarching account of why there was a Third Sector at all, but he did not see them as being relevant to changes in the welfare state. The Big Society, by contrast, is explicit in embracing certain kinds of mutual organisations as well as voluntary ones. This was less evident in the Manifesto, which notes rather vaguely that '[w]e will strengthen and support social enterprises to help deliver our public service reforms' (p. 37), but the commitment was made more explicit after the election. On its formation, the coalition stated in May 2010 that it would 'support the creation and expansion of mutuals, co-operatives, charities and social enterprises, and enable these groups to have a much greater involvement in the running of public services'. The Green Paper published subsequently by the government then expanded on their possible role.[5]

A national citizen service

Douglas had had nothing to say about how the state might provide pro-grammes that would train people in skills to facilitate volunteering in neighbourhoods, but this was another key part of the Manifesto's agenda for the Big Society. The plan was to focus on the young. It was an idea that had already been enacted in a small way by the federal government of the United States in 1990 but after its enactment, and unlike the earlier Peace Corps, that project had sunk completely without trace.

All three of these initiatives were politically astute, in that they were an attempt to broaden the Conservatives' loyal electoral coalition, because none of them was explicitly identifiable with conservative political ideas. Tradi-tionally, British Conservatives wanted to leave a wide range of issues to be resolved locally because it was at that level of politics that social elites could most easily exercise influence. However, the idea of something resembling local democracy was always a left-of-centre notion. Of course, it had come in Britain to be taken as a synonym for local government, but in political thought outside the United Kingdom the idea of an extreme form of decentralisation of power territorially was taken seriously during the 1970s. For example, in 1970 Robert Dahl, then the most famous political scientist in the world, published *After the Revolution?* in which an explicit case for some form of neighbourhood control was made as one of the means of extending demo-cracy.[6]

The proposed use of mutual associations took the Conservatives even further into traditional left-of-centre political territory. In the early nineteenth century various kinds of mutual bodies had been at the heart of local working-class movements. As well as trade unions, these had included:

- friendly societies, providing insurance mainly against costs associated with death for their members;
- building societies (of the original, non-permanent kind), in which members pooled their money and their own labour to build in sequence each of them a house, with the completion of the last building prompting the society's dissolution; and
- consumer cooperative societies, of which the famous original exemplar was started in Rochdale in 1844.

In general, however, producer and worker cooperatives were to play only a small role in Britain compared with other countries including, for example, Spain. This was partly because there was no peasant-farmer class in Britain, and it was that social group that usually benefitted most from this form of organisation. Again, the link between British socialism and mutualism began to weaken in the later nineteenth century as the influence of Marxist ideas increased among socialists, and also because the changing scale of industrial and urban Britain required that socialists focus more on the central state in their strategising. Even though by 1945 much of the link to its mutualist past was usually just a sentimental one for British socialists, by embracing cooperativism as a mechanism for social action the Conservatives today could be seen to be crossing a political boundary. The idea of employee-owned cooperatives, outlined in *Modernizing Commissioning*, could thus be understood as the party trying to expand beyond their original political base. Finally, the idea of national citizen service could be linked just as easily to republican political theory, and the centrality it accords to the political community, as to nationalist ideas of an obligation to defend the nation-state. Here, too, there was no particular connection, therefore, to earlier conservative ideas in Britain, so that it could be presented as a proposal that might appeal across the political spectrum.

The Big Society project has been subject to a number of criticisms, three of which I will briefly mention here, but which I will not discuss further.

- Taking the development of local empowerment seriously could involve massive expenditure to set up the necessary infrastructures, and that may not be possible in the aftermath of the world financial crisis. Whatever its merits, the policy will likely fail in the present era because it will be under-funded.
- The resources required for voluntarism to become an important component of welfare provision in the United Kingdom are too unevenly distributed territorially for the policy to succeed throughout the country. In a minority of communities it may be possible for some local service provision to be taken over from local governments, but those are likely to be places with populations that have higher incomes and more leisure time.
- Although the government intends to reduce so-called 'red tape' to facilitate local provision, it is far from clear how communities can be freed from the requirements of safety legislation, third party insurance, and so on. There are far more laws affecting service provision now than there were a few decades ago, and ensuring compliance with them will greatly complicate attempts at delivering services locally.

Avoiding these sorts of criticisms, the remainder of this chapter focuses on whether, even if they could be ignored, the Big Society constitutes a coherent policy. In particular, it considers two questions that are prompted by the first of its two aims that the government identified in the Green Paper. That aim is to transfer 'power away from central government to local communities.

Improved commissioning practice will encourage a flourishing civil society, increasing community involvement in activities which were previously the almost exclusive domain of the state.'

One of these questions, and arguably the more important one, is whether local communities could be effective *loci* of power in contemporary Britain. For that to happen, it is necessary that neighbourhoods have: first, relatively stable populations from which communal identity can be derived; second, patterns of interaction between residents in those places that can form the basis for joint action by them; and third, sociopolitical institutional structures there through which a collective identity can be developed in the future. The argument presented here is that these conditions are not met in many parts of Britain today.

The other question is whether, from the perspective of neighbourhoods, there is any particular advantage in encouraging charities or cooperatives to bid for contracts for local service provision—beyond the obvious possible advantage that a greater number of potential bidders may enhance competition for public benefit. It is not obvious that, even when there are benefits, they could be offset by disadvantages for those supposedly benefitting from the development of a Big Society.

Neighbourhoods, collective action and identity

Even in the twenty-first century neighbourhoods are still not like hotels, one principal characteristic of which is the high rate of turnover of their occupants. (Nevertheless, the advent of large student ghettos in many university towns has created areas that have some of the attributes of hotels.) Equally, though, they are not like the neighbourhoods of the industrial era when the territory in which people lived really was the main focal point of their lives. Many then were trapped by economic circumstances into living close to where they had been born, and in those communities there were few opportunities for activities outside of working hours that took them much beyond that territory. What happened in their local territory, therefore, dominated people's lives outside the workplace. While this did not, of itself, generate collective action on behalf of all living in that territory, and while it might not have occasioned pride in, or identity with, the territory, it did provide a *necessary* condition for communal action. Local identities were what lay behind the later support, primarily on the left, for some form of local democracy. Territory mattered. As noted above, for some political scientists including Robert Dahl and Jim Sharpe, it mattered until several decades ago. Today it matters less.

During the twentieth century the revolution in private transportation had made it possible for most Britons to move much more outside their neighbourhoods for purposes such as shopping and entertainment. In the twenty-first century the Internet, mobile phones and so on have provided a variety of ways for people to interact in virtual communities; these compete with territorially defined communities for the attention of a high proportion of them. 'Real' community activities are in decline; the Football Association, for instance, reported a fall of over 10 per cent between 2005–6 and 2010–11 in the number of adult, male, football (England's supposedly national sport) teams in England. Many of these teams would have had links to particular villages, suburbs or pubs. It is a British example of Putnam's 'bowling alone' phenomenon.[7] The relevance of the subsequent 'social capital' debate to the discussion here is that it is the territorially defined local community that is most exposed to changes in how people interact with each other. A person cannot get away from the ill-repaired road outside their house, nor can those living near them, but the time each of them may be willing to spend complaining about it, and hence away from Facebook or whatever, may now be more limited. Campaigning takes time, and with individuals having fewer institutional links to their neighbours, this is likely to restrict contributions to any collective action to resolve a matter.

The British experience is not unusual. Even before the electronic social networking revolution began in America, Theda Skocpol (writing in 1999) noted just how much social and political engagement there had changed. Amongst the areas of decline was interaction with the local community:

Since the 1960s, Americans have dramatically changed their ways of associating for civic and political purposes. A civic world previously centered in locally rooted and nationally active membership associations . . . has gone the way of the once-popular television program, 'Leave it to Beaver'. There may still be re-runs but they seem rather quaint. Much of America's civic life has moved into new venues and new modalities.[8]

There is a quaintness, too, to the Big Society idea because it is based on an older view of the role of territory in shaping identities and political action. It is quaint in the same way as John Major's notion, expressed in 1993, that: 'Fifty years on from now, Britain will still be the country of long shadows on cricket grounds, warm beer, invincible green suburbs, dog lovers and pools fillers and, as George Orwell said, "Old maids bicycling to holy communion through the morning mist".' At least, though, no specific policies were following from Major's view of Britain, whereas the Big Society is programme-driven.

Of course, the Internet does increase the potential for all kinds of collective action, and the massive transformation in how American election campaigns have been organised since 2004 is just one example of that. Nor are territorially based interests excluded in any way from that potential. Those wanting to object to the introduction of a new high speed rail line, for example, can now communicate with supporters far more quickly than they could have earlier. The coordination of mass political action thereby now presents a greater populist threat to any government taking unpopular decisions, as it has in Greece during the summer of 2011, than earlier. When clearly defined interests are threatened mass mobilisation has arguably become easier, therefore. However, this is largely irrelevant to the more mundane issues with which the current British government is hoping people in neighbourhoods will become involved as a consequence of its Big Society policies. For those kinds of matters, the Internet and social networks have served to weaken even further the strong claims that territorially defined communities used to have as sources of identity for the individual during the industrial era.

Furthermore, in most of Britain there are not now well-defined local territories that could become a source of a future shared identity in any new era of community action. The prospect for this would be most promising in rural areas with their civil parishes becoming the unit for such identity. However, only about 35 per cent of the population of England live in places where there are such councils. In the absence of well-defined sociopolitical units that could constitute 'neighbourhoods', or from which subneighbour-hoods could be derived, the possibility of developing popular identity with a particular community is reduced. In turn, this raises the problem of who has the legitimacy to speak or act on behalf of an alleged community.

The problem is akin to those facing proponents of regionalism in Britain in earlier decades. Some parts of the country were prime candidates for creating or developing further a regional identity—notably Scotland and Wales. For a few other parts of the country (for example, the southwestern peninsular of England) geographical features offered at least the possibility of a popular identity being created over time. However, in many heavily populated areas of Britain (such as the 'South East' or the 'Midlands') there was neither a history of any regional identity nor any prospect of getting many people to appreciate it. Mercia might have been a recognised entity in Britain for part of the Anglo-Saxon period, but it has had virtually no resonance with anyone since that era. Perceiving that one lives in a place that has recognised boundaries, separating it from other places, is a precondition for establishing an identity through which collective action can then be established. While this is present in some localities in Britain, in many it is not. In a world in which it is unlikely that you will be working for the same employer as those living in the same, or an adjacent, street to yours, developing intermittent action with them is unlikely—at least in the absence of a clear threat to all, or if you happen to live in one of the minority of places where there is a pre-existing sense of neighbourhood identity.

In one respect the assumption lying behind the Big Society—that in the future there really could be well-defined entities throughout Britain called 'neighbourhoods'—is the opposite of Margaret Thatcher's beliefs about social action. Famously she observed that were only individuals and families interacting with each other:

There is no such thing as society. There is living tapestry of men and women and people and the beauty of that tapestry and the quality of our lives will depend upon how much each of us is prepared to take responsibility for ourselves and each of us prepared to turn round and help by our own effort those who are unfortunate.[9]

Thatcher thought there were not societies; by contrast, David Cameron seems to believe that there are neighbourhoods everywhere. Ultimately, the Big Society project rests on the assumption that the individuals and families living in places we call 'communities' and 'neighbourhoods' have both the capacity and the incentive to act together in those entities; the Big Society sees there being some macro-structures beyond the individual where Thatcher had seen none. And, of course, there are some places in Britain where they do exist. What the Big Society policy omits is any realistic assessment of how these kinds of social structures might be constructed in places where they do not.

Those most likely to both participate in and benefit from action at the neighbourhood level are retirees; they have more time to volunteer and are more likely to require services as they get older, some of which might be deliverable at the neighbourhood level. Crucially, though, they are less likely to move out of a neighbourhood than others. This makes them prime candidates for community-based volunteerism. Here self-interest could be harnessed to collective action. It does not take too much imagination to see how a short course on opportunities for volunteering for those who become eligible for the state pension, attendance at which might be linked to one-off additional payments to that pension, could be an obvious way of increasing voluntary effort. Yet the emphasis in the Big Society is not on retirees, but on the young, who typically have less to gain from community-based collective action and are more likely to leave the territory.

Even if a well-funded programme of national citizen service were developed, and even it did stimulate a volunteering ethos among many young people, there is no reason for believing that these results would be directed primarily to work at the neighbourhood level. Nearly all the gap year students that I have encountered who have undertaken volunteer work during the year before university have done so in far more exotic places than their own home towns. Why be a volunteer in a school in Bromsgrove when you can fly cheaply to Botswana to be one there? Furthermore, as just noted, the young are far more likely to leave their original places of residence than the retired. For an ethos of volunteering among residents to be locally oriented, locality has to provide a stronger pull than other possible objects of that drive, and having a stake in a specific place is undermined by geographical mobility. In any case, locally directed voluntarism depends on there being local structures through which it can be channelled. However, in those places in Britain where there are no pre-existing structures which help define a particular neighbourhood that 'pull' of locality is unlikely to be strong. To use Skocpol's phrase, a 'locally rooted' civic world is one in which there are formal and informal structures that focus activism onto the local community. In their absence it is unclear why much of twenty-first-century Britain could really develop in the ways the Big Society proponents seem to want. Even if, improbably, the National Citizen Programme did have similar results to those traditionally claimed by Jesuits in having a grip for life on the values of those subjected to their education, cashing out commitments to voluntarism at the local level still requires there to be structures within neighbourhoods for the commitment to be realised at that level.

There is a Cheshire-Cat-like quality to neighbourhoods and local communities in Britain—the cat is disappearing, but the smile remains. Local shops and pubs continue to close in the face of competition from outside. Housing redevelopment and the prospect of jobs elsewhere, albeit often in the same region, means that compared with a century ago fewer people now live in the neighbourhood in which they grew up. At the same time, people still think of themselves as living in a neighbourhood—after all, each person must be living *somewhere* specifiable. The problem with the Big Society project is that, in those places where neighbourhood identity and neighbourhood structures are weak, it is difficult to see how these 'loose' notions of 'the neighbourhood' could be a sufficient basis on which to build a system of social action locally. Being serious about localism—reintroducing the Cheshire Cat—would involve a far more extensive, expensive and long-term policy than is being proposed currently.

Of course, one of the reasons why the Big Society programme could be advanced by the Conservatives after the 2010 election was that it seemed to mesh with the localist approach to politics that had been practised since the 1960s by the Liberals who, as Liberal Democrats now, are their partners in the coalition. That party had built up its electoral base by becoming competitive in some local government areas through emphasising service to those they were representing. However, the Liberal Democrats' experience exposes the weakness at the heart of the Big Society programme. They were able to generate action because they worked to be effective within the structures of local government; by seeking to improve the quality of refuse collection, for instance, they could provide reasons for people voting Liberal Democrat—at least in local elections. It was the relative strength of local government, compared with now, that had made the Liberal Democrat strategy so effective. However, if power is to be further transferred away from local authorities to 'communities' that lack the kind of institutional framework that these governments have had, the capacity to mobilise people in 'communities' will be much reduced, for the reasons outlined above. In the absence of such a framework it is difficult to see why social action would develop—except in the face of a serious local crisis.

Mutuals and charities in the Big Society

I argued earlier that linking its localist programme to institutions such as mutuals, which historically had been more associated with their political opponents, was a shrewd strategy on the part of the Conservatives. I now want to address the nature of the possible benefit to communities that might derive from extending service provision through the encouraging of bids from mutuals and charities. It is the benefits accruing to those living there that are relevant. I will take it as given that actually increasing the number of qualified bidders for contracts is beneficial in itself, and I now want to address the 'added value' that these types of organisations might provide. Here it is important to consider mutuals separately from charities.

The Green Paper states that the government will introduce:

> rights to provide for public sector workers to take over the running of services, including a right for civil servants directly employed by departments to form mutuals. This builds on the commitment in *Our Programme for Government* and the Spending Review 2010 to 'give public sector workers a new right to form employee-owned cooperatives'. . . . Given the variety of public services and departmental requirements, these rights will not be uniform, but will be as far reaching as possible. This work will open up new areas of public service delivery to competition and the involvement of a diversity of providers.

However, it is an interesting question as to what public benefit there might actually be from the diversity that employee-owned cooperatives would bring. The central point about the original early nineteenth-century mutuals is that they were formed because either the market worked to the disadvantage of the interests of particular groups, or did not function at all in some areas of activity. Their *raison d'être*, though, was that they benefitted their members directly.[10] There could be, and indeed were, public benefits from their activities. Friendly societies helped to reduce the costs of burials on parishes; building societies improved housing stock in given communities; and the competition provided by consumer cooperatives in the retail market benefitted non-members, though not as much as members. No one doubts that an employee-owned cooperative may well benefit its members. Now most such cooperatives would probably take the legal form of a company limited by guarantee, and such companies cannot distribute profits to their director/members. Yet absence of a profit motive does not mean they are publicly oriented. Any profit accrued from trading can be distributed to the members in the form of higher salaries and so on in future years. It is easy to see how the members of a cooperative could benefit from the Big Society, even in the absence of profits that can be distributed directly. The real issue is what, if any, is the possible public benefit?

If there were to be a public benefit, it would not actually have anything directly to do with the fact that it was cooperatives that were doing the providing. Thus, the possible smaller scale of these kinds of providers might conceivably mean that they were more efficient in provision, and, because of that, also more attentive to complaints made by users. On the other hand, that would depend also on how competent the members of a specific cooperative were at their jobs. Moreover, with some service provision there are economies of scale; with such services those advantages might outweigh the benefits that smaller-scale supply could bring. Small is not always beautiful. Nor does small necessarily have anything to do with a supplier's commitment to a locality. The service providers may well not live in the community they are servicing. Clearly, the government is correct in arguing that the diversity of potential suppliers works to the public advantage—assuming that it is possible to decide in the case of specific services whether scale matters or not, and if so how. But that mutual organisations are being encouraged to become suppliers is, in itself, largely irrelevant. The problems of the incentives facing the suppliers of public services are essentially the same whether those suppliers are for-profit organisations or producer/worker mutuals.

Obviously, the situation with charities is wholly different, which is one reason why James Douglas had relatively little to say about mutuals, once he had developed an analytic framework for understanding his supposed Third Sector. The *raison d'être* of a charity is to provide a particular kind of public benefit—or at least a benefit that has been defined in law as being such. Expanding the use of charities in the delivery of services raises two problems however. The first is that the more activity there is by charities, especially in providing services for fees or contracts, the more extensive the regulatory regime of charitable organisations has to be. The public has to be protected from fraudulent, inefficient and wasteful charities. However, the Charity Commission is one government agency that has been woefully under-resourced for decades.[11] The number of potential institutions with which it might have to intervene is enormous by comparison say with the organisations dealt with by Ofwat, Ofgen or other regulatory bodies that have been created in the decades since Douglas published his book. Any major increase in the use of charities in service delivery would require a similar increase in the capacity of the British state to provide effective regulation.

The other problem is related to one of the most common complaints made by charities—that their increased involvement in activities previously undertaken by government agencies results in their often being expected to do so on the cheap. In effect, they end up subsidising, from their other resources and in the interests of some beneficiaries, particular activities that they have felt compelled to help facilitate or supply. In meeting needs the charity often is unwilling to make the calculation that a for-profit firm or a mutual has to: can we cover our costs in doing this? Despite the Manifesto's pledge to ensure 'a competitive return for providing services', there is a long history of successive governments taking advantage of charities. Charities' desire not to let particular needs go unmet within a community, or in society more generally, has meant that they have tended to get drawn in when state supply is being reduced or abolished. Their subsidisation of such activities has to be at the expense of others to which they might have committed their resources.

For neighbourhoods the problem this poses is that, when other kinds of suppliers might be more willing to withdraw from rebidding for those services from which they cannot make a profit, charities might feel compelled to make a bid to prevent those who depend on the services from being left un-provided for. Some provision may be perceived as better than none at all. One effect of this can be to weaken the potential for the use of 'voice' against the government. It is much more difficult to generate support and publicity for a service that is just not very good, by comparison with one that is being threatened with outright removal. Of course, charities themselves are a useful vehicle for 'voice', but there is a danger that indirectly they can let central government 'off the hook' from protests, when at least something is being supplied by them to the recipients. At the same time, their own resources will be diminishing.

The Big Society and political power in Britain

There is an interesting difference between the Labour party's attempt in the 1990s to find a new approach to running services, its Third Way, and the Conservative's approach, the Big Society. It was always difficult for supporters of the Third Way to explain precisely what was distinctive about their approach because it seemed a highly amorphous notion. However, advocates of the Third Way were like those for the Big Society in that they too wanted to offload state responsibilities onto charities. In May 2004, the Blairite Alan Milburn, in between one of his two stints as a Cabinet Minister, made a speech in favour of a much expanded role for charities in delivering public services. Predictably the response to this from charity organisations themselves was mixed. One of the fears of some charities was that they would continue to subsidise public services. Rather than a possible partnership with government, it was thought that they might be used as a crutch by it.

While there is greater specificity to the Big Society than there was to the Third Way, the assumptions it makes about social institutions and how social action is generated do not correspond with how they are known to work. Even if David Cameron were to continue to prioritise the Big Society within the government's overall programme, it is difficult to imagine that it will revolutionise social provision in Britain. At best, it is likely to be seen by future generations as merely an extension of ideas within the Conservative party, and more recently the Labour party, that long pre-date it.

Like the Third Way, though, the Big Society represents an attempt by a major political party to solve a longstanding political problem. In the case of the Conservatives, however, there were two, linked, problems. One was how to devise a plausible model for welfare provision in which the central state was not dominant in both funding and delivering services. The other was more general: how to prevent the central state becoming all-dominant in Britain in respects that went beyond social welfare. The origin of this second problem can be traced back to the late 1960s.[12] The period between the 1920s and the 1960s was dubbed the 'ancient regime' by Jim Bulpitt, who argued that politics was divided into 'high' and 'low', with the former being controlled by the centre and the latter left to the localities to deal with. This suited the Conservative party, who relied on local social elites to protect Conservative interests in governing Britain at that level.

By the 1960s those arrangements ceased to be effective for the party, and it would be Edward Heath's administration that introduced the first major reform of local government since the late nineteenth century. That legislation killed off what remained of the informal mechanisms through which governing in the Conservative interest had been maintained, without generating any offsetting political benefits to the party. With the virtual elimination of Independent and Ratepayer councillors, the protection of the Conservative interest in local affairs now rested firmly with the party itself. This made it easier for their erstwhile opponents, including the Liberals (and its successor party), to influence local matters throughout the country.

Having been a party that favoured forms of devolved power, the Conservatives did a 180 degree turn under Margaret Thatcher. Sources of intermediate power in Britain—local government included—were to be stripped of many responsibilities, so that the main actors in British society would be a strong central government and citizen-consumers. Unfortunately, as a long-term solution to replacing the *ancien régime* it failed to meet the three requirements that were jointly necessary for it to be a successful replacement: providing regular parliamentary majorities for the party; compatibility with the traditional values and goals of core Conservative supporters; and a satisfactory fit with the present structure of British social institutions. Ultimately, the Thatcher experiment failed because the party could not deliver standards of service in a whole series of policy areas that were acceptable to a significant element of the British electorate. In other words, the first condition was not met.

In seeking to rectify that failing, the supporters of the Big Society have tried to move the party away from a framework in which there are claimed to be no significant actors apart from citizen-consumers and the central government. In some ways it can be seen as a move back to a much older Conservative tradition of treating localities seriously. Unfortunately, it is not well-grounded in what the localities have become and it has to operate in a post-Thatcher world in which intermediary institutions have been partly dismantled. Thus it can be seen as representing a halfway house between Heath's attempt to revive the local dimensions of the British state by reforming local government, and the Thatcher approach of dismantling it. Further power is to be transferred away from local governments, but to amorphous local entities with few structures through which effective social action could possibly be conducted. It comes no nearer than any of the earlier attempts to resolving the long-term difficulties of how to govern a large population that no longer inhabits the well defined territorial units through which traditional sources of power had been exercised earlier.

Arguably the Conservative party has more at stake with the Big Society than New Labour had with the Third Way. Because of its massive majorities, Labour could both afford for the Third Way not be treated very seriously by academics, commentators or anyone else and for it to be quietly abandoned as an idea later. Its electoral position after 2010 means that failure and abandonment of the Big Society is less of a luxury for the Conservative party. And if it is abandoned, it is not clear where the party could turn next in resolving its dilemma about how to provide for social welfare in ways that minimise the role of the state. Supposedly 'big ideas' can generate good electoral politics in the short term, but not necessarily in the long term, and they can also make for unsuccessful public policies if their assumptions are unsound. The prospects for the Big Society project being seen by future generations as a major turning point in Britain's social provision do not seem that good.

Notes

1 J. Douglas, *Why Charity? The Case for a Third Sector*, Beverly Hills, CA, Sage, 1983, pp. 146–7. Although not an academic himself, he was well connected to elite intellectual communities through his wife, the distinguished anthropologist Mary Douglas.

2 J. Posnett, 'A profile of the charity sector', in *Charity Statistics 1983–4*, Tonbridge, Charities Aid Foundation, 1984, pp. 56–7.

3 *Charity Statistics 1985–6*, Tonbridge, Charities Aid Foundation, 1986, p. 138.

4 Conservative party, *Invitation to Join the Government of Britain: The Conservative Manifesto 2010*, London, Conservative Central Office, 2010.

5 Cabinet Office, *Modernising Commissioning: Increasing the Role of Charities, Social Enterprises, Mutuals and Cooperatives in Public Service Delivery*, London, Cabinet Office, 2010, http://www.ncvo-vol.org.uk/sites/default/files/commissioning-green-paper1.pdf

6 R. A. Dahl, *After the Revolution? Authority in a Good Society*, New Haven, CT, Yale University Press, 1970. In Britain, the equation of local democracy with reform of the existing framework is evident in L. J. Sharpe, *Why Local Democracy?*, Fabian Pamphlet 361, London, Fabian Society, 1965.

7 On football, see http://www.bbc.co.uk/danroan/2011/06/tough_times_for_grassroots_foo.html; R. D. Putnam, *Bowling Alone: The Collapse and Revival of American Community*, New York, Simon & Schuster, 2000.

8 T. Skocpol, 'Advocates without members: the transformation of American civic life', in T. Skocpol and M. P. Fiorina, eds, *Civic Engagement in American Democracy*, Washington, DC, Brookings Institution Press, 1999, p. 461.

9 Interview given in *Woman's Own*, 31 October 1987; the version quoted comes from the transcript issued by the Margaret Thatcher Foundation.

10 Moreover, a spirit of comradeship was often a factor in the formation of mutuals; A. Ware, *Between Profit and State: Intermediate Organizations in Britain and the United States*, Princeton, NJ, Princeton University Press, 1989, p. 40.

11 A. Ware, 'Introduction: the changing relations between charities and the state', in *Charities and Government*, Manchester, Manchester University Press, 1989, p. 22.

12 J. Bulpitt, *Territory and Power in Britain*, Manchester, Manchester University Press, 1983; see also 'Special Issue on "Territory and Power"', *Government and Opposition*, vol. 45, 2010.

Freedom, Free Institutions and the Big Society

JASON EDWARDS

IN THIS chapter I intend to treat seriously the idea of the Big Society as a political philosophy. Undoubtedly many will be unconvinced by this claim as they see the Big Society as a programme of government relatively unbound by abstract ideas, or perhaps as a cynical marketing campaign to rebrand the Conservative party as the 'Not-so-Nasty party'. But I think the claim is worth taking seriously for two reasons. First, some of the major advocates of the Big Society—most prominently Phillip Blond and Jesse Norman—themselves make the case for it. They engage with ideas from political philosophy and the history of political thought to map out a view of the Big Society as organised around a set of normative principles. Second, I would argue that the Big Society does mark an important break in conservative ideology with the beliefs that informed Thatcherism. In a significant way this change has been occasioned by a reflection on general values and in particular a reassessment of the idea of freedom and the role of free institutions in society.

Part of my task then is to try to give an overview of the idea of freedom and free institutions in Big Society thinking and the way in which it departs from previous conservative thought. I then want to go on to address the Big Society view of free institutions from the perspective of republicanism in political theory. I mean 'republicanism' here not in the classical sense of a system of government that rejects monarchy, but rather in the more philosophical sense of a body of ideas concerning the character of the liberty of citizens and the political conditions necessary to secure such liberty. In recent times in political theory, republicanism has, broadly speaking, appeared in two forms. The first draws on the ideas of civic humanists who, often citing Aristotle as the classical authority, claim that active membership of a political community is central to human freedom. The second, which has been developed most significantly in recent years by Quentin Skinner and Philip Pettit, focuses on a tradition in the history of republican thought that treats freedom as non-domination or as freedom from subjection to arbitrary power. The argument for freedom here is, at the same time, an argument for independence. I will focus on this second conception of republicanism as I think it points to important problems at the basis of Big Society thought from which may well stem its limitations as a programme of government.

Part of the reason for this engagement with republicanism is that at first sight the Big Society conception of free institutions looks to have a republican character. In some moments of its defence, Big Society thinkers have invoked the Aristotelian ideal of civic virtue. But at the same time, and perhaps more

Published by Blackwell Publishing Ltd, 9600 Garsington Road, Oxford OX4 2DQ, UK and 350 Main Street, Malden, MA 02148, USA

importantly for my purposes, the explicit repudiation of 'Big Government' we find in Big Society thinking and its celebration of the value of local institutions, mutual and cooperative enterprises, and other organisations outside of the state charged with economic and welfare functions, seems to involve an appeal to the independence of the institutions of the Big Society. Indeed, in the presentation of the key principles of the Big Society, the idea of freedom from the state as independence from the state stands out. More than this, however, it is striking that Big Society thinkers do not simply reject the state as having *any* role in the establishment of the freedom of the institutions of the Big Society. Quite to the contrary, the state is seen as important in providing the conditions for the flourishing of free institutions. In this regard there might appear to be an overlap with the kind of republican political theory that places independence at the centre of freedom but sees such independence as sustained by a civil order invigilated by the state. However, I will argue that the independence granted to civil institutions in Big Society thinking is entirely conditional and licensed by the state to meet substantive social and economic ends—namely the ends of 'responsibility'.

The Big Society's view of freedom and free institutions, therefore, is not consistent with the republican ideal of freedom as independence. This is because Big Society thinkers fail to recognise the real source of the dependence of civil institutions on the state in contemporary Britain. Their dependence lies not in the existence of a centralised administrative state per se, but rather in the character of the political system that establishes and maintains the administrative domination of the state over these civil institutions. The creation of truly independent civil institutions requires a radical and fundamental transformation of the British political system in which their independence is given in a civil constitutional order that at the same time empowers them to invigilate the state in its role as invigilator.

I will proceed as follows. In the first section I chart out the conception of freedom and free institutions in Big Society thinking and emphasise its distinctiveness from the notion of freedom that characterised Thatcherite conservatism. In the second section, I provide a brief examination of the ideas of two often cited ancestors of Big Society thinking—Adam Smith and Edmund Burke—to highlight an important difference in their thought that relates to Smith's greater sensitivity to republican considerations of independence and Burke's dismissal of them. Burke's understanding of free institutions, it turns out, is much more consistent with the Big Society than Smith's. In the third section I examine the key problems that arise from a consideration of the Big Society from the perspective of the republican idea of freedom as independence.

Freedom and responsibility in the Big Society

In his Hugo Young Lecture of 2009 on the Big Society, David Cameron uses the word 'freedom' just three times. 'Liberty' makes no appearance. In contrast, the word 'responsibility' occurs on no less than 22 occasions. The promotion of responsibility—both individual and social—appears as the goal of the Big Society and in turn is a vehicle for the tackling of poverty and social inequality. 'Big Government', which Cameron claims to have grown substantially under Labour since 1997, has undermined personal and social responsibility and encouraged dependence on the state, while failing to meet the aim of reducing social inequality. The displacement of Big Government by the Big Society involves not simply the 'retrenchment' of the state, but a 're-imagined role for the state' in which power is redistributed to individuals and local communities via 'social entrepreneurs' and 'community activists'. The state's promotion of 'social action' is the key to mending a society that has become atomised, polarised and uncivil.[1]

There is a clear sense here that 'responsibility' means self-reliance and this appears to be a very Thatcherite theme. But the lack of attention to the notion of individual freedom or liberty in Cameron's speech is not just incidental. For Thatcherites, the protection of individual freedom, understood in the classical liberal sense of an absence of interference in the life of the individual by the state, was the paramount goal of policy and for the most part involved a commitment to the idea of rolling back the frontiers of the state (even though the reality was the strengthening of many of the state's powers over the individual under Thatcherism). In contrast, it is the promotion of personal and social responsibility—not individual freedom—that is seen to be the goal of the Big Society. The effect of the kind of social action that the Big Society seeks may be to enhance individual freedom, but this is its by-product—not its immediate aim.

There is little question that this view of freedom and responsibility marks a significant departure from Thatcherism. 'Social action' in the Big Society requires the recognition and empowerment of collective agencies between the state and individual that are charged with economic and welfare functions of the kind that Thatcherites believed should be left to the market, or where the market could not provide, the state. Economic liberals, of the Hayekian variety, stipulated that any state interference with the choices of agents on the free market would lead to inefficient allocative outcomes as well as threatening individual liberty by empowering collectivist bureaucracies.

Thus in principle there is no commitment to the value of non-interference in Cameron's vision of the Big Society. In fact, it involves the enjoinment of various kinds of state interference in the organisation of social life and the conduct of individuals. Thus since the election of the coalition in 2010, the government has selected and funded 'social enterprises' to deliver public services either directly or through agencies such as the Big Society Investment Fund. With respect to individual conduct, in the Hugo Young lecture

Cameron spoke about government 'going with the grain of human nature' to influence behaviour, citing favourably Sunstein and Thaler's idea of 'nudge'.[2] Of course, such evaluations of the 'grain of human nature' are far from politically neutral. 'Nudge' is not non-interference because it resets the range of options that are available to individuals and groups in a way that presupposes substantive views about what constitutes their good. A nudge is not a command, but a sequence of nudges of sufficient strength amounts to a push.

It follows from this that Big Society thinkers cannot claim that the freedom they value is a freedom from state interference in the lives of individuals and non-state organisations. Unlike neoliberals, Big Society thinkers seem to suggest that interference is in principle a good rather than a necessary evil. What makes it a good is its directive effects. Interference is designed to promote certain attitudes and behaviour both in organisations and individuals according to the commitments that are entailed by the Big Society's image of the good society. This vision of the good society departs from neoliberal conceptions—or rather the view that 'there is no such thing as society'—but at the same time, as I will argue, it is inconsistent with a robust defence of the independence of civil institutions that emerges from an engagement with the republican idea of freedom as freedom from arbitrary power. In the next section I will set out some of the grounds of the Big Society's view of 'independent' institutions, and its difference from republican-oriented conceptions, by going back to the birth of the Big Society in the late eighteenth century.

Two visions of the Good Society

Advocacy of the Big Society would make no sense unless it was viewed by its advocates as, at the same time, the 'good society'. In turn, that presupposes we can specify 'society' as an entity that is distinct from and related to the state. This conceptualisation of the specificity of society in relation to the state emerges in the eighteenth century and takes a decidedly 'moral' form, in the sense that we can only consider whether the actions of the state demand approbation or disapprobation in light of the more general character of the society in which they are enacted. Big Society thinkers have themselves traced the origin of Big Society thought to this discovery of the 'moral sciences' in the late eighteenth century. Norman has written that the 'Big Society is ultimately derived from the ideas of Edmund Burke and Adam Smith, who emphasise not rampant but limited markets; not the over-mighty state but free and independent institutions; not personal greed but trust and sympathy'.[3] However, I will argue that in fact Smith and Burke offer us quite different conceptions of what constitutes the good society on the basis of distinct pictures of the historical source and the social role of independent institutions in relation to the state.

Smith and Burke were writing in a political and intellectual context that turned around the problem of the relationship between society and economy, and in particular the question of the limits of the state as the public power. This question is formulated by the emerging discourse of political economy as one that is to be addressed by statesmen who are charged with the protection of the public interest. At the beginning of Book IV of *The Wealth of Nations*, Smith describes political economy in the following fashion:

Political economy, considered as a branch of the science of a statesman or legislator, proposes two distinct objects: first, to provide a plentiful revenue or subsistence for the people, or more properly to enable them to provide such a revenue or subsistence for themselves; and secondly, to supply the state or commonwealth with a revenue sufficient for the public services. It proposes to enrich both the people and the sovereign.[4]

Political economy therefore appears as a 'science' of government oriented towards the improvement of the population as a whole, as a result of their own activities, with a recognition of the necessity of a revenue for the sovereign that allows it to meet its obligations to provide public services. But as *The Wealth of Nations* unfolds, it becomes clear that the form of the state is all important for maintaining the independence of the people in the provision of their own subsistence. In other words, the conventional picture of Smith as drawing a clear line between economics and politics, the market and the state, is in error. Smith's concern with the character of the economic life of the people is, indeed, political for the reason that he is exercised by the question of the good society. While the market functions on the basis of self-interest a good society is one that must promote virtue and civility. A virtuous and civil society is one that must have clean political institutions—that is, institutions that are free from the taint of corruption and uphold the independence of citizens and the associations they form.

As historians of political thought such as J. G. A. Pocock and Donald Winch have shown, Smith's concerns are couched to a significant degree in the language of civic humanism.[5] His regard for the problems of political virtue and the corruption of public office is classically republican in orientation. However, Smith's modernism lies in the fact that he neither asks nor expects citizens in commercial society to participate extensively in the life of the political community in order to be free. Their freedom lies, as Pocock puts it, in the *commercium* rather than the *politicum*. The role of independent institutions in commercial society—and 'commercial society' in this respect refers not simply to the market but to a wide range of civil associations—is both economic *and* political. It is political in the sense that the state is invigilated by the free institutions whose liberty it is charged with protecting.

It is important to see that for Smith the market is no 'natural' order. If the famous 'disposition to truck, barter, and exchange' that he takes as the engine of the division of labour may be seen as instinctual, the particular forms in which it is expressed are given by custom, convention and law. The independence of institutions in modern commercial society is therefore only possible because of the particular attitudes and forms of conduct that are provided for in the symbiotic relationship between economic and political institutions. The question of the uses and abuses of power in this relation is therefore central to Smith's argument. The freedom and opulence allowed by a commercial society are only potential—whether they are realised is a matter of the conduct of individuals in commercial society and the conduct of those who occupy public office. In both instances, the probity of conduct is determined by the strength of a society's free institutions in the invigilation of their own members and the state.

If we turn now to the Burkean conception of society, there is on the face of it an affinity with Smith's account of commercial society. Smith himself said that he and Burke were at one on matters of political economy, though this has been conveyed to us in an anecdote of Burke's own telling.[6] If we understand this broadly to mean that both Burke and Smith argued for the value of free institutions and the limitation of state power, then they indeed appear as one. But the rationale for 'free' institutions is quite different in Burke's thought. While Smith does not see the market order of a commercial society that sustains independent institutions as natural, Burke sought to naturalise the market. His argument against state interference in matters of production and consumption, witnessed in his vehement rejection of the government's plan to provide wage subsidies to agricultural workers struggling through a series of poor harvests in the early 1790s, invokes the idea of the laws of commerce as natural.[7]

This naturalisation of the market stems from Burke's commitment to the idea of the 'ancient constitution' which, as Pocock has shown, was central to his thinking.[8] In the seventeenth century, the idea of an ancient constitution that protected the rights and liberties of free-born Englishmen prior to the Norman yoke developed as a means of opposition to the threat of Stuart absolutism. For Burke, the justification for a commercial society of the kind that had emerged in England, with the guarantee of personal property rights and the free exchange of property on markets, was in fact to be found in the customs and manners of the chivalric order that characterised ancient society. The independent institutions of modern commercial society are thus inscribed in an ancient natural order, the sanctity of property and private exchange within that order is divinely ordained, and both property and political power are differentially distributed according to rank.

Burke's appeal to the 'little platoons we belong to in society' is often invoked by Big Society thinkers, particularly Phillip Blond,[9] to stand for active, self-governing civil associations, but we should be aware that for Burke these appear more as communities of fate rather than communities of choice. His use of 'little platoons' takes place in a passage of the *Reflections on the Revolution in France* where he is excoriating the representatives of the clergy in the Third Estate for their role in the Revolution. For Burke, they 'could hardly be the most conscientious of their kind, who presuming upon their incompetent understanding, could intrigue for a trust which led them from their natural relation to their flocks, and their natural spheres of action, to undertake the regeneration of kingdoms'.[10] In other words, such men should know their limitations and pay regard only to their natural relations and 'spheres of action': they have no quality that could allow them to determine affairs of state with any wisdom. The idea of the 'little platoons' is not, therefore, intended as a call for civic activism and the independence of civil institutions, but is rather employed to defend the value of a society bound by rank and immemorial social practice. The term is a reflection of a view of the divine ordering of nature into social groups differentiated according to function in an organic unity.

My intention here is not to claim that Burke is really a conservative thinker while Smith is not. Smith, after all, was hardly a revolutionary, associated openly with Tories in his later years, and had little critical to say about the British constitution. At the same time, there is a great deal in Burke's work that is in no straightforward sense 'conservative'. However, a consideration of Smith's and Burke's view of what constitutes the independence of free institutions in the good society reveals rather different perspectives. Smith's understanding of the independence of citizens and their associations in commercial society as a product of the interaction between economic and political institutions points to the importance of the invigilation of its members and the state by civil institutions. While Smith believes in the public benefits of deference to political authority, there is a strong suggestion in his work that such deference in modern societies is owed only to the 'natural' aristocracy versed in the science of the legislator. In contrast, the deference to authority that Burke demands is founded in the hierarchy of an ancient chivalric order. At the centre of the free institutions of this society are the church and the nobility. Burke's moral aristocracy is thus a self-invigilating political authority—it checks itself against religious commitments that demand social responsibility, but remains constitutionally unconstrained by the society over which it rules. The good society is a society governed by chivalrous gentlemen, not by independent institutions that grant authority to legislators on the condition that they act to preserve and extend the freedom and wealth of those institutions.

Independent institutions in a republican civil order

It turns out that the Big Society's conception of free institutions is much closer to the view outlined by Burke rather than Smith with his quasi-republican instincts. As I have already indicated, I think that republican insights into the character of freedom can give us an alternative understanding of the freedom of independent institutions that poses a serious challenge to Big Society thinking. Skinner and Pettit have characterised republican liberty as freedom from domination or freedom from subjection to arbitrary power.[11] On this view interference by an invigilating authority in the conduct of individuals or organisations is not detrimental to freedom insofar as the interferee authorises the interference or the conditions in which interference is licensed. This creates a distinction between a republican conception of freedom and the famous notion of 'negative liberty', proposed by Isaiah Berlin and embraced by neoliberals, that claims that liberty is violated whenever one is interfered or impeded with. Cameron, as we have already seen, has no truck with neoliberals on this front, for his account of the Big Society makes a *prima facie* case for interference by the state.

The question is what is taken to be the purpose of interference, and to what degree it is licensed by the interferees, in Big Society thinking? Free institutions, to be free in the republican sense of independence, would necessarily have to license state interference and interference could only be justified on the grounds that its purpose was to defend a system that upholds the independence of civil institutions. But the express purpose of government in the Big Society is not to interfere in order to defend or protect the political freedom of civil institutions, but in order to meet the specific socio-economic goals set out in broad terms by Cameron in his Hugo Young lecture—that is, the promotion of personal and social responsibility. The Big Society has some very thick moral ends and the role envisaged for mutuals, cooperatives and voluntary organisations is essentially moral in character. The function of these organisations is to act as the agents of the state in the mending of the 'broken society'.

Cameron presents a picture of a social and moral order presided over by agencies that have the character of 'social action projects'. The most important of these are the 'social entrepreneurs'—those with 'a proven track record' are to be 'franchised' by the state and directly funded from existing budgets. The role of the individual social entrepreneur is crucial in this: 'If we find the right people, a relatively small number can make a huge difference.' The language of entrepreneurship employed here sits uncomfortably with the idea of inclusive civil institutions. Entrepreneurs, by definition, are not ordinary but extraordinary citizens, who undertake risks at their own cost in the attempt to secure substantial returns. Most citizens have neither the means nor the disposition to risk that would allow them to act as social entrepreneurs. In Cameron's view this is 'the majority of the population' who can only be nudged towards volunteering and charitable giving, or who can be encouraged to sociability by support for 'local shops, the post office and the town hall'.

This emphasis on the role of social entrepreneurs and community activists should lead us to question how big the Big Society really is, but the more significant problem concerns the extent and kind of authority they exercise over citizens. The question becomes particularly acute when the lines between social and commercial enterprises become blurred—one of the reasons why many of its critics have simply taken the Big Society as a smokescreen for the privatisation of public service provision to the profit of large private companies such as Serco and A4e. Yet even if it were the case that most Big

Society agents were charitable and non-profit organisations with laudable social and economic aims, this would not displace the concern for the arbitrariness of the power exercised by and the quality of the invigilation of such organisations.

The reality is that most of the Big Society actors are not self-governing associations of citizens but rather quasi-public agencies, private firms, and charities who are licensed and contracted by the state to provide certain public services. Despite the currency of the notion of a 'post-bureaucratic age' in Big Society thought, in practice the policies are oriented entirely towards issues of public administration. The priorities concern effective 'delivery' and 'value for money', rather than the foundation of a new political order. The neoliberal problematic remains firmly on the agenda—that is, social and economic governance through non-state agencies, which for the most part means large private and quasi-public bureaucracies that remain hidden from public view.

However, as I claimed at the outset it is important to take the Big Society seriously as a departure from the neoliberal and Thatcherite conceptions of freedom and free institutions. If the coalition agenda looks more and more like a neoliberal stripping down of the state and the hiving off of its economic and welfare functions, this is not in spite of the values of the Big Society, but precisely because of them. The Big Society is framed as a moral project, the regeneration of a broken society that is to be carried out by the responsible in the promotion of responsibility. But just as Burke's criteria for free institutions depended on a prior political evaluation of their moral virtue, so the Big Society rests on the selection of who and what is to count as a responsible agent by the state. The institutions of the Big Society are 'free' only in the narrow sense that they are given—within the constraints of the requirements for tackling the broken society—managerial autonomy.

I have raised the issue of republican approaches to the freedom of institutions because they point to the problems with the Big Society approach as a political philosophy. Critics of the Big Society have found the idea elusive and at times difficult to contest, as most people agree with 'the aspiration of helping people to come together to improve their own lives'. In a political system that is widely recognised as highly centralised there is bound to be an attraction to the idea of 'putting more power in people's hands—a massive transfer of power from Whitehall to local communities'.[12] The problem that critics of the Big Society have can be seen in this kind of characterisation of its agents. The vagueness of the idea of a 'local community' stems from the apolitical perspective Big Society thought holds on the constitution of society. There is the recourse here to a Burkean organicism, the notion of spontaneous community that demands the leadership of a natural aristocracy: the *noblesse oblige* of the modern social entrepreneur and community activist. The subjects of the Big Society thus appear as dependent communities, objects for paternal aid provided by the state via its empowerment of the socially active.

Free institutions in a republican civil order must be able to exercise freedom in the sense that they are not subject to the arbitrary power of other institutions. At the same time, truly voluntary institutions are communities of choice, not fate. There are traditions in the history of political thought that emphasise the value of alternatives to the central state and the market as the providers of economic security and social welfare, while maintaining a republican concern for freedom as genuine independence. They seek to conjoin the freedom of civil institutions from arbitrary power and the freedom of the individual to choose one's associative commitments. On this view, the purpose of voluntary associations, mutuals, cooperatives and other civil associations in modern societies is neither narrowly utilitarian nor prescriptively moral, but rather political. They operate in a civil order that recognises and protects their independence and difference, invigilating the public power and limiting opportunities for its corruption. To be sure, a civil political order must at the same time be a moral order in which citizens recognise shared norms of conduct and practice self-restraint and responsibility. But, as Adam Smith recognised, such conduct is not the precondition of a society of free institutions, rooted in immemorial practice, but is rather fostered within a civic and political culture of independence and non-domination.

As Rodney Barker argues elsewhere in this volume, any judgement we can make about the value of the institutions of the Big Society should be reserved until we have a clear view of their internal constitution and purpose. I have claimed in this chapter that Big Society thinking tends to see these institutions in the Burkean sense of the composite units of an organic social whole. The jettisoning of a certain liberal view of freedom as freedom from interference is entailed by this view, but I would argue that at the same time this involves a repudiation of the understanding of the relationship between the individual and society that informed this liberal conception of freedom and which is a reflection of real and ineradicable social relations in modern society. This view, articulated in the work of thinkers such as Tocqueville, Durkheim and the English political pluralists, recognises that the ascriptive bonds of organic unity characteristic of the old world have been irrevocably broken by the advent of democracy, capitalism and industrial society. Yet the individualism necessarily fostered by our modern condition does not eradicate the possibility of civil association, but makes its achievement and sustainment of pressing importance. There is no chance, however, of retrieving these associations from the past, from a mythical golden age of free institutions, precisely because these institutions demanded the kind of servility from their members that is unacceptable to the moderns. Most people who regard themselves as citizens desire to be free to choose and believe that their choices are in some important sense authored by themselves, not imposed on them by the dictates of individual and social 'responsibility' and state-appointed and sanctioned social entrepreneurs and community activists.

Notes

1 D. Cameron, 'The Big Society', Hugo Young Lecture, 2009, http://www. conservatives.com/News/Speeches/2009/11/David_Cameron_The_Big_ Society.aspx

2 R. H. Thaler and C. R. Sunstein, *Nudge: Improving Decisions about Health, Wealth and Happiness*, New Haven, CT, Yale University Press, 2008.

3 J. Norman, 'Hands off our Big Society', *Guardian*, 1 October 2011.

4 A. Smith, *The Wealth of Nations, Books IV–V*, London, Penguin Books, 1999, p. 5.

5 J. G. A. Pocock, *Virtue, Commerce and History*, Cambridge, Cambridge University Press, 1985; D. Winch, *Adam Smith's Politics: An Essay in Historiographic Revision*, Cambridge, Cambridge University Press, 1978.

6 D. Winch, 'The Burke-Smith problem and late eighteenth-century political and economic thought', *Historical Journal*, vol. 28, no. 1, 1985, pp. 231–47.

7 E. Burke, *Thoughts and Details on Scarcity*, London, 1800. See F. P. Locke, *Edmund Burke, Volume II: 1784–1797*, Oxford, Clarendon Press, 2006, pp. 515–21.

8 J. G. A. Pocock, 'Burke and the ancient constitution: a problem in the history of ideas', in *Politics, Language and Time: Essays on the History of Political Thought*, Chicago, IL, University of Chicago Press, 1989.

9 P. Blond, *Red Tory*, London, Faber & Faber, 2010.

10 E. Burke, *Reflections on the Revolution in France*, London, Penguin, 1986, p. 134.

11 Q. Skinner, *Liberty before Liberalism*, Cambridge, Cambridge University Press, 1998; P. Pettit, *Republicanism: A Theory of Freedom and Government*, Oxford, Oxford University Press, 1997; C. Laborde and J. Maynor, eds, *Republicanism and Political Theory*, Oxford, Blackwell, 2008.

12 http://www.cabinetoffice.gov.uk/big-society

From Burke to Burkha: Conservatism, Multiculturalism and the Big Society

RICHARD KELLY and ROBERT CROWCROFT

IN THE literature produced about the Conservative party under David Cameron, specifically his devotion to the 'Big Society', writers have not been slow to pinpoint the influence of Edmund Burke, whose *Reflections on the Revolution in France* (1790) is widely seen as the foundation of Conservative philosophy. Indeed, David Marquand has acclaimed Burke as the 'Patron Saint of the Big Society'.[1] However, to date little attempt has been made to argue that the Big Society—or 'neo-Burkeism'—might also prompt a reappraisal of the party's attitude towards multiculturalism.

In fairness, such a reappraisal would not have been encouraged by Cameron's explicit rejection of it in early 2011. This chapter, nevertheless, will seek to make two relatively novel arguments. First, from a 'descriptive' angle, it will argue a strong, if latent, connection between the prescriptions of Edmund Burke and the practicalities of multiculturalism. Second, from a 'normative' angle, it will argue that the connection is one today's Conservatives might usefully honour, especially if they are serious about bringing the Big Society to fruition. As a result, the chapter hopes to advance, albeit in rudimentary form, a new subdivision of political ideology: conservative multiculturalism.

Multiculturalism and Conservatism: the traditional problem

Emerging in the 1970s and developing in the 1980s, multiculturalism is seen by some as not so much an ideology as a 'political space', where more established doctrines can flourish. By definition, multiculturalism's exponents scorn the idea of a single homogenous culture, and instead extol a society promoting a range of lifestyles, philosophies, religions, practices and codes. Likewise, they are reluctant to accept the superiority of one culture over another, and underpin their argument with a fundamental belief that cultural diversity enriches society.[2]

Although it has attracted some criticism from the liberal-left, multiculturalism is generally seen as an extension of liberal-left thinking. Yet while textbooks routinely refer to the 'liberal' or 'pluralist-socialist' models of multiculturalism, there is a conspicuous absence of any 'conservative' version. Insofar as conservatism features at all, it is usually linked to the various critiques of multiculturalism, leaving readers with the clear impression that conservatism and multiculturalism are mutually exclusive.

This is unsurprising given the Conservative party's traditional and overt opposition to a multicultural Britain. Unlike their liberal-left opponents, Conservatives have been generally critical of moral relativism, drawn towards moral prescription, inclined to see multiculturalism as a threat to social cohesion (or 'one nation') and fearful it would erode their (allegedly atavistic) perception of the British character.

Such attitudes relate to the fact that, since the Second World War, immigration and resulting cultural change have posed ongoing problems for Conservative politicians. During the 1960s, a number were flagrantly hostile to any diversification of Britain's ethno-cultural character—the most notable, of course, being Enoch Powell who effectively argued that multiculturalism would lead to civil war. Powell's views were scarcely eccentric in Conservative circles; a study of Conservative conferences in the late 1960s and 1970s showed that Powell's views were enthusiastically endorsed by up to half of constituency party representatives.[3]

Though less incendiary, senior Conservative figures since the 1960s have still conveyed disquiet about immigration and its cultural consequences. Margaret Thatcher observed in 1978 that Britons felt 'swamped' by 'alien cultures'; Norman Tebbit spoke in 1988 of a 'cricket test' designed to show that many black Britons owed principal allegiance to other nations (as demonstrated by their support for the West Indies et al. at Test matches); and William Hague claimed in 2000 that many British voters felt like 'strangers in a foreign land'. Predictably, the aftermath of 9/11 did not spark any huge change in the party's view. During the second Blair government, Conservative leaders generally supported New Labour's belated enthusiasm for 'British values' and its equally belated contention that immigrants should be vigorously assimilated. In other words, as New Labour retreated from multiculturalism, there was no sign that Conservatives would fill the vacuum.

Cameron's u-turn

David Cameron's emergence as Conservative leader in 2005, however, was thought to mark a possible break with the party's previous approach. His support for greater inclusiveness and tolerance, linked to a strategy of 'detoxifying' Conservatism, raised questions about whether Conservatives were now more equivocal about multiculturalism.

As opposition leader, Cameron fuelled this idea by often lauding the contribution of black and minority ethnic (BME) voters to national life. Sometimes, this involved praising their absorption into mainstream British society, thus confirming Conservative distaste for multiculturalism. But sometimes, as well, Cameron saluted the new ingredients that BME citizens had brought to British society. The 'A-list' of fast-tracked Conservative candidates, backed by Cameron after 2006, also deliberately featured a significant number of BME politicians, of whom 43 were selected as parliamentary candidates by 2010. It is worth recalling that 11 of these were duly elected to Parliament—the highest number of BME Tory MPs so far—while Sayeeda Warsi later became Co-Chair of the Conservative party and the first female Muslim to sit in Cabinet.

By the time of the 2010 general election, some BME spokesmen assumed a symmetry between Cameron's zeal for racial tolerance and his 'big idea' of a Big Society—an idea pointing to the decentralisation of decision making, the diversification of civic engagement and a more pluralist approach to public policy. For some BME spokesmen, this appeared the logical prelude to an acceptance of multiculturalism. As a group of Muslim activists told BBC Radio Manchester in April 2010, they were 'prepared to welcome Cameron's Big Society' on the grounds it might 'firm up our culture', 'validate our different-ness' and 'underwrite the sort of communities we already live in'.

Yet, within a year of entering Downing Street, Cameron seemed eager to de-couple multiculturalism from his Big Society. In February 2011, while delivering a speech in Munich, he explicitly attacked multiculturalism, linked it to terrorism and the suppression of civil liberties, demanded 'muscular liberalism' from politicians and public alike, and stated 'that everyone coming here must be ready to embrace certain core values'. Cameron was generally applauded by Conservative commentators. For them, the Prime Minister had simply come to his senses, and was voicing the sort of views expected of anyone with normal conservative instincts.

Beyond Disraeli, back to Burke

Yet the relationship between Conservatism and multiculturalism is potentially quite complicated, due mainly to the roots of Conservative philosophy. It is often assumed, of course, that traditional Conservatism involves a visceral British nationalism and a passionate stress on shared national identity. Yet this analysis implies that Conservatism dates only from the 1860s and 1870s, the period when Benjamin Disraeli linked the Conservative party to imperialism and an enfolding sense of British-ness.

Of course, there can be no doubt that Disraeli's initiative was inspired, and played no small part in the Conservative dominance of the next century. But, as indicated at the start of this chapter, Conservative philosophy has a much older pedigree—hence the routine claim that Edmund Burke (1729–1797) was 'the father of conservatism'.[4] What is yet to be considered, however, is whether the father of English conservatism might also be the midwife of British multiculturalism.

Burke: no reactionary

When exalting Burke, modern Conservatives often forget that he was neither a nationalist nor a Little Englander. As a Whig MP, he was not even consistently conservative. He expressed support for Adam Smith's *The Wealth of Nations* (whose iconoclastic capitalism shocked insular aristocrats). He supported the American colonists against the imperial persecution of George III's ministers. He demanded the impeachment of Warren Hastings, Governor General of Bengal, for alleged extortion and injustice against the people of Hindustan. And he championed Irish Catholics in their battle with rapacious, Crown-friendly landlords. These causes suggest that, prior to his critique of the French Revolution, Burke was anything but an implacable reactionary. Instead, his politics seemed to be a fascinating blend of four themes: empiricism, organicism, evolutionary change and (to borrow a modern Conservative term) localism.

In terms of *empiricism*, Burke argued that society must be looked at as it is: objectively and factually, not in accordance with abstract theories, and mindful of what he termed 'the crooked timber of humanity'. In terms of *organicism*, he argued that communities tended to change naturally and in a way that defied the contrivances of statesmen. In terms of *evolutionary change*, Burke argued that, though inevitable ('a state without the means of change is without its means of conservation'), rapid revolutionary change was at odds with the subtleties and mysteries of an organic society. And, in respect of *localism*, Burke argued that the statesman should generally allow local discretion and local governance while respecting local differences and local customs—even when (as in the case of Burke and Hindustan) they were not the customs and preferences of the statesman himself. It was this latter insight that produced Burke's most enduring metaphor: the 'little platoons'.

Beyond nationalism: the little platoons

It is often forgotten that, despite its stress on *égalité* and *fraternité*, the French Revolution was also the birthplace of nationalism and the nation-state. Critically, the Revolution's preferred unit of organisation was neither the rooted kingdoms of the *ancien régime* nor the diverse communities of the former American colonies, but the 'French nation', acting centrally in the name of a supposedly homogenous 'French people'. So although leftists today often sneer at nationalism, it was the progeny of what many see as the original leftist revolution. And, in a further irony, one of its most famous opponents was the supposed father of conservatism.

For Burke, the new French nation-state augured a monolithic, top-down, repressive society—not so different to the stifling imperialism he had denounced in Ireland, India and America. Burke's retort was a defence of the society he perceived in England; one comprising a multitude of small, diverse and organic communities based on families, local communities and local networks. Each would have its own peculiar hierarchies, attitudes and rules; and each would impose restraint, responsibility and status upon the individuals within them.

Burke described these variable communities as the 'little platoons', claiming that 'to be attached to the subdivision, to love the little platoon to which we belong in society, is the first principle, the germ as it were, of public affections'.[5] He further argued that these 'platoons' were the vital guardians of individual liberty, without which nothing would stand between vulnerable individuals and a tyrannical sovereign. Events in the new French Republic—particularly the 'Terror' and its symbolic guillotine—gave a swift vindication of Burke's thesis.

Multiculturalism and Conservatism: towards a new analysis

Before considering whether Conservatives *would* champion the idea of a multicultural society, it is worth clarifying how Conservatives *could* without appearing to commit ideological apostasy. With this in mind, we shall re-examine Burke's four key principles in direct relation to the debate about multiculturalism.

A useful starting point would be to claim that Britain's multicultural society is one that has emerged organically, rather than being engineered by misguided social scientists and politicians. At local government level, there have certainly been examples of positive discrimination favouring minority cultures (Ken Livingstone's Greater London Council, in the early 1980s, being the most brazen). But at the national level, and in the bulk of local authorities, the theme of public policy for almost half a century has been one of liberal integration: in other words, blending immigrants into the 'mainstream' liberal culture while offering them protection against racial discrimination.

As Roy Hattersley remarked, while a Home Office minister in the mid-1960s: 'Integration without limitation (of immigration) is impossible. Limitation without integration is indefensible.'[6] These sentiments have since given traction to the Race Relations Acts of 1965, 1968, 1976 and 2000, and the various watchdog bodies (such as the Commission for Racial Equality) set up to enforce the Acts and generally promote a multiracial—but not multi-cultural—society.

As a result, Conservatives would be entitled to contest that the liberal-integration project was a huge, anti-organic exercise that took no account of the profoundly distinctive cultures shaping many postwar immigrants: cultures that could not be easily reconciled with the postwar *zeitgeist* of humanism and moral permissiveness. Equally, Conservatives could now argue that the experiment has inevitably failed. Today, there are distinctive and enlarged ethno-cultural communities in numerous urban areas, blatantly defying the 'muscular liberalism' of the Race Relations laws, vindicating the Burkean belief that human communities cannot be regimented (apart from through tyranny) and proving that human communities are organic entities with dynamics irrelevant to politicians' wishes.

In support of this conclusion, a *YouGov* poll in 2005 found that, forty years after the first Race Relations Act, over 40 per cent of British-born Muslims favoured the introduction of some Sharia law into their communities, while a further 42 per cent of British-born Asians professed 'no principal loyalty to the United Kingdom'.[7] The intercommunity riots of 2001 in Burnley, Oldham and Bradford, the Islamist attacks on London in 2005, plus the numerous thwarted attacks since, offered further evidence that liberal-integration had been at best naïve and at worst dangerously simplistic.

This leads to the second connection between Burke's philosophy and multiculturalism: that whereas an integrated, multiracial society was a liberal-utopian vision, the exponentially diverse, multicultural society we now have is an empirical fact. As O'Hara wrote in a generally sympathetic study of modern Conservatism: 'Britain is a multicultural place. No getting round that, and silly to try.'[8] That, in turn, leads to a question that touches upon the *raison d'être* of Burke's *Reflections*: how might altered circumstances be accommodated without the need for violent, revolutionary upheaval?

As Kirk's study of Burke observed, 'conservatism is never more admirable than when it accepts changes that it disapproves, with good grace, for the sake of a general conciliation'.[9] And although Conservatives might resent the legacy of immigration—and its consequence of a multicultural Britain—the pragmatic, empirical politics bequeathed by Burke implies that they should accept it, and then build policies that reflect it. As Paul Kelly suggests elsewhere in this collection, this would have probably been the conclusion of Michael Oakeshott—perhaps the greatest conservative philosopher of the last century—whose analysis often portended that advanced by Parekh and other theorists of multiculturalism.

If Conservatives do wish to 'move on' in the way Oakeshott might have prescribed, they would be helped by a further connection between multiculturalism and Edmund Burke—*viz*, localism. Given that multiculturalism involves accepting and promoting a range of localised customs, codes and values, it could also be depicted as the modern manifestation of Burke's 'little platoons' and an ally of Cameron's Big Society. Nonetheless, this particular effect of localism and this particular version of the Big Society pose stern and unavoidable challenges for Cameron's vision of the Conservative party.

Little platoons not liberal platoons

Although the Big Society was a flagship theme for Cameron in opposition, a more important one has been liberalisation—a political journey designed to make the party acceptable to centrist voters who previously found Conservatism repellent. In the course of that journey, Cameron apologised for the Thatcher government's Section 28 (forbidding the 'promotion' of homosexuality in schools), took a more 'sociological' approach to delinquency (hence the tabloid phrase 'hug a hoodie'), burnished environmental concerns ('vote blue, go green') and, at the 2011 Conservative conference, supported same-sex marriage. It is unclear if such measures endear Cameron to BME communities; in respect of many British Asians, there are reasons to think the reverse.

Cameron has not been slow to praise Burke's little platoons or see their relevance to the Big Society. But neither has he acknowledged any likely tension between his support for liberalism and his concurrent support for localism. This tension was compounded in early 2011 by Cameron's bracing denunciation of multiculturalism, implying that BME 'little platoons' were often extremist, reactionary and a menace to public order. Put simply, Cameron suggested that certain little platoons could not be relied on to be liberal platoons. Cameron thus became just the latest liberal to treat non-liberals illiberally.

Cameron would be wise to remember, though, that the Conservative party has never existed simply as a home for surrogate liberalism; nor has its durability been attributable simply to echoing the policies of liberal-left parties. He might also remember that the Conservative party, dating as such from the early nineteenth century, has a DNA fusing two distinctive political traditions from the eighteenth century. On the one hand, there is the 'Whig-liberal' tradition, stressing individualism, capitalism and liberty. On the other, there is the 'Tory' tradition—pessimistic and sceptical, and thus stressing tradition, authority, religious morality, established institutions and localised paternalism.

With this in mind, Cameron might have recognised that many of the BME communities he threatened to alienate with his Munich address exhibit many 'Tory' attributes. Furthermore, recent economic history suggests that Britain is moving in a direction where 'Tory' as opposed to 'liberal' values have currency—and where the Tory values enshrined in many BME communities could be valuable to a Conservative leader seeking public support.

Red Tory: multicultural Tory?

The economic ruptures since 2008, and the corresponding crisis of global capitalism, have been widely depicted as an indictment of free-market, neo-liberal thinking. Indeed, the resulting pessimism and fear, and the apocalyptic warnings stemming from numerous economists by 2011, are at odds with liberalism generally. In such a climate, the quest for individual ambition and individual fulfilment—two quintessential liberal goals—normally give way to a yearning for communal support and communal solidarity. Put into Conservative language, the Whig perspective tends to get eclipsed by the Tory perspective.

Progressives might argue that today's crises are an indictment of conservative politics per se, while exonerating the leftist belief in a strong and democratically centralised state. But if central state intervention is also discredited, as even some on the left admit (*vide* 'Blue Labour'), then localised voluntary arrangements, of the sort associated with Toryism and Edmund Burke (a maverick Whig) become germane. These arrangements might also allow a recalibrated Conservative party, drawing upon its Tory as opposed to Whig elements, to engage more effectively in the politics of austerity while reconciling itself to new forms of communal action.

Such notions were touched upon in 2010 by Phillip Blond, who advanced the case for 'Red Toryism'. In his book, Blond argued that both big business (inspired by neoliberalism) and big government (inspired by social democracy) were responsible for the erosion of community, and thus called for conservatives, as well as leftists, to indict the social and cultural effects of globalisation.[10] Within a year of publication, Blond's diagnosis of social breakdown seemed compelling; the riots of 2011 were widely portrayed as a grotesque example of amoral individualism, spawned by a liberal society that was materially comfortable but morally bereft. But the riots also highlighted something Blond did not consider—namely the possibility of a synthesis between conservatism and multiculturalism.

In the wake of the 2011 riots, Cameron spoke of how certain sections of society were 'sick'. Yet this diagnosis scarcely applied to the BME communities he had effectively condemned six months earlier. Indeed, many of these communities—like the Kurdish community in Haringey, the Sikh community in Southall, the Bengali and Somali communities in Whitechapel—were among those that appeared to stand up most effectively to mob violence, while still respecting the rule of law and the status of the police.

In the days that followed, those same communities were duly exalted in many Conservative-supporting newspapers. On account of their determination to protect property and small business, and to shield families and communities, these communities were duly hailed as the unlikely tribunes of conservative values—a development made more poignant by the death of a British Muslim, who had confronted rioters, in a Pakistani district of Birmingham. As Cristine Odone noted in the *Daily Telegraph* on 10 August:

Across the country, ethnic minorities have emerged as the heroes of the week's riots . . . they have shown themselves to be not just as law-abiding as the Anglo-Saxons but more inspiring. In the tight-knit societies peopled by Kurds, Sikhs, Poles and others, a strong sense of community survives which makes state assistance almost redundant . . . and it is mutual obligation, not government incentives, that motivates their members. Marriage is the model they live by and aspire to; divorce is almost nil; single motherhood ditto; extended families living together are routine. . . . Strong immigrant families support their children and also provide them with a moral compass. Can the natives measure up?

Such comments suggested that, in the space of a few nights, the perception of BME communities had been transformed from terrorist enclaves to bastions of Toryism. In the process, a new political climate seemed to emerge: one in which England's conservatives and England's immigrants seemed to have common cause. The resulting question for Conservatives was whether they should build on this unexpected rapprochement.

By the autumn of 2011, there were signs that some, at least, were doing so. Working with the Church of England's 'Near Neighbours' programme, co-

Party Chair Baroness Warsi argued that, unlike New Labour, the modern Conservative party should indeed 'do God' and encourage religious charities to deliver welfare services, via (for example) faith-based schools, hospices and rehabilitation programmes. A month later, Phillip Blond argued that, for the Big Society to succeed, it would need the backbone of 'Christian values'—'mutuality, subsidiary, solidarity, reciprocity and mediation'—thus suggesting that some of Britain's Afro-Caribbean communities were exemplars of a new, 'civic conservatism'.[11]

Baroness Warsi, however, went further. Arguing that any religious dimension to the Big Society should be multifaith rather than exclusively Christian, she claimed that such an approach would spawn greater tolerance, exploit the energy of faith-based BME communities, and thus nurture the philanthropic localism sought by the modern Conservative party. The notion that ethno-cultural diversity should not just be recognised but promoted is nothing new: it has long been at the heart of multiculturalism. What was significant was that it was now being endorsed at the highest level of the Conservative party.

During 2011, there were other emerging overlaps between applied multiculturalism and modern Conservatism. For example, as part of their wish to encourage diversity, multiculturalists usually defend positive discrimination and affirmative action—schemes traditionally dismissed by Conservatives as 'politically correct'. Yet, during 2011, Warsi's approach to events in Pakistan was less than predictable. She had discussions with Paul Bhatti, brother of the assassinated Christian politician Shabaz Bhatti and now 'minorities adviser' to Pakistan's prime minister, praised Bhatti's creation of a new Ministry of Harmony (devoted to the 'celebration' of non-Muslim religions), applauded the Pakistani Senate's allocation of seats for religious minority representatives, and voiced the classic multiculturalist mantra: 'unity through diversity'.

All this suggests that the modern Conservative party's approach to multiculturalism is not as unequivocally negative as Cameron's Munich speech indicated. In short, the Conservative approach to multiculturalism evolved quite significantly during the course of 2011—with the August riots proving a likely catalyst.

From problem to opportunity: a Conservative *leitmotiv*

In this chapter, we have suggested that that there could be a much stronger alliance between the Conservative party and Britain's ethnic minorities and a fresh Conservative approach to multiculturalism. We have also suggested that such an approach would chime with the Burkean aspect of conservative philosophy, the Tory aspect of Conservative archaeology and the Big Society aspect of Conservatism today.

The main obstacle to such an outcome remains the party's association with moderate British nationalism (not for nothing do various studies of the party have titles like *We, The Nation*). With reference to conservatism's founder,

Edmund Burke, we have therefore made a particular effort to show that Conservatives are not inevitably wedded to nostalgic forms of nationalism or abstract concepts of British-ness, and that they might rework their patriotism into something more localised. But that still leaves the crucial and complex question for all advocates of multiculturalism, Conservative or otherwise: how can radical, cultural pluralism avoid the 'balkanisation' of the state and the fragmentation of Britain's wider society?

Here again, a glance at Conservative history might help those who advocate a Conservative version of multiculturalism. For this history shows a party that has adapted to widely varying social and economic conditions; one that has had an infinitely flexible view about who is 'one of us'; and one capable of audacious reinvention. In fact, one of the recurrent themes of Conservative party history is its tendency to see certain groups/concepts as initially beyond the pale, but eventually to absorb those groups/concepts into both its own pantheon and the political mainstream.

Having initially been the party of the established Church and opposed to Catholic emancipation, it was a Conservative government that abolished the Test and Corporation Acts in 1828–29, thus admitting non-Anglicans into official political life (a move which, in the context of the early nineteenth century, was itself 'multicultural'). Having initially feared universal adult suffrage and the attenuation of property as a criterion for voting, it was a largely Conservative coalition that abolished the property qualification in 1918 (with the party going on to be the most popular party among working class voters in the interwar era). Having initially opposed female suffrage, it was a Conservative government that gave women equal voting rights in 1928 (with the party going on to be the most popular one among women voters for most of the twentieth century). So having under-performed with BME voters for so long, despite BME and Conservative values being far from inimical, the time may be right for another example of daring Conservative reinvention— one that could well lead to another surprising extension of Conservative support.

Conclusion: no end of a lesson

The Conservative party's durability, as a force for promoting both itself and an uneven yet cohesive society, owes much to its historic pragmatism and versatility. This side of Conservatism has already been exploited with some success by David Cameron. But the party's protean nature may now have to be exploited further and much more boldly if Britain's 'broken society' is to be mended, the values of BME voters accommodated, and the party's role in a cosmopolitan society secured.

As his biographer noted, Edmund Burke 'taught English statesmen how to meet change with courage and dexterity and how to soften its consequences'.[12] In respect of multiculturalism, it remains to be seen whether Burke's lessons can be learnt by today's Conservative leaders.

Notes

1 D. Marquand, 'Patron saint of the Big Society', *Prospect*, no. 175, 2010.

2 See, for example, W. Kymlicka, *Multicultural Citizenship*, Oxford, Oxford University Press, 1995; B. Parekh, *Rethinking Multiculturalism*, London, Palgrave Macmillan, 2005.

3 R. Kelly, 'The party conference', in A. Seldon and S. Ball, eds, *Conservative Century*, Oxford, Oxford University Press, 1994.

4 R. Kirk, *The Conservative Mind: from Burke to Eliot*, Washington, DC, Regnery, 1983, p. 20.

5 P. Buck, ed., *How Conservatives Think*, Harmondsworth, Penguin, 1975, pp. 48–52.

6 Z. Layton-Henry, *The Politics of Immigration*, Oxford, Blackwell 1992, pp. 49–50.

7 Quoted in *Sunday Telegraph*, 31 July 2005.

8 K. O'Hara, *After Blair: David Cameron and the Conservative Tradition*, London, Icon Books, 2007 pp. 243–50.

9 Kirk, *The Conservative Mind*, p. 47.

10 P. Blond: *Red Tory: How Left and Right have Broken Britain and How We can Fix It*, London, Faber & Faber, 2010.

11 *Daily Telegraph*, 25 November 2011.

12 Kirk, *The Conservative Mind*, p. 46.

The Big Society: Post-Bureaucratic Social Policy in the Twenty-first Century?

BENJAMIN WILLIAMS

THIS chapter seeks to explain and analyse the development and evolution of the concept of the 'Big Society' as a specific strand of David Cameron's attempts to modernise and revamp the Conservative party's social policy agenda since he secured the party leadership at the end of 2005. It also seeks to analyse the role of the state within this policy approach and in turn assesses how realistic are attempts by the Cameron-led government to provide a comprehensive and stable range of public services and social policy initiatives within a smaller state model and a less bureaucratic structural framework. The sociopolitical term, 'The Big Society', has subsequently evolved into a high-profile element of the wider approach of Conservative party 'modernisers' to create a revised social policy agenda that particularly promotes a fresh vision of social justice for the right-of-centre of British politics, seeking to adhere to Conservative traditions yet also pragmatically accepting the significant socio-economic developments of the New Labour era from 1997 onwards. This policy approach was a culmination of Cameron's focus on the broader sphere of social policy since becoming party leader, and it came to evident fruition in the prolonged lead-up to the 2010 general election, becoming a flagship Conservative policy proposal in the process. As opinion polls suggested an appetite for change among the dissatisfied electorate and the likelihood of a return to power for the Conservatives after thirteen years in the political wilderness, Cameron's specific Conservative remedy to deal with his identification of the country's social and welfare-related problems (originating from various policy reviews) materialised in the form of a policy agenda that was clarified and condensed into three words: 'The Big Society'. Such a succinct and well-marketed title was part of a broader attempt by Cameron to instil some vision, direction and an ethos of 'social justice' into his distinct brand of socially orientated Conservatism, and to increase levels of social activism and volunteering as a legitimate and more flexible alternative to uniform state provision, while also instilling a moral streak into social policy in the process.

However, in its evolution in the period that has followed, the brevity of its title has created confusion and uncertainty, and this social and moral vision has been somewhat blurred and misunderstood as both a concept and practical entity by significant sections of the media, the political classes and the wider general public. The specific term of the 'Big Society' had been

Published by Blackwell Publishing Ltd, 9600 Garsington Road, Oxford OX4 2DQ, UK and 350 Main Street, Malden, MA 02148, USA

developing and germinating from an early phase of Cameron's leadership, but it was firmed up towards the end of 2009 at the Hugo Young Memorial Lecture, when Cameron sought to explicitly create a distinct and alternative model for a better functioning and more efficient civil society to replace the stuttering and 'broken one' his policy reviews had identified. In doing so he emphasised the need for a bottom-up approach to social policy, involving enhanced levels of citizen involvement, along with a bigger role for cooperatives, private service providers and voluntary groups in the delivery of key social policies. All of which were key components of his vision of public policy provision that rejected the hegemonic and prominent role of the centralised and bureaucratic state that had been the dominant model and means of providing core public services for most of the postwar era. In essence, Cameron was arguing for a revised 'rolling back' of the state from a twenty-first-century perspective, which would in turn create localised communities with greater autonomy and the power to initiate, influence and organise public activity including the provision of social and welfare policies.

In order to illustrate this burgeoning concept of an enhanced sense of civil society and individual morality released from the ostensible shackles of an overbearing state, in subsequent months Cameron progressively formulated it as a dynamic and indeed 'vigorous' doctrine, which in its practical application would promote voluntarism and generate a wider collective social conscience as a means of rebuilding Britain's wider cultural and social fabric:

Cameron's pitch is that British society is broken, not just parts of it; and the underlying causes are cultural not economic. Taking his cue from the Social Justice Policy Group, the Conservative leader argues that British society is broken because of what he terms the decline in 'responsibility' and 'social virtue'. Civil society has become a lot less civil. By extending the powers and reach of the state, and taking responsibility away from individuals and communities, the Labour government has added to this social fracture.[1]

This emphasis on 'social virtue' and on the reinvigoration of a 'civil society' within the renewed and remodelled sociopolitical structures of the twenty-first century has therefore been at the heart of the Conservative party's social agenda in the Cameron era. Such a revised Conservative social and welfare policy outlook was initially encouraged by the party hierarchy on an internal basis while in opposition, evident in the 'self-help' social action projects that many Conservative politicians and parliamentary candidates were encouraged to develop in the build-up to the 2010 general election (and to continue beyond in some cases), although which were dismissed by political opponents as gimmicks. Such schemes were deliberately targeted at a grassroots level in order to provide model examples of how to respond to some genuine needs in terms of welfare provision, while being notionally free from as much 'statist' bureaucratic control and regulation as is possible, and in political opposition they were used by the Conservatives to illustrate the effective role of voluntarist, non-state bodies in delivering vital areas of public policy. Indeed, in early 2007, Cameron was keen to outline the importance of the 'Third Sector'[2] in his plans for a Conservative government, and this sector was from an early stage identified as key component to be encouraged in such schemes, again as a means of finding more efficient alternatives to uniform and monolithic state provision, and which in the process rejected the notion that the state has the answer to all of society's major socio-economic problems.

There does however remain a consistent public undercurrent of doubt and scepticism as to the viability of such an approach, with opinion surveys indicating that the public ultimately retain greater faith in the power of the state to most effectively administer and deliver social and welfare policy. This has resulted in a somewhat quixotic public mood, given that for all the inflated levels of public spending yet questionable service delivery under New Labour from 1997 onwards, there remains 'little public appetite for an expansion of private sector provision . . . (and) deep divisions over the delivery of services by other organisations in the voluntary and third sector'.[3] Nonetheless and despite such wider public doubts, the 'Big Society' social policy ethos has appeared on the political horizon to argue that by promoting and developing public service delivery schemes that fuse a reduced role for the state along with voluntary activity and greater community-level involvement, this in turn leads to a sense of greater social responsibility and civic virtue being instilled back into those who participate, along with better value for money for both the taxpayer and the government.

With the overall ethos of this concept focusing on a reduced role for the state and an enhanced civic and even moral benefit for those involved in such community activities, Cameron's refocused brand of Conservatism has therefore sought to offer a robust critique and coherent solution for Britain's 'broken society', with the promise of providing distinct alternative policy approaches in the process. This is particularly in relation to the funding and overall strategic approach in delivering welfare provision in the United Kingdom, broadly recognised as a rising source of expense for all governments both now and in the future, and particularly so during a period of recession and austerity. Alongside a greater emphasis on civic and community-based activity as a means of delivering a distinct Conservative vision of social justice, such an approach is however not supposed to mark a return to the 'rugged individualism' promoted during the Thatcher era, but instead provide a more diverse, responsive, compassionate and flexible range of decentralised community-focused services and support structures for the vulnerable members of society to utilise.

During the 2010 general election campaign there was much dispute and political debate as to what the somewhat ambivalent term 'The Big Society' actually meant, with one political commentator describing the term as having the power 'to send voters into a state of catatonic indifference' and with some Conservative candidates citing confusion about its meaning as an issue on the doorstep when canvassing for votes.[4] Critical voices cited it as a factor why Cameron failed to achieve an overall parliamentary majority despite Labour weaknesses, accusing him of failing to connect with both his party and the wider public about the fundamental problems facing Britain, with the coalition with the Liberal Democrats as an eventual compromise settlement as a means of the Conservatives being restored to national power. However, Cameron appeared undeterred and continued to promote the specific values and agenda of the Big Society once he had been elevated to the position of Prime Minister, albeit within a coalition framework tinged with political expediency. In one of his first high-profile press conferences with his Liberal Democrat Deputy Prime Minister Nick Clegg, he indicated how the concept was central to the party's coalition agreement and aims for coalition government, with Clegg appearing to endorse this position in the process.

The official Cabinet Office document that supported the policy affirmed the essence of this specific policy agenda as follows:

Our Conservative-Liberal Democrat Government has come together with a driving ambition: to put more power and opportunity into people's hands. We want to give citizens, communities and local government the power and information they need to come together, solve the problems they face and build the Britain they want. We want society—the families, networks, neighbourhoods and communities that form the fabric of so much of our everyday lives—to be bigger and stronger than ever before. Only when people and communities are given more power and take more responsibility can we achieve fairness and opportunity for all.[5]

Despite such cross-party support for this localist and decentralised political agenda being proposed to run through the heart of the coalition government's decision-making and policy process, debate over the precise meaning of the term has continued postelection. Some political observers subsequently claimed that despite Cameron's buoyant rhetoric, during the first six months of his premiership from May 2010 onwards, this high-profile policy stuttered along and hovered on the brink of collapse. In response, David Cameron has consistently and vigilantly argued that this policy agenda represented a remoulding of a more compassionate form of Conservatism for the post-bureaucratic political era, essentially replacing Labour's 'big government' model with the Conservatives' Big Society alternative. Within such a framework, Cameron has sought to utilise figures such as the social entrepreneur Baron Wei and his focus on enhanced 'social capital' and innovative social activity, alongside the academic Phillip Blond as prominent supporters of this sociopolitical agenda. They in turn have been dubbed Cameron's 'Big Society gurus', broadly endorsing the coalition government's critique of Labour's state-heavy approach during its thirteen years in power from 1997, and instead seeking to generate greater social energy and community activity from a bottom-up rather than a top-down model of political action.

Blond has particularly been a key influence behind the ideas that have shaped the 'Big Society' blueprint, and as the founder of the think tank

'ResPublica' he has emerged as the architect of the 'Red Tory' vision that espouses a more compassionate and less individualistic form of Conservatism, yet which rejects a powerful state within such a desired formula. An original Conservative-minded thinker, Blond has echoed the sentiments of David Willetts in arguing for a focus on civil society and community as alternatives to the state in the provision of public services. Blond's argument is both anti-statist yet concerns community cohesion, rejecting the bureaucracy of New Labour and the postwar model of welfare delivery, while also desiring '"red Tory" communitarianism, socially conservative but sceptical of neoliberal economics'.[6] Such a viewpoint rejects the perceived supremacy of the markets in influencing policy formulation (as espoused by the New Right), but instead demands a paternalistic and community-led approach to shaping social policy, aligned with greater government efficiency, a more streamlined state and a focus on a more diverse range of service providers to deliver wider social policy improvements.

In further developing this argument, Cameron has proclaimed that this new political approach would represent a 'big advance for people power', and that it will 'turn government completely on its head' due to the creation of a less 'statist' model of government as a consequence. Blond has gone on to argue under the cloak of his think tank that the role of collective and 'community' action should indeed be an important feature of modern and rebranded Conservatism, and this focus has appeared to represent an apparent rejection of the Thatcherite 'New Right' individualist analysis of society. In claiming that the policy is 'pro-poor', this appears to contradict broad perceptions of post-1979 Conservative policies that ostensibly seemed to promote a free-market model of government featuring a 'rolled-back' state and low taxation that created a sociopolitical scenario which broadly appeared to favour the better off members of society.[7] This twenty-first century approach on the back of three successive general election victories seeks to broaden the party's electoral appeal while maintaining a general Conservative suspicion as to whether the state has the definitive answer to all of society's sociopolitical problems, broadly adhering to the right-of-centre viewpoint which remains sceptical of the merits of public spending. Nevertheless, the viewpoint of Blond explicitly argues that both the neoliberal 'market-state' of the 'New Right' under Thatcher's guidance and the more socially liberal and interventionist tendencies of 'New Labour' under the Blair-Brown axis, have ultimately failed in addressing the inherent socioeconomic needs and demands of the wider population.

From an academic perspective therefore, Blond has sought to consolidate and bolster Cameron's attempts to shape and influence a Conservative political agenda with an ideological anchor and an enhanced social policy focus and emphasis, promoting a sociopolitical model that values the importance of society and community, yet one which is not exclusively dominated by the power of the state, and which actively seeks its withdrawal from some aspects of everyday life.

Public response to the Big Society and the austerity agenda

In terms of the Conservative party at grassroots level, the appeal of this concept has been its ability to rebrand and remarket some core Conservative values, and in this context the Big Society agenda is complementary to Conservative party traditions of the small state, localism and the empowerment of the individual. However, despite claims of the Big Society having an ideological coherence and consistency with the Conservative party's overall localism agenda of recent years, parts of the media, the political commentariat and indeed the wider general public have continued to be increasingly frustrated and confused at the perceived fuzziness of what it actually means in practice, requiring further detail in the process. In this context, approximately a year after Cameron became Prime Minister, two opinion polls in May 2011 suggested public confusion over the concept. One recurring concern has been the broad belief, as expressed in opinion polls and British Social Attitudes surveys, that despite a steady short-term growth in public worries about the levels of government spending as the New Labour era progressed, long-term opinion trends suggest that certain key social and welfare policies continue to be viewed as the fundamental responsibility of the state, calling into question the likelihood of sustained public support for the Conservative idea of the Big Society.

Along with a sceptical public, even Big Society prophets and ideologues such as David Willetts have appeared to acknowledge that the overall policy approach and the emphasis on community-led voluntarism lacks some practical realities in terms of policy delivery and implementation. A key cross-party report published exactly one year after the launch of 'The Big Society' subsequently claimed that the government 'has failed to properly explain it . . . amid fears it will be concentrated in wealthy suburbs and leave the poorest parts of the country behind'.[8] Such apparent failings of communication have exposed the Cameron-led government's inability to effectively transmit the primary focus of the government's message in relation to this high-profile policy—a particularly notable failure in this instance given that it is the poorer parts of society that the Big Society was primarily supposed to focus upon.

In response to such wider public confusion, Cameron was forced to promote what was claimed to be the fourth relaunch of the flagship policy in May 2011, again emphasising the need for greater voluntarism and charitable activity stemming from community-based activity rather than the unerring control of the state, and in doing so offering a revised and softer version of modern Conservatism in rhetorical emphasis at least, being somewhat detached from both the New Right's individualist neoliberal focus but also resistant to the perceived 'statist' tendencies of New Labour in government. However, further criticism of 'The Big Society' policy emerged in autumn 2011 when the House of Commons Public Administration Committee reaffirmed such practical concerns, declaring that such devolution and decentralisation of power would not work without radical and significant structural reforms to the Civil Service in order to meet the demands of the new policy. Further critical comments came from the same committee at the end of 2011, when it declared that the public and voluntary sectors remain confused about the Big Society's implications, with the Chair of the Committee, Bernard Jenkin, adding that the government's ongoing focus on greater localism and devolution within political decision making would take time to impact on broader public perceptions of this policy.

Such concerns followed claims from both political opponents and erstwhile allies that government spending cuts were further hampering the implementation of this policy ethos, and that indeed the whole approach was in fact a smokescreen to mask the significant public spending cuts being pursued from May 2010 onwards. This was even partially acknowledged by Blond, who in early 2011 pointed to the danger of public spending cuts for the overall Big Society agenda and who later in the year claimed that the policy was being undermined by the depth and scale of the government's retrenchment agenda, amidst rumours of a cooling of his level of influence over the Prime Minister. There followed reports that the charitable sector, the ostensible cornerstone for the delivery of the Big Society agenda, was facing massive cuts in government funding and subsidies as part of the coalition government's determined attempts to drive down the national deficit from mid-2010 onwards. It has also been argued that many people are too busy either maintaining or seeking employment during a difficult economic period to have the time or commitment to engage in the sort of community-based voluntarism envisaged by the Big Society's approach to public policy. Some critics and bodies such as Volunteering England have even claimed that charities are being exploited and the unemployed are being targeted in the name of work experience within a Big Society narrative, both being expected to provide their services free of charge as a means of reducing the costs of private work programme providers.

Given such an unconvinced wider reaction towards the policy amidst an atmosphere of public spending cuts, the government has been regularly forced on the offensive in promoting it, with further attempts to clarify the precise sentiments of the Big Society made by Cabinet members on a regular basis. Other serious thinkers from the modernising wing of the Conservative party have also attempted to define its apparent vague meaning into a more concrete political entity, and have sought to distance it from being an explicitly partisan or 'party political' entity in the process. Such sentiments clearly imply that in an era of less adversarial and less explicitly ideological politics, the Big Society project could be comfortably pursued by either a Conservative or Labour administration, and in autumn 2011 the ResPublica think tank lobbied the Labour party conference amid claims that some senior Labour figures wanted to save the Big Society agenda. Many reformers and advocates of this agenda within the Conservative party are, however, wary of Labour embracing the Big Society, primarily due to the belief that it is essentially opposed to and in conflict with the statist or centralising instincts of Labour governments.

This viewpoint therefore argues that the Big Society's essential localism and personal empowerment rejects both the 'statism' of the left and the 'neoliberalism' associated with the free-market Thatcherism of the 1980s, and is essentially a modern, original and mainstream idea in tune with traditional Conservative philosophical instincts (as well as the 'localist' agenda of the Liberal Democrats), and aligned with the instinctive communitarian tendencies evident across broader society. However, its failure to launch and effectively capture the wider public, and indeed Conservative, imagination could perhaps be seen in that it failed to make the formal agenda of the 2011 Conservative party conference.

Reaction to the 'Big Society' from left and right

There are various left-of-centre figures who have been critical of this new Conservative-led agenda and who have been sceptical of claims that the policy does not have right-wing or 'neoliberal' implications. This viewpoint is also fearful of how the Big Society's emphasis and reliance on voluntarism and localised schemes could potentially affect the overall provision of key public services. In its rejection of the hegemony of the state as a public service provider, this has raised fears that the policy could initiate a return to the mentality of the Victorian era when state welfare provision, the effective regulation of standards and the assurance of 'safety nets' for recipients of key social policies were limited, and both public and charitable welfare provision was far more arbitrary and less uniform in nature. Such a voluntarist emphasis has therefore been lambasted by many political and academic figures on the centre-left who have claimed that the term 'Big Society' is merely a vague euphemism for the justification of savage public spending cuts and a massive shrinking of the state's size and its egalitarian scope and remit, regardless of David Cameron's soothing vocabulary and renewed focus on 'society'.

Having said this, in the wake of the 2010 general election result Labour politicians have been forced to adapt and respond to the Big Society agenda, with concerted efforts being made to mould rival and distinct political messages in order to both contribute to and challenge the narrative in relation to social justice and the welfare state, but framed with a left-of-centre political hue. This has been evident in the appearance of alternative yet similar concepts based on localised and cooperative activity such as 'Blue Labour', 'The Purple Book' and the 'good society', and has witnessed the Labour party under Ed Miliband's leadership from September 2010 onwards, promoting a vision of government (influenced by Lord Glasman in particular) that also offers a reduced reliance on the role of the state, an embracing of popular capitalism and a return to the pre-1945 focus of Labour governments with a greater emphasis on utilising voluntarist and cooperative activity to deliver public services where appropriate. Although the Labour left can cite the various failings of pre-1945 Labour governments as a reason not to hark back to their distinct ethos, this reciprocal development on the political left-of-centre could be used as evidence for a degree of success in Cameron's promotion of a new and innovative social agenda for the Conservative party and the need for political opponents to adapt accordingly. From another ideological angle however, there has been some right-wing criticism of David Cameron's abandonment of the economics-driven, individualist, neoliberal focus of the Thatcherite era, consolidating the mainstream criticism that the policy is vague and unclear.

Such internal party criticism has generated concerns that today's Conservative party has abandoned traditional and hard-won political territory that it seized after 1979, and the emphasis placed by Cameron on an enhanced and revitalised social policy agenda that stresses the importance of cooperation and the benevolent 'mutualism' of relationships within 'society', has raised suspicions from the right that the 'dead hand' of the state will continue to be unerringly and prominently present within such an approach. Such suspicion has perhaps been justified in policy terms in the form of Cameron's explicit reluctance to cut taxes or make savings in key public services such as the National Health Service, which the Conservatives pledged during the 2010 general election would be ring-fenced from any future spending cuts, despite a common right-wing complaint that it is an inefficient and excessively bureaucratic organisation. Although there is a fierce political debate about the true nature of Cameron's controversial NHS reforms, Cameron's counter-argument to internal party critics from the right is that his own specific vision of an increasingly voluntarist, 'rolled-back' yet benevolent state model is actually consistent with one of Thatcher's greatest political and philosophical inspirations: 'The virtues these people possessed [the British] . . . were independence and self-reliance, individual initiative and local responsibility, the successful reliance on voluntary activity . . . and a healthy suspicion of power and authority.'[9]

Hayek's claim (above) is notable for its explicit rejection of the 'collectivist' state whose growth was said to unerringly accelerate under left of-centre governments, and which established what has been described by Blond as 'the rotten postwar settlement of British politics'.[10] Hayek's sentiments can therefore be said to be wholly consistent with the support for such a voluntarist approach and the vision for reduced statist welfare provisions as espoused by both Cameron's Big Society gurus and recently established bodies such as the Centre for Social Justice. Cameron's revised welfare and social agenda has therefore sought to maintain a delicate balance of preserving some inherent Conservative traditions while simultaneously developing a new and more refined social dimension to the party's contemporary image, involving enhanced levels of citizen involvement and empowerment associated with the ideas of compassionate conservatism and post-bureaucratic politics. Such desire for a more compassionate Conservative image has been reflected in Cameron's rhetorical focus on society, and which appears to be an implicit rejection of the tough yet somewhat uncaring reputation the party had been associated with in relation to its social policy attitudes during its sustained period in power between 1979 and 1997, and this formed part of Cameron's wider strategy to 'detoxify' the brand. His renewed focus on a refreshed and revised approach to social policy and its associated issues can be linked back to the period when he was striving to establish himself as an effective Leader of the Opposition, and he promised to adopt a distinct policy focus in the process, stating that he was going to be as radical a social reformer as Margaret Thatcher was an economic reformer.

However, despite some on the right of politics speaking about a 'post-bureaucratic state' and pushing for a perceived logical conclusion that entails a radically reduced level of reliance on state-provided welfare and the need for greater 'marketisation' of its core services, there has been a broad acceptance among the modernising 'Cameroons' that the state has a key function in its provision of coordinating, if in a less cumbersome and top-heavy manner, the delivery of important social policy provision. So whereas the Thatcherites of the 1980s desired a strong state yet a limited role for government to deliver the necessary conditions for the 'maintenance of a free economy', somewhat neglecting the innovation and initiation of social and welfare policy in the process, twenty-first-century Conservatives acknowledge that the markets alone are not sufficient to tackle the country's 'broken society' and wider welfare needs. Their Big Society analysis therefore argues that the state's framework can be effectively used in instigating and formulating generic social policy goals and then devolving the process to allow innovative and 'localised' policies to flourish that are most appropriate to tackling specifically challenging social conditions and associated problems, with the state ultimately stepping back from such policies' direct implementation. By supporting and promoting the different and variable dimensions of government-initiated activity, a more detached state role can therefore be fused with 'Third Sector' charities and localised bodies within a proposed model of 'creative' policy delivery that divides and fragments the role of providing core public services while also consolidating individual 'social ambition', ostensibly saving money and liberating individuals from excessive and centralised government intervention in the process. In this respect, the politics of Cameron's modern-day Conservatives ultimately appear to be distinct from the libertarian, free market and more ideological agenda of the neoliberal Thatcherites, arguing that despite talk of *a* post-bureaucratic state, the state must continue to play a proactive role in fixing the broken society.

Given the focus on austerity and financial savings as the driving force behind many key government decisions from May 2010 onwards, some critics from Labour and the centre-left of the political spectrum have questioned whether Cameron's vision of a more 'enabling' and devolved welfare state, with an increased focus on self-help and the support of variable 'voluntarist' providers as opposed to direct state provision, is actually a genuine and original post-Thatcherite policy development or merely an extension of the economic and social priorities of the 1980s and the mood of economic austerity often associated with aspects of this historical period. Replacing direct state provision with greater voluntarist and charitable involvement is by no means guaranteed to provide a more solid basis for innovative and sustainable social policy development, and indeed, in the worst case scenario it could create serious risks to both the sustainability and the comprehensive and regulatory aspects of the British welfare state and its historic focus on protecting society's most vulnerable citizens. This is because by reducing the hegemonic influence and role of the state as part of the 'Big Society' agenda, yet at the same time pursuing a programme of fiscal retrenchment and eroding some of the support for charitable institutions that often bolster state provision and which are expected to have an enhanced role under the original Big Society model, this potentially increases the prospect of vulnerable individuals being excluded from its 'non-universal' and fragmented welfare provision. Such a scenario directly conflicts with the more generous 'social democratic' welfare model that has been dominant for most of the postwar period in Britain, and it is in this respect that the Big Society proponents have struggled to convince the sceptical public.

Overview of the Big Society

In the context of developing a critique and a background narrative to the evolution of the party's new social policy agenda and its overall approach to administering a streamlined and genuinely reformed welfare state provision, David Cameron has specifically sought to distance the contemporary Conservative party from its explicitly neoliberal socio-economic agenda of the past, revising its relationship with the party's Thatcherite legacy in the process. This has subsequently led to a more 'compassionate' Conservative analysis of a 'broken' or 'atomised' society that needs to be genuinely healed in the long-term, and such 'compassionate conservatism' appears to be a distinct contrast to the short-term punitive outlook and broad lack of sympathy aimed in the direction of long-term recipients of the welfare system, as was the tendency of some right-wing Conservative politicians during the 1980s. Cameron's difficulties in selling his specific analysis of society to both his political party and the wider public has however been hampered by the fact that many politicians—notably some Conservative ones—have rejected the somewhat simplistic Big Society analysis implying that all aspects of British society were broken and required a radical overhaul when the Conservative-led coalition came to national power in 2010. For example, London Mayor Boris Johnson has openly questioned the mantra, rejecting its arguably simplistic conclusions as 'piffle'.

In his affirmation and emphasis as to just how 'broken' Britain was when the Conservatives have found themselves back in national office in 2010, some have criticised Cameron for simplistically exaggerating the social problems that Britain faces in the early years of the twenty-first century. Certainly there are significant enclaves of poverty and deprivation throughout British society (exacerbated by rising levels of unemployment amidst the prolonged economic recession), many of which are long-established and which have been sustained under governments of different political stripes. However, those that are hostile to Cameron's critique of broken Britain, situated on both the left and right of British politics, argue that its analysis is too primitive and its message too gimmicky, and that it needs to be grounded in greater practical realism, without distorting or exaggerating the state of contemporary society in order to generate hysteria for party political benefit. Ultimately, if such an analysis is to be constructive, effective and be able to carry the necessary weight and subsequent public support, it requires appropriate intellectual rigour and practical reality behind it. Iain Duncan Smith's experiences with the Centre for Social Justice since 2004 and his subsequent thorough analysis of proposed sociopolitical remedies appears to have the potential to instil a greater degree of realism and credibility into the Big Society agenda, although the nature and effectiveness of his actual proposals in this key area of public policy remain to be seen. Thus, in the context of a post-Thatcherite and a speculative post-bureaucratic model of governance as identified and alluded to by contemporary academics and political thinkers, there has developed some significant further analysis of the key socio-economic issues and problems that exist within modern society and how best to address them, with the Big Society a prominent and innovative example of how a revised vision of social justice can best be achieved within a reconstructed social policy and welfare agenda. Cameron has been a central figure in this debate since his accession to senior political office from late 2005, but his arguments for a future post-bureaucratic vision of government and its capacity to effectively deliver key social policies have yet to convince both the political community and the wider British public.

Notes

1 S. Driver, '"Fixing our broken society": David Cameron's post-Thatcherite social policy', cited in S. Lee and M. Beech, eds, *The Conservatives under David Cameron: Built to Last?*, Basingstoke, Palgrave Macmillan, 2009, p. 88.
2 The 'Third Sector' broadly incorporates the charity, voluntary and fund-raising sectors within society.
3 A. Defty, 'The Conservatives, social policy and public opinion', cited in H. Bochel, ed., *The Conservative Party and Social Policy*, Bristol, Policy Press, 2011, p. 76.
4 B. Wheeler, 'Big Society: more than a soundbite?', *BBC News*, 14 February 2011, http://www.bbc.co.uk/news/uk-politics-12163624
5 See 'Building the Big Society', Cabinet Office document, 18 May 2010, http://www.cabinetoffice.gov.uk/sites/default/files/resources/building-big-society_0.pdf
6 P. Blond, 'Rise of the Red Tories', *Prospect*, 28 February 2009, http://www.prospectmagazine.co.uk/2009/02/riseoftheredtories/.

7 See H. Young, *One of Us*, London, Pan Macmillan, 1989, p. 607.

7 *Powerful People, Responsible Society: The Report of the Commission on Big Society*, 16 May 2011, http://www.acevo.org.uk/page.aspx?pid=191&nccsm=21&_nccscid=28&_nccsct=Free+Downloads&_nccspID=1077

9 F. A. Hayek, 'Material conditions and ideal ends', in *The Road to Serfdom*, London, Routledge, 1944, Chapter 14, p. 235.

10 Blond, *Rise of the Red Tories*.

Free Schools: Big Society or Small Interests?

ADAM LEEDER and DEBORAH MABBETT

Introduction

A FLAGSHIP policy of the coalition government is the introduction of Free Schools. In September 2011, 24 Free Schools opened their doors across England, and many more applications are in the pipeline for September 2012. The aim of this contribution is to work out what Free Schools tell us about the Big Society agenda. To what extent do they rest on enhancing the role of neighbourhoods and mobilising local effort? Does the engagement of local initiative in education signal a politically pluralist agenda, in which different providers bring the social capital of their communities into a relationship with the government which has elements of policy making as well as 'delivery'? Or is the principal-agent structure of the education quasi-market maintained, with the government deciding the regulatory terms on which it will release funds and schools scrambling to compete for pupils and their vouchers? And, if the latter, what should we make of the relationship between parents and schools? Is this a productive form of engagement with public services, or does it just create scope for parents to make anti-social choices?

The resources of Free Schools come from contracting with central government, which puts it in a powerful position to shape the way that Free Schools develop: so much so that we can see them as creatures of the government's making. Yet this does not render claims about local empowerment and pluralism entirely nugatory. The Green Paper on 'Modernising Commissioning'[1] argues for changes to contracting to promote more innovation and diversity of provision, and less centralised hierarchical control. The reason for government to give up control is instrumental: it seeks to achieve its ends by exercising less power over the means. International comparisons suggest that educational attainment is promoted by school 'autonomy'. The Organisation for Economic Cooperation and Development (OECD) shows that countries that delegate managerial discretion to head teachers and school governing bodies often have higher educational attainment.[2] It notes that autonomy can mean different things, from variation in educational content and the subjects taught at one end of the spectrum to budgetary and administrative devolution at the other. Thus lessons from the apparent relationship between autonomy and performance are hard to draw. Nonetheless, both Labour and the coalition have embraced the idea that school autonomy should be promoted, while bringing different bits of baggage to the table in working out the details.

An education system can apparently reconcile the goals of equality of access and autonomy in provision by operating a quasi-market in which parents have vouchers for the education of their children. In the United Kingdom, successive reforms by both Labour and Conservative governments have allowed an education 'quasi-market' to emerge. The first steps were taken by the Conservatives with the introduction of grant-maintained schools. By the late 1980s, some 80 per cent of education funding was being distributed according to the number and age of pupils, as it would be if each pupil carried a voucher. Grant-maintained schools received this money direct from central government. Open enrolment (without catchment areas or ceilings on numbers) was promoted in order that schools would compete for pupils and the funding they brought with them. Labour returned grant-maintained schools to local authority control, but the voucherisation of funding remained in place, and the promotion of autonomy re-emerged with the introduction of Academies.

This chapter proceeds as follows. After briefly introducing the basic regulatory arrangements, it discusses in turn the governance of Free Schools and their operation in a competitive education quasi-market. The governance arrangements are designed to use the voluntary engagement of parents and other socially concerned people to ensure that a school is run well. It is argued that these arrangements are liable to atrophy through time, leaving either teachers or for-profit education providers in charge. Choice in an education quasi-market is meant to provide an alternative, competitive mechanism for maintaining school quality, but, we argue, this is only unambiguously the case if parents' view of quality is the same as that of the government. A government concerned with promoting the public interest should be more concerned about adverse neighbourhood effects and ideology in schools than parents will be.

The regulatory framework

This section outlines the main institutional features of Free Schools, specifically the powers the school can exercise within the regulatory framework established by the government. As the word 'Free' implies, schools established under the Free Schools initiative are not subject to close day-to-day control over their activities. They enjoy various 'autonomies', both by being outside the control of local education authorities and by being exempt from various central government rules and regulations.

Free Schools have freedom over the curriculum, subject to the requirement to teach a 'broad and balanced' curriculum that includes English, Mathematics, Science and Information Technology. They set the pay and conditions of their staff, and their teachers are not required to have Qualified Teacher Status (QTS).[3] They manage their own budget, made up of funds disbursed by the Young People's Learning Agency, mainly distributed in the form of notional vouchers attached to pupils. They can vary the length and organisation of the school day and year, subject to some regulatory reserve powers (see below).

On pupil numbers and admissions, Free Schools have some autonomy in setting their target numbers but little autonomy in selecting students. Target numbers are specified in the school's funding agreement with the Department for Education (DfE). The Department funds the capital cost of establishing the school, so has an obvious interest in ensuring that this cost is proportionate to the number of students who will be educated. If schools fail to meet their targets, they will receive a lower grant, and their management plans have to show how they will cope with this eventuality. In recruiting students, Free Schools are expected to have inclusive admissions arrangements and to participate, as with all other schools in their local area, in the Local Education Authority's coordinated admissions process. If Free Schools are oversubscribed, they must have published oversubscription criteria that comply with the government's admissions code of practice (schools for students aged 16–19 are exempt from this).

Undersubscription has serious consequences for the viability of the school, which implies that their autonomy is constrained by the need to attract customers in the education quasi-market. Free Schools are required to provide data for school league tables, and more generally 'to submit . . . to monitoring and moderation of [their] assessment as required by the Secretary of State'.[4] This means that Free Schools will not be free of the pressures that exist for teachers to divert their effort towards key indicators of results unless they have a self-selected high ability intake or are sufficiently oversubscribed by parents who are interested in criteria other than league tables.

The government has retained various regulatory powers over Free Schools. While not required to employ teachers with QTS, Free Schools have to satisfy the DfE that teachers are of requisite ability. The curriculum must be 'of an appropriate standard' (a provision which might safeguard against the teaching of Creationism, for example). Regulatory powers are exercised pursuant to the School Funding Agreement, which also provides for mandatory Ofsted inspections both prior to, and within two years of, a school's opening. In addition, Free Schools are required to permit reasonable access on to their premises for the Secretary of State, his agents and officials. The DfE can suspend the right of any Free School to operate if the terms of its School Funding Agreement are not met.

Governance

We can think of Free Schools as operating under a contract with the government: they receive government funds and in return they provide a service. However, the contract is not specified in great detail, and the regulator's role in monitoring the school's day-to-day performance is limited. Instead, it falls to two processes—the quasi-market and the school's governance arrangements—to ensure that the school provides a good quality of education. This section reviews the governance structure.

The regulations provide that the formation of a Free School is initiated by proposers who can establish a company limited by guarantee or a charitable trust. Any social entrepreneur can propose a school: in practice parents and faith-based groups dominate. Employees of the school (teachers) should not normally be proposers: thus the employee mutuals which the Green Paper promotes in other areas are not advocated for schools. The proposers then have to prepare a plan for the school. While there are different models for running the school, as discussed further below, it is clear that successful applications call for a considerable amount of donated labour on the part of the proposers. Parents have been engaged not only in planning the management of the school but also in finding suitable properties and contributing to their renovation. Thus Free Schools are apparently a model of voluntary endeavour, which is reflected in their non-profit constitution.

In the first wave of the Free School initiative, only outline plans needed to be presented to the DfE, which then provided funding for the development of a fuller plan. Subsequently the Department changed the procedure to request a more extensive proposal at the outset, in response to high demand. A charity called the 'New Schools Network' has been funded by the Department to help proposers through the planning stages. In the course of the process, the proposers must demonstrate that they have a workable plan for the school, including premises, staffing and evidence of adequate demand for places. One consequence of the high level of work involved in meeting these criteria is that specialist companies have entered the field to develop plans on behalf of parents. The DfE maintains a list of approved suppliers of services for setting up Free Schools. Most of these are not-for-profit organisations, but the for-profit company Edison Education—a large provider in the United States—has obtained approved status.

The New Schools Network suggests that there are three models that proposers can adopt for running the school. The 'sponsor model' envisages that proposers form a partnership with an existing charitable education provider. This provider takes over the task of sponsoring the application through the DfE, with the proposers having the role of campaigning for the school, helping the sponsor to prove that there is adequate local support and demand, and constituting the governing or advisory board of the school. The sponsor will have an established model for running a school (such as ways of promoting a school 'ethos' and an established curriculum), so proposers have to decide whether their own preferences are aligned with this model. Parents who wish to propose a school but leave its running to an existing provider can also seek to establish a local authority maintained school on this basis.

By contrast, under the 'promoter model', proposers make the contract with the DfE and undertake the day-to-day running of the school. Those using this model have to demonstrate that the governing body has sufficient expertise in education management and finance to recruit the teachers and manage the budget. Some procurement of services from other organisations (for example, property management companies) is possible, but the core activities are managed by the governing body.

The third model is the 'school provider' model, where the proposers establish the school but then contract out the running of it to one or more organisations with specific expertise. As with the 'promoter model', the proposers are the parties to the funding agreement with the DfE. They engage in a process of open tendering to find suitable providers. A particular feature of this model is that a contract can be made, to run the school in all its aspects, with a for-profit provider. The party to the contract with the DfE cannot be a for-profit organisation, but the organisation responsible for the day-to-day running of the school, the appointment of staff, management of property and design of curriculum can be for-profit. A recent example is the Breckland Free School, which has contracted with IES UK—a subsidiary of a Swedish for-profit provider.

The presence of for-profit providers at one remove raises the question: how important is the not-for-profit condition imposed on the proposer/ sponsor? There is a well-established account of the reasons why governments might prefer to contract with not-for-profit rather than for-profit firms for the delivery of public services. The argument is that not-for-profit firms are less likely to reduce the quality of provision in order to cut costs. They have weaker incentives than for-profit firms to cut costs because the owners cannot take profits out of the firm due to the 'non-distribution constraint'. This argument implies that the government party should weigh up the risk of quality 'shading' against the (loss of) incentives to cut costs. If relevant qualities can be specified and monitored, then for-profit providers with their strong incentives may be preferred, assuming that the government can share the benefits of their cost-cutting. Where quality is difficult to contract for and monitor, then the less sharp incentives of the not-for-profit provider may be preferred.

In the case of Free Schools, the government has deliberately reduced the contractual provisions that appear to guard against reductions in quality. As noted above, Free Schools are allowed to substitute less-qualified for more-qualified teachers, vary the curriculum and change the school day. The implication of the 'autonomy' arguments rehearsed above is that writing detailed contracts to maintain quality is possible, but apparently not desirable. Instead, a different mechanism for preventing quality shading is envisaged. It is that the governing body of the school retains the residual control rights to monitor the performance of the contractor and insist that key qualities are maintained. But will governing bodies be able to do this, and what is the significance of their own not-for-profit constitution?

One scenario is that the governing body is active and made up of people who want to maximise all possible dimensions of quality. One can imagine a body of parents who are all concerned with obtaining the best service for their children. No one on the governing body has an incentive to reduce costs, whereas higher quality has non-pecuniary benefits for parents. However, this seems to be a recipe for a good deal of conflict. We can imagine that the for-profit provider will only enter this arrangement if it thinks that the governing body can be kept in its box, and prevented from interfering with decisions that will make the school profitable. At least one past experiment with private school management has foundered on the provider's concerns about its lack of autonomy to make decisions.[5]

Another scenario is that the governing body is not very active, or has different preferences. A parent-based governing body has a lifecycle problem: there is a risk that the first wave of activist parents withdraw when their children leave school, and are not replaced by equally involved new parents. This would suggest that a for-profit provider must endure a few difficult years but will eventually enjoy considerable autonomy. DfE guidance states that Free School proposers must show how the governing body will be viable in the long term, and advises that having trustees who are not current parents will demonstrate this. These trustees might be altruistic volunteers: the question mark about them is whether they will invest enough effort in monitoring a for-profit provider with incentives to cut costs.

One possible response to these issues is to argue that the governing structure does not matter because the school will have to compete in the education quasi-market, and so it cannot cut quality too far. This argument is discussed in the next section. For the moment, note that it implies that the presence of a not-for-profit intermediary is not important for ensuring school quality. For-profit firms could as well directly enter funding agreements with the DfE. However, the intermediary may be a useful smokescreen for the DfE: in the event of a major failure in quality, the trustees can be blamed, rather than the government.

Many of the existing Free Schools have adopted the 'promoter' model, rather than contracting-out the management of the school to an established provider. Can we say that this model provides the most robust governance, with trustees able to take the key decisions in the best interests of the pupils, without coming up against the profit motive of a provider? Yes and no. While Free Schools are not labour-managed firms, they are likely to be subject to a high level of teacher influence (particularly of head teachers). Sponsors have only a part-time interest in the school, while teachers are fully engaged, and, as in the contracting-out case, the commitment of parent sponsors may fade through time. As in many areas of public administration, expertise and information asymmetries favour the employees over the users. If external stakeholding weakens, the school will become a type of labour-managed firm. The workers can then evade the non-distribution constraint and appropriate benefits for themselves in the form of shorter working days, easier conditions and higher salaries.

There is a different scenario based on the theory of donated labour, which goes like this. Teachers who embrace their school's mission and remain on good terms with the governing body will be highly motivated, which will boost their productivity. Grout and Yong[6] consider the situation of employees who are committed to the organisation's goals to the extent that they are willing to work beyond the formal limits of their employment contract. They give the example of nurses staying beyond the end of their shift; teachers remaining at school at the end of the day present a similar example. They argue that workers' willingness to 'donate' labour in this way depends on the governance structure of the organisation. Specifically, the presence of a for-profit provider sharply undermines donated labour, as the workers can see that their motivation can be exploited to raise profits, perhaps by keeping the organisation perennially understaffed. This suggests that the in-house pro-poser model for a Free School is superior to the contracted-out model in its effect on teachers' donated labour. Note, however, that the in-house trust can undermine its own good effect by giving senior management performance-related pay because this is a form of 'distribution' that potentially has the same effect on teachers' donations as the presence of a for-profit provider.

There is a further potential limit to teachers' donations. As Ware notes in his contribution to this volume, there is a long history of successive govern-ments taking advantage of voluntary endeavour to reduce the cost to the state of providing services. At first sight, Free Schools are far from being exploited. They receive not only the per-pupil 'voucher', but also the 'Local Authority Central Services Equivalent Grant' (LACSEG) to compensate them for the loss of LEA services. On top of this, capital grants have been given, sometimes at the direct cost of planned works at neighbouring schools. However, there are some political risks attached to the funding arrangements. In a less favourable political environment, Free Schools could find that donated labour is captured in the reduction of discretionary government grants, although the pupil voucher would seem to be secure. Grout and Yong argue that the exploitation of donated labour by the government in its contracting arrangements could have just the same detrimental effects on motivation as the presence of an owner extracting profits.

Competition and choice

We have little information about the criteria that the DfE has used to evaluate Free School proposals. One requirement, however, is clear: the proposers must demonstrate that the school will attract students. The DfE invests in Free Schools by providing capital grants, and it wants to be satisfied that the buildings will be occupied for the foreseeable future. Once begun, Free Schools, like other schools, may have to manage a fluctuating current budget which is dependent on pupil numbers, and the sponsors' plans have to show how they will cope with lower than expected numbers.

The nature of the education quasi-market means that parental choices will drive the allocation of resources, once the basic architecture of eligible schools is established. In the following discussion, we assume that the government is interested in financing education that enhances pupils' skills and thereby increases their potential earning power. Its focus is on the attainment of the educational standards seen as necessary for economic success. This orientation to skills and competences is reflected in international comparisons of educational attainment, which measure the functional skills that have been identified as contributing to a productive workforce. For the sake of clarity in the argument, we rule out the possibility that the government has ideological objectives in addition to these economic objectives. The question we ask here is: will parental choice produce the higher standards the government seeks? Are there conflicts between the empowerment of local parent or faith groups and the attainment of central government's objectives?

To answer these questions, we first outline the competitive strategies that Free Schools can be expected to use in the education quasi-market. We focus on their possible 'technologies' for improving educational attainment, although it cannot be ruled out that a school can compete with services that bring lower attainment, such as a free relaxed environment and advanced leisure facilities.[7] We show that the technologies for improving attainment present two potential problems. One is an adverse 'neighbourhood effect'. Advocates of competition in the education quasi-market argue that it will 'raise all boats': neighbours will respond to the entry of a high-quality competitor by improving their own performance, but this might not happen. The other is that parents' choices may be influenced by ideology. Following a theory developed by Kremer and Sarychev,[8] we suggest that this can lead to higher attainment for their children, but lower economic success overall.

Consistent with its 'black box' approach to much contracting out of public services, government documents say little about the technology that Free Schools might bring to improve educational outcomes, instead alluding vaguely to the 'innovations' that result from 'autonomy'. However, the education literature gives us several fairly clear ideas about what the key elements of a successful technology might be. Education is an 'associative good' so peer group effects are important: children surrounded by high attainers tend to reach higher levels of attainment themselves. This points to a technology dependent on cream-skimming. We see this in the most successful schools in the English system—the independent fee-paying schools. It is clear that this way of achieving high levels of attainment comes at a high cost in (not) pursuing the public interest in equitable education provision. There is evidence that the government does not want to facilitate cream-skimming in the regulations governing admissions.

The drive to cream-skim is related to, but potentially mitigated by, another process which seems to be important to outcomes, which is about identification. Students' performance is affected by their peer group at school, but a school may have more than one possible peer group. The student population is likely to be divided into subgroups, some of which identify with the school and its goals, while others reject it. Where a school has a strong ethos, students have a choice between identifying with the school and rejecting it.

With rejection comes low effort and low attainment. Where the ethos of the school is less defined so that staff tolerate less conformist behaviour and pupils have more choice about the subjects they study and the way they approach their studies, the risk of rejection and failure is lower. However, the high attainment that can come from strong identification with the ethos of the school is also foregone.

Akerlof and Kranton[9] summarise a large quantity of American research that suggests that public schools in the United States have opted for tolerance and student choice, partly because of legal constraints which in turn reflected previous patterns of rejection and failure, particularly as experienced by black students entering white-dominated schools. Private schools, in the meantime, are noted for their strong prescriptions about student behaviour and the effort they put into establishing a unifying ethos. One feature of the successful private initiatives is an emphasis on parental involvement, which may reduce the social distances that see students rejecting the school's ethos. The art is to establish an ethos but also minimise the number of students who are unable to share it. The key management decision is to decide the share of resources that will be put into direct teaching and the share that will go into creating a school community: the assumption is that an autonomous school will choose a higher share for the latter.

The establishment of a distinctive ethos in a Free School might have positive or negative neighbourhood effects. Negative effects might flow in two ways. First, the Free School may attract applications from the most concerned and engaged parents, creating an indirect form of selection. Second, if there is a surplus of places in the area, competition may push other schools into decline, with insufficient pupil numbers to maintain a good range of classes and facilities. Conversely, positive effects might arise if all schools are moved to mobilise active parental choice and engagement. Machin and Vernoit's study of Labour's Academies programme found that they appear to have achieved performance improvements, and 'there is some limited evidence of positive spillovers to neighbouring schools'.[10] However, Academies under Labour were established in a selective way: schools that were underperforming and in deprived areas were taken over and put under new governance arrangements. The new range of Free Schools and Academies are not being established under these conditions.

One hazard of allowing parental choice to allocate education funding is that parents' preferences might not be fully aligned with those of the government. Parents might have other goals than maximising the future earnings of their children. Bear in mind that the case for public funding of education rests in part on the idea that, left to themselves, some parents will not invest enough in their children's education. This may be because they are not able to, due to low incomes, but it may also be because they do not value education as much as the government, or value different aspects. This could, in theory, lead to schools competing for vouchers by offering parental 'backhanders' that allow finance to be diverted into private consumption that is valued more highly by parents or children than education to enhance skills. Rewards for joining, like free electronic gadgets, could fall into this category. Schools that offer long teaching hours could arguably be attracting pupils by maximising parents' private benefits rather than focusing on the quality of time spent in education. Schools could also attract students by offering enjoyable 'consumption' activities rather than educational 'investment' activities.

These ways of creating private benefits out of public education funding can presumably be controlled by regulation. However, there is one class of private benefit which presents a dilemma in regulation, and that is ideology. We use the term here in the broad sense found in the education literature, to refer to belief systems that may affect attitudes to different groups in society, views about scientific knowledge and understanding, or concerns for the environment, as well as loyalty to the nation-state and religious adherence. The dilemma is that ideology could provide the basis for creating a school ethos and promoting active parental engagement, which in turn might lead to higher educational attainment. In other words, rather than being a private substitute for the public good of education, it could be a complement.

The usual way of thinking in economics about ideology in education is that ideological qualities are a private benefit to the ideologues. This type of increment in quality is not valued by the government, so an ideological Free School is diverting and privatising public money. However, parents may be attracted to the ideology, increasing their engagement and commitment to the school's ethos. (Alternatively, ideological teachers could offer parents private benefits, such as long hours at low cost, because of their commitment to disseminating their views.) The most obvious problems with ideology arise if parents value the ideological conformity of their children to the extent that they are willing to sacrifice their academic attainment, but even without this level of 'extremism', ideology presents a public policy problem. Suppose that a school adopts an ideology that forms the basis of its ethos and is specifically designed to appeal to a particular group of parents. As noted above, this could help to produce higher educational attainment in the school. For a government which is instrumentalising school autonomy in the interests of attainment, this suggests that a benign attitude to ideology should be adopted. The Blair government advanced this instrumental account of its encouragement of faith schools. As Kelly and Crowcroft point out elsewhere in this volume, the orientation of such schools towards authority, morality and paternalism conforms to a Tory tradition, and thence to the embrace of a conservative form of multiculturalism.

However, the instrumental uses of ideology have limits. The Burkean image of small and organic communities that impose restraint on the individuals within them conflicts with the prevailing economic order, which emphasises the gains from trade. An efficient market economy is meritocratic and nondiscriminatory, providing diverse economic opportunities and not ghettoising communities into a limited range of occupations or closing their lines of exchange with other communities. Kremer and Sarychev argue that ideology may enhance identification and learning, but can also reduce the value of skills in the economic marketplace. Their argument is that members of different ideological groups might not trade readily with each other, especially in long-term high-trust trades like employment relationships. Thus school success can produce economic failure, or at least failures of economic integration.

This does not mean that the government cannot instrumentalise ideology, but it does suggest that it will have to limit the ideological range of schools to those which do not have divisive economic consequences. Established churches might fall into this category because their own hierarchical controls constitute a restraint on the extremism of the ideology they teach. But this implies that some ideological Free Schools should be approved and not others—a policy which has proved difficult to implement in the past, with Muslim groups protesting about discriminatory refusals.

Conclusion

Free Schools could potentially mobilise the resources of concerned parents to support teachers in creating schools with a strong ethos, that work to the benefit of the great majority of those who attend them. The channel that Free Schools offer for parental involvement seems, on the face of it, to be preferable to the current situation, where concerned parents exercise choice through their housing decisions or indeed by exiting the public system and paying fees to private schools. These ways of exercising influence are only available to wealthy parents, and they have antisocial effects.

However, the contribution of Free School governance to school quality may well be limited. The wave of enthusiasm that carries a new Free School into existence is likely to fade over time, leaving them with no better or worse governing bodies than other community schools (many of which already engage parents and mobilise donations of time and money). The more profound effects of Free School formation are likely to come through their role in expanding choice in the education quasi-market. Here we have suggested that deviations between private and public interests may prove all too salient. Education is publicly funded not just because some parents are too poor to finance their children's education themselves, but also because parental preferences over education are not fully aligned with the public interest. The central problem in applying the idea of a Big Society to education is that it requires that the public interest can be pursued just by aggregating numerous private interests. This could produce an education system even more divisive than the present one.

Notes

1 http://www.trusteenet.org.uk/files/Modernising%20Commissioning%20 Green%20Paper.pdf

2 OECD, 'Raising the quality of educational performance at school', *Policy Brief*, 2004, http://www.oecd.org/dataoecd/17/8/29472036.pdf

3 The material in this and the next paragraph is drawn from C. Gillie, 'Free Schools', *House of Commons Library Standard Note* SN/SP/6058, 2011.

4 Department for Education, 'Free Schools model funding agreement', 2010, p. 16, http://www.education.gov.uk/schools/leadership/typesofschools/freeschools/ a0074737/free-schools-model-funding-agreement

5 BBC, 'Private bid for state school withdrawn', *BBC News*, 27 January 1999, http:// news.bbc.co.uk/1/hi/education/264180.stm

6 P. Grout and M. Yong, 'The role of donated labour and not for profit at the public/ private interface', CMPO Working Paper 03/074, Bristol, Centre for Market and Public Organisation, 2003.

7 For some signs of these strategies in the Swedish case, see R. Orange, 'Doubts grow over the success of Sweden's Free Schools experiment', *Guardian*, 10 September 2011, http://www.guardian.co.uk/world/2011/sep/10/sweden-free-schools-experiment

8 M. Kremer and A. Sarychev, 'Why do governments operate schools?', Economics Department, Harvard University, 2000, http://www.economics.harvard.edu/ faculty/kremer/files/Governments_Operate_Schools.pdf

9 G. Akerlof and R. Kranton, 'Identity and schooling: some lessons for the economics of education', *Journal of Economic Literature*, vol. 40, 2002, pp. 1167–201.

10 S. Machin and J. Verniot, *The Effects of Moving to More Autonomous School Structures: Academy Schools and Their Introduction to English Education*, London, LSE Centre for Economics of Education, 2010, p. 1.

The Big Society and the 'Mutualisation' of Public Services: A Critical Commentary

JOHNSTON BIRCHALL

Introduction

The attempt to devolve public services to 'employee mutuals' is one element in the political agenda known as the 'Big Society'. This specific policy initiative by the coalition government is surrounded by a broader interest in the idea of 'mutuality' or 'mutualism' as a new political principle encapsulating the idea of a revised relationship between the state and civil society. The promoters of the idea refer back to a time before the welfare state when 'mutuals' such as friendly societies provided a radically different approach to meeting the needs of citizens based on self-help and mutual aid. For instance, in his Hugo Young memorial lecture in 2009, David Cameron described how an 'ethos of mutuality' was present when the welfare state was created, a 'vibrant panoply' of civic organisations such as cooperatives, friendly societies, building societies and guilds. He drew from this the lesson that the state had subsequently squeezed out self-help and mutual responsibility, and that it has to become an instrument for giving power back to society.

Despite the insistence of the writers of the Big Society narrative that they are reacting against a centralising, authoritarian Labour government, this emphasis on mutuality shares a lot in common with a 'new mutualism' that was espoused by the previous government, and that led to the promotion of foundation hospitals. Here, a similar historical narrative was drawn on that emphasised a loss of the mutual ethos: for instance, in the introduction to the legislation setting up foundation trusts they were described as being modelled on cooperative societies and mutual organisations. They were required to offer membership to local patients, the public and employees, and to set up a board of governors mainly elected by these members, who would then appoint, and call to account, a board of management. Previously, trusts had had only one board, whose non-executive directors were appointed by an Appointments Commission acting on behalf of the Secretary of State for Health. This fundamental change in the governance of health provider organisations was justified by the then Secretary of State for Health, Alan Milburn, as a switch from top-down control by national government to control by 'local communities'.

Going even further back, we can see that the idea of devolving provision of public services to organisations owned variously by employees, service users

Published by Blackwell Publishing Ltd, 9600 Garsington Road, Oxford OX4 2DQ, UK and 350 Main Street, Malden, MA 02148, USA

and local communities had been on the political agenda since the mid-1980s under the previous Conservative government headed by Margaret Thatcher and then by John Major. The transfer of state schools to 'grant-maintained' status began in 1988, with direct funding from central rather than local government and with an enhanced role for parent governors. The transfer of hospitals to semi-independent providers called 'health trusts' began in 1991. The narratives used to explain and justify these policies were quite different from those of the later 'compassionate conservatism'; they included faith in the 'new public management' and a neoliberal belief in the efficacy of markets. Central government wanted to create a market in which services would be provided on contract and consumers would have a choice among providers. As a precondition for this, they had to devolve management to more independent providers.

Also, the transfer of local authority staff to new provider agencies with substantial amounts of employee ownership had also begun a long time before Big Society. In 1988, local authorities began to transfer their housing stocks to new housing associations. The main reason was so that as private sector organisations they could borrow on the strength of their assets and do major repairs and renovations to old housing stock, but there was also a rhetoric of freedom from council control, greater engagement of staff and tenant participation. In 1993, under increasingly strained budgets local authorities began to transfer the management of leisure services to new leisure trusts that had substantial employee ownership built into their governance. Here the rhetorical justification was very similar to that used to justify the transfer to employee mutuals in the Big Society. The freedom to manage and to innovate, combined with the engagement of employees, were expected to lead to substantial efficiencies and a more responsive attitude to customers.

So what makes the current policy different from previous ones? Have we really been here before or is this something genuinely new? How important is the policy, how coherent is it, and most importantly will it succeed? The aim of this chapter is to answer these questions through providing a critical commentary. Such a commentary may be analytical or normative. A normative commentary would also include comparison with an alternative script or prescription based on different values such as equality or fairness. But the intention here is more modest. This chapter provides a descriptive analysis, using a simple model of a four-stage policy process that this author has used before in relation to devolved public services: emergence of the idea, development of the policy, implementation and impact.[1]

However, before this two short excursions are necessary. The first is a discussion of what is meant by a 'mutual'. This will provide a yardstick against which to measure the use of the term by policy makers, and in particular against which to understand the governance structures of the new 'mutuals'. The second is a discussion of the significance of the 'old mutuals' that flourished before the welfare state was founded in the late 1940s. There is an assumption among promoters of the new public service mutuals (shared by their predecessors in the previous Labour government) that the history of mutuals supports their reintroduction into social policy. However, it is difficult to make this argument stick; the old mutuals existed in a totally different institutional and policy environment, and they had their own problems (not least from interference from governments). It is useful to consider this before starting to evaluate arguments for the 'new mutualism'.

What do we mean by a mutual?

Mutuals are part of a class of organisations (also including cooperatives, credit unions, friendly societies and other economic associations) that have one common feature: they are membership-based. While public agencies exist to serve the public in general (or some part of the public that citizens in general wish to serve), and private, investor-owned businesses exist to increase the profits of their investors, mutuals exist for the benefit of their members. Benefit implies ownership and ultimate control, which is why mutuals do not have outside shareholders; they put people before capital, and so usually work on the principle of one-person-one-vote. In this, they can be called 'people-centred' organisations.[2] Of course, the larger and more complex they become, the more they rely on professional management, and so they are as vulnerable as other organisations to being diverted from their original aims by the self-interest of managers. They are also subject to the isomorphic pressures of market forces, and so can sometimes become almost indistinguishable in their business practices from their investor-owned competitors. However, no matter how far they detach from their membership base, ultimately the members are the owners; in a proposed demutualisation member-owners have to vote to allow it to go ahead, and sometimes they vote down the proposal.

There are various historical reasons why member-owned businesses are known by so many different names, which it would be tedious to go into in this chapter. Briefly, the label 'mutual' has only been applied consistently in life insurance societies, but even here there are businesses that call themselves cooperatives. Member-owned banks are called 'mutuals' in France and 'popular banks' in Italy, but are grouped together in a European Co-operative Banking Association. In the rest of the world they are called credit unions! In the United Kingdom, friendly societies and building societies are now generally referred to as 'mutuals', and they are seen as complementary to, but separate from, the cooperative sector. This may change, because the International Co-operative Alliance has recently decided to allow mutuals as members. However, in the London-based political culture in which policy is made, the term 'mutual' has tended to become a catch all for all member-owned businesses, including employee-owned.[3]

There are strong and weak sets of principles associated with being a mutual. The strongest are found in the cooperative tradition, which stresses the

'Rochdale Principles' that include: voluntary and open membership; democratic member control; member economic participation; autonomy and independence; education and training; cooperation among coops; and concern for community. Organisations wishing to be known as cooperatives have to sign up to these principles, which in many countries are enshrined in cooperative business laws. However, not all cooperatives practise them, and in the United States agricultural cooperatives have signed up only to three basic principles: member ownership, control and benefit. Many mutuals, notably in insurance and banking, do not even adhere to these, and have minimal contact with their members; drastic failures in governance have sometimes resulted—notably in Equitable Life. In this sense they could be said to be mutual in name only. Hansmann points out that in this case they approximate more to another type: the non-profit firm that is not owned by anyone. [4]

There are three issues that are particularly important to the design of new mutuals. The first is whether the members have the right to dissolve the society and split the proceeds. In some countries (notably Italy), mutual or cooperative law states that the distribution of assets on winding up the society should be transferred to another society or to a charity. This is in recognition of the principle that the society does not belong entirely to its existing members, but that it has moral obligations to previous generations of members who have foregone benefits to build up the business. When it comes to conversion of existing public sector organisations to mutuals, the new mutualism often requires this principle: a lock on assets that prevents a public service mutual from ever being broken up for the benefit of members.

A second issue concerns the distribution of economic surpluses. In conventional mutuals, this is entirely at the discretion of the members; they can allocate funds to reserves or distribute them to members in proportion to the use they have made of the business—the well-known consumer coop 'dividend' is a good example. However, a public benefit mutual has wider purposes, and so the new mutualism tends to adopt a 'non-surplus distributing' principle.

A third issue concerns who can become a member. In the conventional mutual usually there is one category of member: the consumer of the product or service (or in the case of a worker coop: the employee). The new mutualism tends to adopt a multistakeholding principle, accepting that more than one category of person benefits from the mutual; in foundation hospitals, for instance, there are three categories of member, each with their own elected representatives: patients, the public and employees. We will return to these issues of definition when considering possible weaknesses in the new mutualism.

The rise and fall of the old mutualism

Briefly, the institutional origins of the British welfare state can be traced to three types of organisation: philanthropic societies, local government and mutuals. By far the most important type of mutual were the friendly societies, which provided sickness benefits to their members, appointed doctors to provide general practitioner services and ran medical institutes, which we would now call 'health centres'. They also provided support to enable members to travel in search of work, acted as social and benevolent clubs, and provided death grants and support for widows and orphans. Their funding came from compulsory health insurance levied on workers and employers and with contributions from the state, supplemented by voluntary payments by members for extra benefits. By the end of the Second World War, there were over 18,000 friendly societies, with 6.5 million members. Also, there were hospital contributory schemes that provided their members with insurance against the cost of hospital care; in 1943, there were 114 schemes with a membership of almost ten million. This mutual welfare system was part of a larger mutual and cooperative sector that included over 2,000 working men's clubs with nearly a million members, over 1,000 consumer cooperative societies with nine million members, nearly 900 building societies with over two million members, 400 trade unions with 6.5 million members, and 87 trustee savings banks with nearly 4.5 million members.[5]

In the founding of the welfare state in the period immediately after the Second World War the emphasis shifted to the provision of welfare services by central government, and earlier forms became marginalised. The role of philanthropy became to add to basic state services and to provide a cutting edge of innovation in service development that, once a need was recognised, the state would eventually take over. Local government lost many of its former services such as health care and unemployment benefit, and, in return for receiving a support grant, became mainly a provider of welfare services required by central government legislation. Friendly societies had already lost their autonomy in provision of health care and sickness and death benefits. From the 1911 National Insurance Act onwards, they had been 'subject to a process of creeping nationalisation', becoming agents for the state's compulsory social insurance schemes.[6]

The 'architect' of the welfare state, William Beveridge, had envisaged a comprehensive social security system, but was against its being delivered by a government agency. He was concerned that the social solidarity generated by the friendly societies would be lost, and recommended they deliver basic state social security, supplemented by voluntary insurance (the option chosen by most governments in Western Europe when they set up their welfare states). The government chose, instead, to nationalise social security, thus marginalising the friendly societies and, in consequence, the whole idea of mutual welfare. The idea of mutuality did not get back on to the political agenda until the 1990s, in relation to two new trends: the devolution of public services, and the demutualisation of much of the building society and mutual insurance sectors.

The new mutualism is meant to restore something 'old', but a closer examination of the strengths and weaknesses of the friendly societies at

1945 provides a mixed picture. Then, mutual organisations proved to be unsatisfactory because of their lack of complete coverage of the population, the high cost of their administration and the inequality in the benefits they provided. They also suffered from lack of member participation, and were not particularly democratic. A Mass Observation study in 1945 found ignorance and apathy among members of friendly societies. There was confusion over the difference between real societies and insurance collecting businesses that were not really societies but were permitted to call themselves such. Two out of five people asked had no knowledge of the term, particularly among the under-forty age group (though of those who did know of it, two-thirds had a positive attitude). There had been a real decline in numbers over time, with negative and resistant attitudes to attending meetings, more pronounced among young people. A case study showed they had lost a lot of members during the war, and that group feeling had deteriorated. Historians of the hospital contributory schemes find a similar picture of low participation; a 1947 study found less than 3 per cent attended meetings.

However, it can be argued that this was not entirely the mutuals' fault. One historian, Noel Whiteside, comments that, while participation had never been strong, the decline was due to central regulation of the societies that had ruined the chance of popular participation.[7] Members had made a rational decision that when government policy continually overruled them there was no point in attending meetings. However, there is a distinction between participation in governance and participation in the social affairs of the society. The fraternal spirit that so impressed Beveridge was still alive.

While the evidence for the effectiveness of the mutuals is mixed, the process of recovering and re-examining their history has enabled policy analysts to question the direction that social policy took. Comparative analysis of health care systems in France and Germany can be used to show what might have happened if Beveridge had had his way and given the mutuals a place in the delivery of welfare. So there is nothing wrong with advocates of Big Society using history as a stick with which to beat the present, as long as they do it carefully without idealising the past.

Emergence of the idea

How do ideas get into policy? It is useful to begin from an account of how mutualism got on to the agenda of the previous Labour government, and then to contrast this with its rebirth as part of the Big Society. In the previous government's espousal of a 'new mutualism' there was a broad intellectual underpinning for the idea from Amitai Etzioni's communitarian philosophy and Anthony Giddens' 'Third Way'. At first, Etzioni was lukewarm about the idea of mutualising public services. He valued communities rather than voluntary organisations, believing that the bonding power of association was too meagre to bear the weight of his prescription for social renewal. He saw the problem in terms of finding a balance between the three elements of market, state and community, rather than, as mutualists do, between market, state and associations. However, in a report for the think tank Demos, he began to show a real appreciation of the new mutualism, saying:

Mutuality-based associations have always existed and have been on the rise in recent years. Still, they need to be greatly expanded, encouraged and furbished with the needed resources in order to carry more of the social burdens in the years to come.[8]

He suggested the BBC should become a mutual owned by its license-payers, and that water utilities and public services such as the London Underground should take a mutual form.

Anthony Giddens parted company with Etzioni in this valuation of community. He believed communities can be exclusive and intolerant, and the broader idea of civil society was preferable. His reform programme was aimed more at the state, and included a process of democracy deepening in which government enters into partnership with agencies in civil society to foster community renewal and development. He used the term 'mutuality' occasionally and advocated that third-sector agencies should play a greater part in providing welfare services, but he rejected the idea of creating markets for service provision. However, like Etzioni, when the idea of mutualisation had begun to catch on he began to see the benefits, suggesting 'a variety of non-state agencies, including mutuals, social enterprises, not for profit trusts and public benefit corporations, can and should be brought into the delivery of public services'.[9]

What had happened to make these two philosophers warm to the idea? Between 1998 and 2003 the Co-operative party commissioned a series of pamphlets from well known journalists that laid the ground work for a more serious appreciation of the cooperative and mutual business models. Then more detailed reports came out from the think tanks Demos, New Economics Foundation and Mutuo—the last two working out in more detail how the health services could be mutualised. Government ministers became involved, and the foundation trust model was promoted.[10]

In the case of the Big Society, a similar idea of mutuality has developed but under slightly different conditions. First, it has been linked from the start directly to David Cameron and so has come with him into the centre of government. Second, it was developed while the Conservatives were in opposition rather than in government, which means that there was time to work it out before implementation. Yet again there are two key thinkers involved, who have supplied the justification for the policy: Jesse Norman and Phillip Blond.[11] Norman comes first with a series of books starting in 2006. He develops an argument that contrasts the 'state first' Fabianism of Labour with the idea of a 'connected society' in which there would be a three-way relation between the state, the individual and linking institutions. He believes that Labour cannot draw on its own mutualist traditions because of this dominant Fabian attitude towards the state (a claim that, as we have seen with the foundation trusts, is not all that plausible). He says that cooperatives, mutuals and employee ownership have been regarded as 'left wing' but are really a conservative idea. He provides a potted history of the Rochdale Pioneers, showing that their success came from self-help, entrepreneurialism and community energy. He is thus able to see cooperatives as an extension of the Big Society project.

Phillip Blond provides a similar analysis, with a graphic description of the 'malaise' that affects the United Kingdom with the collapse of British culture and the disappearance of civil society. Again, he looks to associations as a source of independent power, and underpins this with a strong argument derived from Hilaire Belloc on the need to distribute property and assets more widely. A modern mutualism means the sharing of assets within genuinely free markets by associations that could create value directly, rather than relying on welfare. Blond explains that in a 'moral market', mutualist structures of ownership and reward have an important place. He applies this to the current situation (after the banking crisis) and suggests that the big banks could be split up into local banks and building societies, and that post offices could become cooperatives operating under a franchise. However, he does not single out employee-owned mutuals in public services, preferring instead some kind of hybrid of employee and consumer ownership.

We can see how these ideas worked themselves into Cameron's speeches while he was in opposition. At first his themes were about 'compassionate conservatism' and 'social responsibility' with no mention of the mutualisation of public services. Then in 2007, in a bold and provocative move, he and Jesse Norman launched a Conservative Co-operative Movement, challenging the assumption that the cooperative and mutual tradition belonged to the Labour party, and paving the way for a new appreciation of the idea by Conservatives. In his Hugo Young memorial lecture in 2009, he talks of a re-imagining of the role of the state, so that it helps to create the Big Society, empowering individuals, families and communities. He describes an ethos of mutuality that existed when the welfare state began, with a 'vibrant panoply' of civic organisations such as cooperatives, friendly societies, building societies and guilds. However, the election manifesto says only that the Conservatives would support social enterprises to help in public service reform. It was not until after the election was won that the idea of encouraging employee mutuals in public service delivery became part of the programme. In May 2010 the coalition government declared its support for 'the creation and expansion of cooperatives, mutuals, charities and social enterprises, and enable these groups to have a much greater involvement in the running of public services'.

Development and implementation of the policy

The implementation of the Big Society follows a conventional route. An Office for Civil Society was set up as part of the Cabinet Office to work across government departments to translate the agenda into practical policies.

Francis Maude MP was appointed Minister for the Cabinet Office and began to chair a government committee on the Big Society, while Nick Hurd MP was given the title of 'Minister for Civil Society' with responsibility for charities, social enterprises and voluntary organisations. The aim of opening up public services was one of three parts to the Big Society agenda, which also included community empowerment and social action. The plan included setting up a Big Society Bank, a national citizen service and a community organiser programme. In August 2010 a list of twelve 'pathfinder mutuals' was announced. It included a diverse mix of organisational types in several different service areas, which illustrated that the government was, as it made clear later, agnostic about what form each mutual should take. Every government department put in place a right for public sector workers to take over the running of their service, except in sensitive areas such as defence and security. The right came with some duties: to meet appropriate guarantees, and to show that services would make savings or improve the quality of services. A modest Pathfinder Programme was begun, with £10 million of funding to help the process, and experts from companies such as John Lewis were asked to advise.

In December 2010, the Green Paper *Modernising Commissioning* was published.[12] It showed awareness of unavoidable complexity in trying to support so many different types of organisations. Referring to mutuals, coops, charities and social enterprises as 'civil society organisations', it then added a caveat recognising that mutuals and cooperatives are profit-making. It reiterated the right of employees to challenge existing provision and to provide it through mutuals, and explained that a Localism Bill would extend this to local authorities. However, it also recognised the barriers to change: large-scale commercial enterprises had the advantage of being able to bear the risks, while the transfer of engagements rules (known as TUPE) might put off employees. It asked commissioners of service to focus on price and value rather than just on costs, and asked that citizens should define what is in the contract. This is a long way from the ruthless compulsory competitive tendering of the last Conservative government of the 1990s.

In February 2011, a second wave of seven pathfinder mutuals was announced. Like the first wave they were a diverse mix of organisational types and service areas, including four providers of various types of social care services, a further education college, a local authority youth and library service and a nurse-led therapy unit. This last was significant because it was the first spinout from a hospital foundation trust.

In May, a thoughtful report was published by Co-operatives UK that provided international comparisons of public service mutuals from Spain, Italy and Sweden.[13] From these it extracted lessons for the United Kingdom, finding that Britain's policy context did not emerge very well from the comparison and that much more needed to be done to create an enabling environment. It identified the key ingredients as being: enabling legal and fiscal frameworks; a positive approach to commissioning and procurement;

access to capital; successful organisational models (including mixed models of employee and user ownership); and specialist business support. The report concluded that it was still early days for the programme, and that with political will obstacles in the way could be tackled.

In July, the £10 million fund was launched; called an 'investment and contract readiness fund' it was earmarked to help charities and social enterprises to develop the skills to win public service contracts. The Bank was to be set up to provide them with capital investment. In the same month the White Paper was published.[14] It emphasised that the reform of public services was a progressive cause, giving people more control as users, opening up provision to new providers, as well as costing less money. The government declared its agnosticism about the ownership form the new providers should take (the organisations competing for the chance to run the service were described rather imprecisely as 'mutual and cooperative social enterprises'). The emphasis was on the values of diversity, choice and transparency, and the underlying dynamic was identified as a 'power shift'—a radical decentralising of power down to the lowest level both in commissioning and provision. The idea was to level the playing field, remove the barriers and then see what emerges.

In September, in a parallel move in education 24 Free Schools opened their doors across England. There were many more applications in the pipeline, mainly from parents and faith-based groups. In this case the guidance on organisational form was more prescriptive: applicants have to be a company limited by guarantee or a charitable trust, and employees were not normally expected to be proposers (no employee mutuals here!). Four partner organisations that were experts in employee ownership published guidance on how to become an employee mutual. They advocated a community interest company or a cooperative model, indirect ownership through an employee trust and an asset lock on ownership. A Mutuals Taskforce was set up under the chairmanship of Julian Le Grand, who drafted a report that provided evidence for the benefits of employee ownership, and showed how a variety of legal forms could be used to achieve this.

The same month, the whole programme received a setback. Government ministers had lauded one well-established mutual, Central Surrey Health (CSH), as a wonderful example of what could be achieved. Begun in 2006 under the previous government, it was a mutual formed by 700 National Health Service staff to provide community health services under a £20 million contract. It bid for a similar contract in North and West Surrey but lost out to Assura Medical, a for-profit company that was 75 per cent owned by the Virgin Group. CSH's own contract is due for renewal in 2012. Despite the assurance in the White Paper that contracts will be let on wider criteria than just cost, there is concern among NHS employees that large, well-capitalised firms may outbid the mutuals, making the whole idea too risky.

Finally, in January 2012, David Cameron announced a bill that will consolidate 17 separate acts into one comprehensive cooperative law. This should make it easier for promoters of employee mutuals and employee/service user hybrids to set up. However, it comes at a stage in the policy process when politicians are beginning to realise that 'spinning out' is not going to be as easy as they expected. What has been the impact so far?

The impact so far

A progress report on the mutual pathfinders published in December 2011 says that out of 21 pathfinders seven have gone live, eight are progressing well, three are in the early stages and four have decided not to go ahead.[15] The conclusion that they have enjoyed significant successes seems rather optimistic. The four who are not proceeding cite uncertainty over future service needs and the impact of restructuring, and the report admits that unless a clear market for a service can be identified, spinning out may not be appropriate. What is happening is that the drive to cut public expenditure is cutting across the mutuals policy, causing a turbulent environment in which employees do not want to take more risks. Trade unions are worried about the effect of the move to the private sector on staff pensions; transfers of engagement rules protect existing but not new employees' pension rights.

The tone of this report is upbeat, linking the empowerment of employees through ownership with redesign of services around the needs of service users, and efficiency gains. However, a report from the House of Commons Public Administration Committee published the same month is more sceptical.[16] Evidence from the charitable sector suggests that small organisations are unable to meet the requirements of tendering to take over public services. Contracting out continues to favour the larger, more commercial suppliers. The independence of the voluntary sector is also threatened by this new role. Francis Maude said 'there is a huge role for profit-making companies in our society' and noted the number of public services already delivered by profit-making companies. A submission from one of those companies, Capita, claimed that it provided 15–30 per cent efficiency savings in local authority contracts. However, trade unions expressed concern that these large companies would create an unbalanced marketplace, through their economies of scale and abilities to run loss leaders. The report concludes that such providers may provide the cheapest option in the first round, and that this may drive out smaller providers who are more local and accountable.

Ministers remain agnostic about which ownership type should run public services. The Public Administration Committee asks them to be clear in their guidance to commissioners—should they prefer the voluntary sector to offers of potentially better value? On public sector mutuals, the Employee Ownership Association's evidence was significant. It suggested that during the early development of a mutual, commissioners should see market-building as a legitimate goal, and that mutuals should have an 'infant protection period'. It said it was imperative to ensure that they 'do not risk losing out the moment they leave the public sector because they simply cannot compete with larger competitors'. The Minister had indicated early in 2011 that the target was to transfer one million public sector workers into mutuals by the end of the Parliament—one-sixth of the total public workforce. Limited progress has been made, with only 45,000 being transferred by the end of 2011.[17]

The Committee identifies the potential loss of the pension scheme as the biggest disincentive, and it suggests the government should develop innovative ways of persuading public sector workers that the benefits of mutuality are greater than the losses. Resistance to the idea by middle managers is also a problem, and in this respect the Committee asks whether the Mutuals Taskforce is equipped to overcome such resistance.

Conclusion

The limited impact to date of the mutualisation of public services under Big Society can be explained quite simply; for most public service workers it is too risky. The gains in ownership and control from converting to an employee mutual (or any of the other options) are offset against the risks and uncertainties of ceasing to operate within the public sector. Conversion offers new rights but also takes away some old ones. It introduces a contractual relationship between purchaser and provider that is no longer a 'quasi-market', but a real market in which providers may expand and flourish or decline and even cease to exist. There are push and pull factors. Employees and service users can be pushed into conversion if the alternatives are seen to be worse. They can be pulled by the example of successful mutuals that are expanding and demonstrating the comparative advantages of the form. If the only alternative is takeover by an investor-owned business, then the risks of not converting will be seen to be greater. Then there will be mass conversion of public service providers to mutuals. On the other hand, if the policy begins to fail, then a government that started out determined to 'release the social energy' of civil society may have to fall back on the more authoritarian policies of its predecessors and force public service providers to be 'free'.

Notes

1 C. Pollitt and J. Birchall, *Decentralising Public Service Management*, London, Macmillan, 1998.

2 J. Birchall, *People-centred Businesses: Co-operatives, Mutuals and the Idea of Membership*, London, Macmillan, 2010.

3 The think tank Mutuo publishes annual statistics that include cooperatives as part of a mutual sector.

4 H. Hansmann, *The Ownership of Enterprise*, Cambridge, MA, Harvard University Press, 1996.

5 Figures from D. Green, *Reinventing Civil Society*, London, Institute of Economic Affairs, 1993; M. Gorsky, J. Mohan and T. Willis, 'From hospital contributory schemes to health cash plans: mutualism in British health care after 1948', *Journal of*

Social Policy, vol. 34, no. 3, 2005, pp. 1–21; W. Beveridge, *Voluntary Action*, London, Allen & Unwin, 1948.

6 D. Mabbett, 'Mutuality in insurance and social security', in J. Birchall, ed., *The New Mutualism in Public Policy*, London, Routledge, 2001, p. 118.

7 N. Whiteside, 'Private provision and public welfare: health insurance between the wars', in D. Gladstone, ed., *Before Beveridge: Welfare before the Welfare State*, London, Institute of Economic Affairs, 1999, pp. 26-42.

8 A. Etzioni, *The Third Way to a Good Society*, London, Demos, 2000, p. 20.

9 A. Giddens, *Where Now for New Labour?*, Cambridge, Polity Press, 2002, p. 65.

10 For references, see J. Birchall, 'The mutualisation of public services in Britain: a critical commentary', *Journal of Co-operative Studies*, vol. 41, no. 2, 2008, pp. 5–37.

11 J. Norman, *Compassionate Conservatism*, London, Policy Exchange, 2006; J. Norman, *Compassionate Economics*, Buckingham, University of Buckingham Press, 2008; J. Norman, *The Big Society*, Buckingham, University of Buckingham Press, 2010; P. Blond, *Red Tory*, London, Faber & Faber, 2010.

12 Cabinet Office, *Modernising Commissioning*, Green Paper, London, Cabinet Office, 2010.

13 J. Bland, *Time to Get Serious: International Lessons for Developing Public Service Mutuals*, Manchester, Co-operatives UK, 2011. Ed Mayo, Secretary General of Co-operatives UK is now working on a 'decision tree' through which those interested in mutualising can find their way to the best kind of ownership structure to fit their circumstances. In a competitive market an employee mutual should be the default option, while in a less competitive market it should be a hybrid employee and consumer owned mutual.

14 Cabinet Office, *Open Public Services*, White Paper, London, Cabinet Office, 2011.

15 Cabinet Office, *Mutual Pathfinder Progress Reports*, London, Cabinet Office, 2011.

16 Public Administration Committee, *Report on Big Society*, House of Commons, 2011.

17 Public Administration Committee, *Report on Big Society*, paragraphs 53, 232, 235.

Beginning the Big Society in the Early Years

LOUISE BAMFIELD

Introduction

THE GUIDING motivation for the Big Society can be simply put: 'the state has grown, is growing and ought to be diminished'. In basic terms, it is a plea against the concentration of state power and resulting waste and inefficiency in human as well as monetary terms. Essentially conservative in outlook and disposition, it is a medley of different strands and traditions—liberal, libertarian, traditionally conservative, moralising, communitarian—which though distinct in their underpinning philosophies, are united in calling for power to be dispersed away from the state. Decentralisation, we are told, is the 'biggest' and 'best' thing that government can do to build the Big Society: in David Cameron's words, it 'gives people the freedom to take responsibility'—for themselves, for their families and for the wider community. What is more, government must not merely cease to *disempower* local communities; it must take steps to *actively empower* them. Power is to be devolved to those 'best placed' to find the 'best solutions' to local needs: elected local representatives, frontline professionals, social enterprises, charities, co-operatives, community groups, neighbourhoods and individuals.[1] Anyone, it seems, is better placed to direct, design and deliver public services than the state.

While the problem—Big Government—is easily stated, what is less clearly articulated or conceptualised is *how far* and *for whom* the alternative will actually be empowering. The influence of different strands and traditions of thought can again be detected in the various proposals. Rather than adhering in a single direction, when it comes to dispersing power away from the state, they may have different implications for how the relationship between state, citizen and intermediary institutions should be redrawn. Two strands in particular appear to pull in different directions: while the communitarian ethic desires to bring people together, the logic of market competition would seem to drive them apart. While some take a gloomy view, fearing that the ethic of individualism is bound to isolate people further whilst favouring citizens unequally, the Big Society is essentially optimistic about this tension, assuming that the efficiencies of the market go hand-in-hand with a flourishing society. According to its proponents, decentralisation helps counter the 'vertical' power relationship between citizen and state by dispersing power within the 'horizontal' relationships in civil society.[2] But the nature of power in wider society is under-theorised, to say the least. Without some account of

Published by Blackwell Publishing Ltd, 9600 Garsington Road, Oxford OX4 2DQ, UK and 350 Main Street, Malden, MA 02148, USA

social stratification, the wilful dispersal of power into a vacuum is surely bound to reinforce existing hierarchies of power, control and resources.

In this chapter, I explore how far citizens and frontline practitioners are likely to be empowered in reality by focusing on 'early years' services for families and young children as a test case for decentralisation and 'community empowerment'. What is striking about the coalition's early years strategy is how well it chimes with the key themes of the Big Society (even more so, perhaps, than its usual poster child, the flagship Free Schools programme) by promising to: streamline the state; devolve control to local areas; 'empower' frontline practitioners to be more innovative, flexible and responsive to local needs; and promote participation at all levels. The analysis that follows briefly charts the journey of discovery and expansion under Labour, as it crossed 'the new frontier of the welfare state'. It then recounts the coalition's efforts to reconfigure early years services in line with 'localism' and 'fairness', pausing to examine three of the main features of the new *modus operandi*: payment by results for Sure Start children's centres; decentralised control of funding in the Early Intervention Grant; and the enhanced role of the voluntary sector by way of 'collaboration' and 'co-production' in the design and delivery of early years service. Beneath the rhetoric, I explore and assess how far a more streamlined and collaborative model is likely to be 'empowering' in reality.

Before turning to our test case, it is helpful first to have a better sense of the specific ways in which Big Government is said to disempower and disconnect citizens and communities and the different accounts of how decentralisation will then be empowering.

The nature of disempowerment

For opponents of 'Big Government', the problem with endlessly crossing new frontiers of the welfare state is that far from liberating or empowering citizens, the pervasive reach and scope of government provision is believed to have a damaging and stultifying effect on people's capacity, initiative and personal agency. Having to rely on state support is said to cast people into a position of dependency[3]—a spectre evoked in David Cameron's 2009 Hugo Young lecture, when he rails against the perverse incentives of an 'ever-present', paternalistic welfare state:

There is less expectation to take responsibility, to work, to stand by the mother of your child, to achieve, to engage with your local community, to keep your neighbourhood clean, to respect other people and their property, to use your own discretion and judgement. Why? Because today the state is ever-present: either doing it for you, or telling you how to do it, or making sure you're doing it their way.

Furthermore, a pervasive and paternalistic state not only infantilises its subjects, it also compounds their lack of freedom and agency by isolating and individuating them:

The paradox at the heart of big government is that by taking power and responsibility away from the individual, it has only served to individuate them. What is seen as an act of social solidarity, has in practice led to the greatest atomisation of our society. The once natural bonds that existed between people—of duty and responsibility— have been replaced with the synthetic bonds of the state—regulation and bureaucracy.[4]

In this sense, Big Government is held to be doubly disempowering, eroding individual initiative and capacity to take responsibility for oneself and one's family, but also destroying the conditions in which people learn to share responsibility for other members of the community as well. Entrenched in layers of bureaucracy, smothered by prescription, a highly centralised state is not only wasteful and inefficient in monetary terms, it is wasteful and costly in human terms too. The critique is directed at every aspect of Labour's command state: the growth in its size and scope in fiscal terms (its expansiveness), the increasing number of areas of our lives into which state power encroaches (its pervasiveness), plus its method and manner of governance (from the level of centralisation, prescription, bureaucracy, to the degree of paternalism and coercion). The proposed remedy is therefore to reverse the concentration and centralisation of power along each dimension, to restore the freedom, independence and responsibility that are lost when the government grows too large.

Following its own blueprint for decentralisation, the coalition has set out the steps it must take to enact a shift from 'Total Politics' to local politics by reversing each driver of Labour's command state: in place of top-down targets and micromanagement from the centre, it must cut waste, bureaucracy and government prescription; in place of highly centralised and complex funding streams, it must increase local control of public finance and greater flexibility in the allocation of resources; and instead of state monopolies, it needs to open up public services to a diverse range of providers, to enhance competition and promote choice for citizens.

From disempowerment to active empowerment

Government must not merely cease to *disempower* local communities, but must take steps to *actively empower* them. As reimagined by Cameron, the role of the state is not simply to disappear: instead of a simple retrenchment of the state, 'strong and concerted government action' is called for to build citizen capacity and rebuild the ties and values of community.[5] Indeed, far from having no role, the state has a vital part to play by galvanising, catalysing, prompting, encouraging and agitating for social and civic renewal. This, in building the Big Society, the state is called upon to correct for the damaging effect of Big Government: instead of destroying initiative and agency, it must rebuild people's capacities and restore their sense of personal agency and responsibility; and instead of eroding community, it must endeavour to recreate the conditions for civic engagement and allow a strong sense of social responsibility to flourish.

The Big Society is therefore based on the twin goals of decentralising and limiting state power, on the one hand, and enabling and extending civic and democratic engagement, on the other. The essential practical steps that must be taken are set out in the *Essential Guide* to the Localism Act 2011. Here, we learn that communities must be 'empowered to do things their way' by 'creating new rights for people to get involved with, and direct the development of, their communities'. Further provisions aim to 'strengthen accountability to local people' by giving every citizen the power to change the services provided to them through participation, choice or the ballot box.

Again, the influence of different strands of thought can be detected in the proposals. But when it comes to empowerment, instead of all adhering in the same direction, the medley of different elements do not necessarily have the same view about the nature of freedom and the conditions for realising it, and so may pull in different directions when it comes to specifying how the relationship between state, citizen and intermediary institutions should be redrawn. A dominant influence is the libertarian or neoliberal strain (akin to Blairite 'new localism', which led to the founding of Academy Trusts and Foundation Hospitals), which points to a greater role for market competition, with a diverse range of providers creating choice for individual consumers of public services. For the coalition, it is not so much a hidden or covert agenda (as is sometimes alluded) as an open political commitment to diversify the supply of public services by ending public sector monopolies, ensuring a level playing field for all suppliers, giving people more choice and so achieving a better standard of service.[6] As such, it is based on a clear libertarian belief in the efficiency of market competition as a mechanism to boost public sector productivity and performance.

Also evident is the communitarian strand, more akin to strong, participatory democracy, which emphasises direct participation and active citizenship as a way of renewing the communal bonds, interconnections and social relationships that give meaning and purpose to human lives. From the communitarian perspective, there is likely to be general value in fostering those types of civic activity which allow bonds to develop over time, in non-instrumental ways. As Thomas Janoski argues, communities and groups tend to be stronger when based not on short-term, one-for-one exchange (as typified in the contractual relationship between consumer and producer in the market sphere), but on longer-term forms of social interaction, which reinforce generalised reciprocity and solidarity. The longer-term, 'generalised' exchange typical of family and friendship groups, church groups and other collective endeavours entails a willingness to delay gratification, to enter into activity without always demanding immediate returns, and also to look beyond one's personal wants to satisfy the needs of others.

From this perspective, we might also look to encourage those types of civic engagement and communal activity which help build bridges between individuals and groups rather than merely promoting bonds within them. As captured in Robert Putnam's classic distinction between 'bonding' and 'bridging' social capital, there may well be value for group members in fostering closer ties and affiliations within a closed social group, but these insular bonds will not necessarily strengthen interaction with non-members and could well exacerbate tensions and intercommunity rivalries. By contrast, participation in groups and associations which are open and inclusive in their membership, which bridge across different communities, tends to create cross-cutting values, norms and relationships that can bring lasting benefit to the wider community. In such cases, the state may be inclined to give active encouragement or endorsement, for example, through public funding or subsidy, or by commissioning organisations of this type to provide public services.

There is, perhaps, a basic tension between the two strands. While the logic of market competition encourages citizens to attend to their individual self-interest, the communitarian ethic points not to restricted, one-to-one connections (as in market exchange), but to generalised forms of exchange and reciprocity, embedding ties and connections over time and forging bridges for people across different social positions and cultural backgrounds, as well as cementing communal bonds between them. In theory at least, the libertarian urge to diversify provision and individualise forms of civic engagement would seem to pull in the opposite direction from the communitarian desire to bring people together.

The distinct logic and appeal of the different strands helps explain why political reaction to the Big Society has ranged widely, from cautious welcome to contemptuous dismissal, with much bewildered silence in between. Amidst the general fog of confusion, we might draw out four distinct ways of viewing the Big Society. In the first camp are those who welcome the libertarian strand, but tend to see other elements as a distraction or irrelevance. To those committed to market reform, the idea of the Big Society is useful insofar as it cements the shift away from public provision, but occasionally distracting in its sentimental attachment to community groups and charitable endeavours. From the perspective of the 'pure' market reform, the Big Society might be viewed as a kind of localism *lite*—a watered down or artificially sweetened version of the real thing. In the second camp are those attracted by the communitarian elements, but who tend to be agnostic or ambivalent about market reform. For this group, community empowerment and civic engagement offer a kind of localism *plus*—an essentially richer and more fulfilling set of human relationships, drawing from a deeper well of philosophical insight than other strands. In the third camp, are the outright opponents of the Big Society, who treat the project with withering scorn. For these critics, of which certain traditional social democrats are prominent examples, the communitarian elements amount to little more than a cynical political ploy: a barely disguised piece of ideological window dressing, designed to distract attention from and soften attitudes towards an otherwise nakedly neoliberal assault on the state.[7] Finally, there is the Big Society camp, comprised of those who see the appeal of both sides (together with other constitutive elements). In this, essentially optimistic view, the efficiencies of a more streamlined state and competitive public sector go hand-in-hand with a flourishing civil society—a strengthened public domain where people come together to pursue common purposes and collective endeavours. The common element, as we have seen, is the critique of an over-centralised state, with its debilitating, demoralising and disempowering effects for individuals and communities.

The philosopher and Conservative MP, Jesse Norman is one in the optimistic camp, who sees the value of both (and other) elements. In place of the vertical relationship between citizen and state, his account of the 'connected society' stresses the voluntary bonds and horizontal linkages that exist between people as citizens, in conditions of basic equality:

People relate to the state vertically: they tend to defer to politicians and bureaucrats as those in charge, and obey them in part through fear of sanction. But society is organic, not official: it cannot be established by law or fiat, but evolves through time and practice. Above all it is delicate. An invasive state disrupts the voluntary bonds between people, linking them upwards to the government rather than sideways to each other.[8]

In this conception, society is a delicate flower, which cannot be artificially manufactured or cultivated, but which must be allowed to evolve naturally, and which risks being trampled upon and destroyed by a big, blundering state. Decentralisation is therefore essential, to release people from the dependency and subservience of a highly centralised and paternalistic state; and to release communal relationships from the danger of the intrusive, pervasive state. What is missing from this account is any mention of the power relations that exist in actual society, rather than the idealised account that is given. Norman stresses the basic conditions of equality in civil society, 'where people identify with each other as equal members of the civic whole, and do things for each other, at least partly, through mutual recognition, mutual respect and goodwill', but is silent about the unequal power, re-sources and status that shape the relationships between members of different social groups and positions. Perhaps for this reason, it is assumed that dispersing power away from the centralised state is equally and essentially empowering for all citizens alike.

The counter view is that giving 'choice' to individual citizens to exercise as consumers of public services will damage the bonds and connections that might otherwise sustain them. Ironically, far from strengthening civic bonds and reinvigorating the civic sphere, it risks deepening the problem of social fragmentation by exacerbating the atomism of the Big Individual. The danger is that people will become *demanding* consumers, rather than more engaged and connected citizens. In pursuing their self-interest and entitlements with-out regard to duty and obligation, the shift to a contractual mode (in restricted market exchange) threatens to destroy an essential part of what was originally valuable in the activity for those involved. By reconfiguring the relationship between members and participants to that of 'service provider' and 'service user', it potentially transforms what was a bonding or bridging activity into a competitive and divisive one. What is at stake, then, is the very essence of citizenship:

If citizens approach their rights and obligations intending to maximise personal benefits, then citizenship becomes commercialised and can no longer protect against the market. This makes citizenship 'writhe in self-contradiction'.[9]

For those of a conservative disposition, such talk may seem rather fanciful, and in any case, beside the point, since inherent tensions and contradiction are encumbrances to be shouldered lightly, not shirked or reconciled away. Conservatism, according to Jesse Norman, is in effect 'a cluster of ideas competing with each other for market share'. Unlike socialism and liberalism, it is inherently instinctive, realistic and sceptical—not theoretical, grandiose or doctrinaire. This does not mean, he assures us, that conservatives do less thinking than their political opponents: no, 'the difference is that they have never settled on a conclusion'.[10] Thus, while the theoretician might blush and the ideologue angrily redden at the evident inconsistencies, the conservative will embrace the disharmony, drawing on his innate common sense to make the appropriate inference or judgement about which element is called for, as circumstances demand.

This innate good sense and sound judgement will doubtless come in handy in building the Big Society, helping ministers and their aides to face the inherent tensions with a clear head. For those less inclined to trust in the art of Tory statecraft, however finely honed, we might press for a clearer account of where and to whom power is to be distributed, for what reason, and with what likely impact on the wider distribution of power and resources. At an abstract level, the matter is of some academic interest: for those so inclined, there is an intrinsic reward and satisfaction in trying to decipher the meaning and significance of the different strands by tracing their origin and historical antecedents in political thought, or by probing the philosophical under-pinnings of each and testing their internal coherence, contradiction and possible reconciliation. For those more prosaically employed, drawing fine-grained distinctions between different categories and conceptions may not be of immediate use or practical advantage. Certainly, the Whitehall mandarins charged with translating the idea into concrete steps have dispatched any such difficulties, sensibly opting to list the main elements of 'decentralisation' and 'empowerment'—choice, voice, voting, direction participation and so on—without inquiring too deeply into their inner meaning or interrelation-ships. It may be useful, then, to consider these issues in relation to a specific area of policy, where the principles of decentralisation and active empower-ment are being applied in practice. It is to this task, and the example of Sure Start children's centres, that our attention now turns.

The 'early years' as exemplar of the Big Society

Heralded as the 'new frontier for the welfare' state, the Labour government oversaw an unprecedented increase in investment for support and services for families and young children, from birth to age five, including the introduction of a network of integrated Sure Start children's centres, beginning in the most deprived areas of England. This interest and investment spawned the first national childcare strategy, a £3 billion roll out of children's centres across the country, and a new national curricular and inspection framework for the Early Years Foundation Stage (EYFS). No doubt with an eye on the coming general election, in 2008 Labour set out to achieve full coverage of the Sure Start programme, with a prime ministerial pledge to open 3,500 children's centres—one for every community in the country. By May 2010 it had succeeded in reaching the magic number (and even surpassing it by a hundred), building up a valuable body of parental support and engagement in the centres along the way.

For the Conservative party in opposition, Labour's 'discovery' of the early years as a political and public policy priority certainly rang alarm bells as new Child Trust Funds or 'baby bonds' introduced the state into people's lives as soon as they were born, while the new Sure Start programme extended the state's influence during their early years. For many Conservatives, reports of 'yummy mummys' flocking for baby massage and aromatherapy were worrying enough, but the spectre of parents off-loading their children into institutional childcare facilities was even more troubling, threatening to erode parents' natural inclination and responsibility to care for their own children at home. Alarmed by the dramatic growth in government activity under Labour, the Conservatives in opposition promised to cut the waste, inefficiency, bureaucracy and prescription that it says had proliferated. Under the principle of 'last in, first out', one of the first places to start, one might have thought, would be the new national network of children's centres.

Over time, however, growing public enthusiasm meant that the Conservatives were obliged to reconcile themselves to the new services. Thanks to Labour's expansionist and colonising strategy, by 2010 the infrastructure had already become too embedded to be quickly unearthed. In the event, while the Child Trust Fund was an early casualty of the coalition cuts, the new government pledged to protect early years investment and retain a national network of Sure Start children's centres. Coalition ministers were persuaded by the solid research evidence for investment as a way of compensating for early disadvantage. Indeed, not satisfied by the wealth of existing data, they immediately set about the task of rediscovering the early years for themselves, commissioning a series of independent reviews led by Frank Field MP, Graham Allen MP, Professor Eileen Munro and Dame Clare Tickell on the topics of poverty and children's life chances, early intervention, child protection and the EYFS. The final reports when they came reaffirmed many of the key messages and findings of previous studies (notably Sir

Michael Marmot's review of the social determinants of health inequalities), whilst also pointing the way towards a more focused, streamlined and targeted system of provision. Across the key Whitehall departments (Department for Work and Pensions, the Cabinet Office, Department of Education), ministers jostled to take the lead on the government's 'fairness' agenda, under which 'early years' policy and provision was embraced as a vital component of the various strategies for promoting social mobility, social justice and tackling child poverty.

Nevertheless, while it pledged to protect and retain Sure Start, the new coalition government had no intention of continuing down Labour's path of expansion towards a genuinely universal service either. Having conceded the principle of government involvement in the early years, ministers moved to redraw the boundaries of state involvement, looking to streamline guidance and prescription where possible, enhance community involvement in the design and delivery of services, and devolve responsibility for key decisions, including public finance, to the local level. Thus, whereas Labour's strategy was geared towards universal provision, under the twin banners of 'fairness' and 'localism', the main goal and emphasis for the coalition is now on devolving power and control to local communities, whilst refocusing effort and resources on supporting the most vulnerable and disadvantaged families, as part of wider efforts to break intergenerational cycles of deprivation and transform the life chances of poor children. Not all are convinced, of course, by the government's rather narrow conception of fairness, focused as it is upon enhancing the relative life chances of the most disadvantaged children, whilst leaving in place an increasingly polarised labour market and wide inequalities in income and wealth.[11] Opponents worry too about the long-term consequences of a more targeted service, since any way of redirecting resources is bound to miss *some* of those in greatest need (who may not live in the most deprived geographical areas, for example), and also because of the longer term political ramifications of more concentrated provision in eroding the electoral bases of support for early childhood provision.

For our purposes, what is striking about the coalition's revised strategy for the 'early years' is how well it chimes with the key themes of the Big Society. At a governmental level, the emphasis is on providing clear strategic direction and oversight from the centre, whilst leaving the detailed planning and delivery to local authorities and service providers. At an intermediary level, it promises to enhance the role of the voluntary sector, whilst opening up provision to a wider range of providers, including mutuals, cooperatives and social enterprises. By cutting red tape and bureaucracy, it promises to 'free' frontline professionals to be more innovative, flexible and responsive to local needs. For local communities, it promises a greater say in how resources are allocated. And finally, for families and children, it promises greater parental engagement, enhanced opportunities for involvement and a stronger sense of local belonging. The government claims that the reforms will achieve three core aims: greater efficiency, fairness and democratic empowerment. To help us examine the claims to efficiency and fairness, and assess whether and for whom the reforms will actually be empowering, it is worth examining three of the main pillars of decentralisation in greater detail: first, the introduction of payment by results for Sure Start children's centres; second, decentralised control of funding in the Early Intervention Grant; and third, the enhanced role of the voluntary sector by way of 'collaboration' and 'co-production' in the design and delivery of early years service.

Payment by results

Perhaps the best example of the new *modus operandi* is the introduction of 'Payment by Results' (PbR): a new system of funding and accountability, which aims to give clearer rewards and incentives to providers to improve outcomes for the most disadvantaged families and children, on which a proportion of funding (5 per cent) will now be dependent, with specific indicators or outcomes to be determined by centre managers in collaboration with the local authority. Central government will therefore continue to set the strategic direction for services, but will deliberately not try to micromanage or interfere in the 'black box' of service design and delivery. On paper, PbR is intended to enhance autonomy for providers, improve outcomes for the most disadvantaged groups (such as parental skills and employment; increased family income; and better health, education and development for children) and hence achieve savings and reduce government spending over time.

Unlike DWP's 'Work Programme' for the long-term unemployed, the model has not yet been implemented across the board, but is first being piloted in thirty local authority areas, with a timetable to roll out to all authorities in England in 2013–14. This is sensible; whether driven by principle or necessity (since there was no working model available to implement in any case), the DfE is to be commended for developing and testing different frameworks before making a final decision. In the spirit of genuine experimentation, however, ministers would do well to resist the temptation to start rolling out the new approach before the completion of the pilots. What is more, they should remain open to the possibility that the main conclusion from the pilots could be that payment by results is not a viable model for the early years after all.

Developing an effective and efficient model of PbR for the early years is problematic for a number of reasons. In the first instance, local authorities will need to ensure that each individual setting (or cluster of centres) has a full record of all the eligible families in the locality in order to identify those who are most disadvantaged or most in need. Centres are heavily dependent for referrals and information about local families on other agencies (especially health practitioners such as health visitors, midwives and GPs), with many areas still struggling to achieve effective partnership working and improve the quality of baseline data collection. A more serious difficulty will be ensuring that there are appropriate systems in place (both within the centre and in partner organisations) to measure progress and developmental outcomes for each child and family over time. As always, the key challenge will be finding ways to capture the most important and meaningful outcomes, as opposed to recording 'outputs' (such as attendance), which are less revealing but easier to measure. Centres will need a framework with the right balance between breadth and specificity of outcomes, whilst also avoiding new perverse incentives to 'cherry pick' families. Further difficulties arise when it comes to monitoring outcomes over time, something that will be particularly hard in areas of high geographic mobility or population transience such as inner city areas, especially since people with improved health or employment outcomes are more likely to move away and thus leave the catchment area for the Sure Start children's centre where they first 'engaged'.

Tracking progress is made harder still because of the length of time it can take for improvements in family circumstances to materialise: a positive labour market 'journey' from worklessness to sustained employment may take many months or years to achieve, especially for people facing additional barriers (such as mental or physical health problems or social isolation). In addition, it will be important to assess whether local providers and centre managers really do have sufficient incentive and resource under the terms of PbR to develop and test innovative new practices and programmes, as intended. When resources are very limited—and the potential gain only slight—centre managers may make the strategic decision to concentrate on existing programmes as this may seem a safer and less risky strategy than experimenting with new approaches.

In practice, the PbR model may well fail to deliver promises benefits either in terms of efficiency or greater freedom and autonomy for providers. As past experience of reform highlights, any new system of accountability and performance management itself runs the risk of creating a new set of bureaucratic processes (as witnessed, for example, in National Health Service hospitals, when previous attempts to replace the relative simplicity of headline targets with a new suite of measures led to an escalating outcomes framework). In practice, frontline staff are likely to be encumbered by a fairly expansive outcomes framework and system of assessment and monitoring—for without this, it is not clear whether local areas will be able to demonstrate the improvements over time upon which PbR depends (and even so, whether it will be possible to attribute improvements in individual or family outcomes to the specific role of the children's centre, as distinct from the multiple other factors which may have had a positive influence over time). Having rejected the burdensome bureaucracy, micromanagement and perverse incentives of a highly centralised state apparatus, it would indeed be ironic if the coalition inadvertently put in place a system which replicated its flaws by creating a costly, time-consuming, wasteful and inefficient process for measuring and monitoring every family who engages with the centre, and charting and tracking their progress through partner organisations

Increase local control of funding

A second important pillar of decentralisation is the reform of public finance, with the aim of simplifying complex funding streams and devolving greater control to local areas. To this end, a new Early Intervention Grant (EIG) has replaced a host of former funding streams, including four separate grants for the early years (the most sizeable of which was for Sure Start children's centres) and eighteen other grants for children and young people (ranging from the Connexions service, to the 'Think Family' initiative, to teenage pregnancy and young people substance misuse).[12] According to ministers, at the same time as increasing efficiency, the changes will enhance local democracy by redistributing power away from the centre. In line with localism, the EIG is not ring-fenced, meaning that local councils and communities are 'free' to decide how best to allocate resources. In principle, the new funding arrangements will 'empower' local authorities and communities to focus on essential services and respond to local needs and priorities in a more strategic way. In theory, it will increase 'fairness', too, both in a procedural and a substantive sense, by increasing local involvement in decision making, whether by aggregative mechanisms (for example, voting), or taking part in local deliberative processes (for example, through extended consultation).

As the name reflects, the DfE also hopes to encourage local councils to invest funds up front in early intervention and preventative services, with a view to saving money over time (though the new grant risks confusing the issue by rolling together so many funding streams, since many of the areas covered by the grant constitute 'early intervention' in only the loosest sense of the term). Councils will struggle to be as strategic as the government may wish, however. The funding allocation for the new EIG (worth £2,222 million in 2011–12 and £2,307 million in 2012–13) has itself been subject to cuts of 11 per cent for 2011–12 and 7 per cent for 2012–13 (as compared to the aggregated total of £2,483 million for the predecessor grants in 2010–11). At a time when funding is being cut across the board (with some councils facing overall cuts in the region of 26 per cent), the removal of the ring-fence means that local councils are under pressure to cut more than this, to meet funding deficits elsewhere in the council budget.

In general terms, there is a strong case for increasing local control of public finance, particularly since local councils have historically had little discretion over funding levels. Under the existing, highly centralised system of taxation, local councils are dependent on centrally levied taxation for the vast majority of local government funding (with council tax making up only 20–25 per cent of the total). But the problem with devolving control for specific budgets in the context of the current system is that local councils are thereby given the responsibility for allocating resources without any real control over funding levels, and with no recourse to raising finance from other sources. Although in theory councils could raise additional finance through raising council tax, in practice this would mean a significant hike in council tax, which is politically unpalatable at the best of times and unthinkable in the current context.

As a result of the spending cuts and removed ring-fence, local councils have faced tough choices about which areas of provision to protect and which to cut. What is clear to all is that maintaining the status quo—continuing to run services as they had previously been configured at 2010–11 levels of funding—is not a sustainable or viable option for any local area. For Sure Start children's centres, it has meant difficult decisions about how to reconfigure provision in order to meet the funding deficit: some local areas have chosen to close centres or to convert them to alternative provision (for example, as a base for children with disabilities and special educational needs); others have opted to keep centres open, but with a skeleton staff, meaning a drastic reduction in the range of services and activities offered. A handful of councils have chosen to commission out the entire provision of Sure Start children's centres to an external provider; other areas have responded by merging staff teams across centres, or by merging the management of centres, which in turn has implications for the quality of provision for families and children and the quality of relationships across the centre.

Thus, the new arrangements are certainly yielding 'efficiencies' or cost-savings in the narrow sense since local councils have little choice but to reduce spending to meet the funding deficit. But whether they will manage to improve social outcomes and achieve better value for money over the longer term is far more doubtful, no matter how strategic local councils manage to be in the very difficult choices that they face. As research has shown, the most important factor affecting children's early years learning in preschool settings is having higher levels of staff training, professional development and qualification: the higher the qualification of staff, particularly the manager of the centre, the more progress children made. Children do best when trained teachers are able to work with them for a substantial proportion of the time, and when a centre is led and managed by an experienced education professional. The big danger for restructuring services is what it will mean for the level of qualification, training experience of frontline staff and managers— and hence, what the impact will be on children's development and outcomes.

Local communities, meanwhile, have had a chance to voice their preferences—and their concerns—to differing effect in different areas. Some local councils certainly appear to have responded to community activism in the form of parent-led campaigns to oppose planned closures. Facing EIG cuts of 11 per cent (and cuts in council funding as a whole in the region of 26 per cent), many local authorities initially announced that some local children's centres were subject to closure. Thanks to proactive lobbying by local parents against the planned closures—including campaigns led by Netmums and other self-organised local groups—it appears that many of the 250 centres originally earmarked for closure then earned a reprieve, with some being merged instead to reduce adverse publicity surrounding centre closures.

Whether it is fairer and more democratic to retain a popular children's centre in response to community activism, or to enforce a strategic decision to close a centre in a less deprived sociodemographic area, is a moot point. Either way, the experience does not bode well for the future allocation of resources. In contrast to early childhood services, those EIG services that have born the brunt of the cuts instead (particularly funding for youth services, which has been severely cut) have not been so favoured with middle-class support. Over the medium term, the clear danger is that as Sure Start becomes more targeted or 'refocused' on lower income families in line with the government's new approach, the more vulnerable those services will become to future cuts as an increasing proportion of local residents will no longer benefit directly from their provision, and as the ranks of disgruntled parents start to dwindle, no longer bolstered by the angry middle classes.

Role of the voluntary sector

A third pillar of decentralisation is to promote collaboration and diversity in the provision of public services. To this end, the Localism Act 2011 will make it easier for services to be outsourced to external providers by giving voluntary organisations, local authority employees and parish councils a new 'right to challenge' local authorities to commission out services, including children's centres. In the case of the early years, the DfE has pledged to work with local authorities to enhance the role of the voluntary sector as part of wider efforts to diversify the provision of services. At the same time, it is taking steps to encourage smaller charities and those with more inclusive governance arrangements—including mutuals, cooperatives and social enterprises—to take part, and has commissioned its strategic partner, *4Children*, to investigate ways of removing barriers in the existing procurement arrangements. The Department has also committed to adopt a new, more inclusive process of 'co-production' for the development of early years policy and strategy. While the leading charities have welcomed the chance to work more closely with ministers and officials, they have already noted that 'old habits die hard' when it comes to consistent engagement, citing the unfortunate omission of any voluntary sector representatives on the new Children's Improvement Board which will oversee provision. If even voluntary sector leaders and chief executives are being denied a place at the 'top table', it does not bode well for smaller charities and community groups, who are even more dependent on central government to ensure that there is a level playing field in commissioning and procurement arrangements and in the 'co-production' of services on the ground.

When it comes to the provision of services, the government has opted for the best of both worlds: on the one hand, the further expansion of provision by large charities and corporations offers the benefit of economies of scale and the stimulus of market competition; on the other hand, ensuring a level playing field for smaller groups and promoting more inclusive governance models offers potential benefits for democratic and civic engagement—with the added benefit of neutralising concerns about the dominance of for-profit corporations. Although based on different underpinning philosophies, the goals of 'diversification' (to promote market competition), 'collaboration' (promoting partnership working across all sectors and settings) and 'community empowerment' (for example, by encouraging citizens and community groups to adopt self-governing models) are not mutually incompatible: it is, after all, theoretically possible to commission out services to big charities or private sector corporations, with the proviso that they will not just sub-contract to smaller organisations, but actively support and sponsor local community groups to develop successful social enterprises and other models of self-governance. In reality, it takes considerable time, money and ongoing commitment at a strategic level to ensure that there is sufficient incentive and resource to devote to 'enabling' smaller bodies. Achieving a genuine mix of providers calls for active management of commissioning arrangements, which crucially depends on having the political will and commitment to do so. Early evaluations suggest that there are (negative) lessons to be learned from the Work Programme in this regard, where many of the 300 voluntary and community sector organisations involved as subcontractors have expressed frustration about the extent to which the prime contractors (two of which are themselves in the voluntary sector) are properly rewarding them.

In any case, it does rather beg the question as to why ministers are committed to enhancing the role of the voluntary sector in the first place. In justifying its approach, DfE pays tribute to the specialist skills and expertise of many voluntary and community groups, especially their experience in working with the most vulnerable and disadvantaged groups of parents and children (where it can be an advantage to be independent of government, since families may be wary of involvement with the social services). However, while there are many highly skilled practitioners in the voluntary sector, there is no monopoly of expertise in any sector. Overall, there is no evidence that voluntary or private sector organisations achieve better outcomes for families and children than the public sector: in the EPPE study, the highest scores in children's development and outcomes were achieved in nursery schools and integrated children's centres (which are predominantly local authority maintained, but also include some private and voluntary sector providers), than in playgroups and private day nurseries, indicating that what matters most is the level of staff training and qualification, rather than the provider per se.[13]

In the current fiscal climate, there is of course the strong motivation to make savings through 'smarter' and more efficient use of resources. As the Department puts it: '[M]any local authorities can see the benefits [of] commissioning out their children's centres or services within them as part of wider strategies to improve efficiency and outcomes.'[14] As compared to their public sector counterparts, non-public providers offer the competitive advantage of lower average wages, typically reflecting a streamlined management structure (with centre managers assuming responsibility for more than one setting) and also lower average qualification levels for staff than in equivalent local authority settings. Contracting services from the voluntary or private sector is therefore likely to deliver services more cheaply—though if efficiency is the main criterion, it would be a mistake for strategic commissioners to give preference to *any* sector since the sole determinant should be which provider is best placed to deliver the service.

While all would agree with the imperative to achieve better value for money across the public sector, including making genuine efficiency savings wherever possible, the key question is whether it will actually be possible to improve outcomes for families and children at significantly reduced cost. Disappointingly, the coalition government's change in direction means that it has moved away from the target in Labour's Ten Year Childcare Strategy to have a graduate-level professional educator in every setting by 2015. While some cost savings will be achieved, there is no evidence to suggest that children's outcomes are significantly improved when the level of qualified staff is reduced.

Empowering citizens and communities

How empowering is the new approach likely to be for local parents and families? First, it is bound to mean greater variability in the type of services on offer around the country. As critics warn, the flipside of decentralisation is that it means fewer guarantees for families and children about the scope and quality of provision available in each locality. Supporters of Sure Start worry that the patchwork of early years provision is already beginning to unravel; and that over coming months and years it will start to look increasingly threadbare.

The opportunity for parents to take part in centre activities, therefore, will clearly depend on the particular configuration of services in their local area. The government has pledged both to retain a national network of children's centres, and to refocus provision on those in greatest need. In practice, the decision about which services to keep, and which to cut, will depend on the particular decisions and priorities of each local council. Ironically, the shift away from universal provision is doubly disappointing because the model of integrated children's centres, open to parents from all backgrounds, actually provides an ideal setting for two key aims of the Big Society: developing individual capacity and promoting a sense of community engagement. From the outset, one of the distinguishing features of Sure Start children's centres has been the platform they provide for parents, carers, children and wider family members to build up levels of engagement and interaction—progressing, for example, from informal, *ad hoc* attendance, such as visiting the playground or drop-in facilities, to regular participation in group activities (antenatal groups, breastfeeding advice, fathers' groups and so on), to more formal types of participation in parenting courses or skills training, in the running of services or activities, or in the governance of local settings. Far from inducing a state of dependency, the best settings have always and continue to provide the basis for agency and independence. Furthermore, what is particularly striking about integrated children's centres is that they are a natural fit for parental engagement (much more so than the much vaunted opportunities for parental engagement in the Free Schools policy). Since their inception, Sure Start children's centres were always intended to act as a 'community hub', offering a range of information, advice and services in one location—health, education, training, employment, financial support, housing services, debt advice—and so acting as a shared resource for families, local groups and the wider community. By bringing new parents together in one place to make use of a range of general and specialist services, centres have provided a chance for parents to meet and offer mutual support to other parents in the locality, including those who may not otherwise get this support from their peers, such as young, first time parents, victims of domestic violence, or parents with substance abuse problems. At the same time, the opportunity to take part in a range of services, activities and classes creates an important bond and connection between people from different social and cultural backgrounds.

Not all settings have realised the vision of the community hub, of course: in many areas there are still many more ways in which parents and other members of the community could be actively involved in the planning, design, coordination and governance of activities. What is so interesting and distinctive about the integrated early years centre is the way it functions as a 'host' or umbrella association, creating space for many different types of group and community to meet, building bridges across communities, as well as strengthening bonds within them. In this sense, it is the very image of the interdependent, overlapping community that is invoked in the Big Society. Far from replacing, in Cameron's words, the 'natural bonds of duty and responsibility' with the 'synthetic bonds' of the state, children's centres have played a valuable role in building and sustaining a community by providing a wealth of occasions and opportunities for people to come together and build strong, supportive relationships, by participating in the life of the centre. As expressed by one woman in a local consultation event recently: '[F]or me, the centre is my family.'

If this is the case, one might wonder why the coalition has not committed to ensure that there will be a centre in every community, or to guarantee a minimal level of service for in every locality. From the government's perspective, it is fairer to focus resources on the neighbourhoods, communities and families who need them most. After all, while nearly all new parents would value the opportunity of meeting and interacting with other new parents after the birth of their child and forming new social networks of support and advice, such activity is not necessarily 'core' to the government. Although highly valued by the individuals involved, conducting a cost-benefit analysis of its value would not necessarily yield a positive return.

Many of the parents who have benefited from the opportunities available in children's centres would not necessarily be classed as 'needing' them, since they could afford to pay for similar services privately. Clearly, any such analysis will be determined by which 'goods' are valued—and, of course, how far they are measurable (putting a price on 'community' being particularly taxing). By devolving responsibility for allocating resources to the local level, the government would also claim that it is giving local communities the power to decide how resources should be allocated—and giving communities the chance to escape the legacy of top-down managerialism that lingers on in Whitehall. After all, if local centres are really at the heart of the community, then local parents and the local council will be aligned in wanting to protect them. We can see here the tension between being 'strategic' and 'responsive': although some local councils have responded to parent-led campaigns against planned closures, presumably this also undermines their capacity to be strategic in the deployment of resources to more deprived communities. If middle-class parents shout loudest, then it may distort the decisions of councils away from more disadvantaged areas.

One way that providers (in all sectors) are looking to balance and retain the different areas of provision is through encouraging the greater involvement of parents and other volunteers in running or assisting with activities and services as a way of freeing up skilled staff to focus and engage on families and children with highest need. While parental engagement and involvement in helping to plan, coordinate and govern children's centres is of considerable importance, there are clearly limits to how far experienced practitioners can be replaced with unpaid volunteers without compromising the ability of early years services to improve outcomes for families and children. A greater reliance on volunteers risks reducing the quality of provision by reducing the capacity of frontline 'staff' (paid and unpaid) to respond appropriately where children are showing signs of developmental delay—for example, by making referrals to other agencies or by knowing how to engage with parents and provide the necessary support. There are also real dangers to consider when it comes to safeguarding, since unpaid volunteers are unlikely to possess the necessary experience and training to be able to identify and respond appropriately to families and children who are at risk of harm.

When it comes to frontline staff, these developments look to be rather more demoralising and disempowering than the government's rhetoric would suggest. The stretching of qualified staff and experienced professionals across centres (which means that workers with qualified teacher status may now have to divide their time between settings), together with the greater reliance on unpaid volunteers, does nothing to improve the pay, status and conditions of the predominantly female early years workforce, which has historically suffered from lower wages and status than other sectors—as a result, it likely to cement low pay and low status. The fear is that it is not just a sticking plaster to cover a temporary funding cut, but will become a permanent trend. Thus, instead of ensuring a decent wage for practitioners and closing the gender pay gap, it could make the problem worse by reinforcing the idea that early years education, family support and childcare can be provided on the cheap or for free. Far from 'empowering' professionals, beneath the government's rhetoric about the importance of the early years, there continues to exist another, powerful set of assumptions about the value and worth of working with families and young children. If the government really wanted to 'empower' professionals to innovate and achieve better outcomes, then it would do well to start by challenging the view that these are not 'proper' areas of employment, worthy of being paid a decent wage—or any wage at all.

As a final point, it is worth reflecting on what the new funding arrangements say about the status and perceived worth of early years education as compared to schooling. Removing the ring-fence on early years investment, whilst continuing to protect the schools budget, not only increases the pressure on local councils to make cuts in non-schools spending, it also reflects the very different value ascribed to each policy area. Despite the strong government rhetoric on the importance of early years investment (and early intervention more broadly) as a vital component of its strategies to promote social mobility and tackle child poverty, in reality it is still a much lower priority than other areas of education. We might reflect back to the main recommendation of the government-commissioned Review of Poverty and Life Chances, chaired by Frank Field MP, which called for the 'Foundation Years' to be established on an equal par with 'Schooling and Higher Education' in terms of status, funding and public recognition—viewed by politicians and public alike as core government provision in the same way as hospitals and schools. The reality of the funding situation for children's centres, as compared to schools, show just how far we are away from this goal.

Conclusion

Just who, then, is being empowered by the coalition's new early years strategy? As expounded by David Cameron, the Big Society aims to correct and reverse the damaging, disempowering effects of Big Government in two key ways: first, instead of destroying individual initiative and agency, it seeks to rebuild people's capacities and restore their sense of personal agency and responsibility; and second, instead of eroding community, it endeavours to recreate the conditions for civic engagement and allow a strong sense of social responsibility to flourish. Ironically, the shift away from universal provision risks undermining both aims since children's centres provide an ideal model of the interdependent, overlapping community, whilst also supporting particular individuals on a journey of personal empowerment. Despite the impressive set of claims to be empowering frontline staff through more innovative and flexible working practices, and providing greater opportunities for parental engagement, the reality of the reforms is that the main act of decentralisation—devolving responsibility to local authorities to allocate funds for a range of child and youth services out of the same pot, whilst cutting the total amount and giving the local authority the 'freedom' to cut more—is not particularly conducive to 'empowerment'. In reality it looks more like off-loading responsibility for making a set of extremely tough choices than a genuine redistribution of power. At the intermediary level, the government has sought the best of both worlds: cost savings and economies of scale through opening up the market to larger providers (in both the voluntary and private sector), whilst stressing the virtue of encouraging smaller community and cooperative groups to prove its Big Society credentials. In practice, the logic of the two models pulls in different directions: a mixed model is possible in theory, but requires active strategic commitment and direction at all levels to ensure that smaller organisations have the resource and capacity they need to enter and successfully compete in the market of provision. From a decentralising perspective, such active management of the commissioning process, contractual arrangements and council funding defeats the point of opening up the market in the first place.

Notes

1 Department of Communities and Local Government (CLG), *Decentralisation and the Localism Bill: An Essential Guide*, London, TSO, 2010.
2 J. Norman, *The Big Society: The Anatomy of the New Politics*, Buckingham, University of Buckingham Press, 2010.
3 Q. Skinner, 'A third concept of liberty', *Proceedings of the British Academy*, vol. 117, 2002, pp. 237–68.
4 D. Cameron, Hugo Young Lecture on the Big Society, 10 November 2009.
5 Cameron, Hugo Young Lecture.
6 CLG, *Decentralisation and the Localism Bill*.
7 R. Hattersley and K. Hickson, 'In praise of social democracy', *The Political Quarterly*, vol. 83, no.1, 2012, pp. 5–12.
8 J. Norman and J. Ganesh, *Compassionate Conservatism: What It Is and Why We Need It*, London, Policy Exchange, 2006.
9 T. Janoski, *Citizenship and Civil Society: A Framework of Rights and Obligations in Liberal, Traditional and Social Democratic Regimes*, Cambridge, Cambridge University Press, 1998.
10 Norman and Ganesh, *Compassionate Conservatism*.
11 N. Pearce, 'Beyond social mobility', *Public Policy Research*, vol. 18, no. 1, 2011, pp. 3–9.
12 Department of Education (DfE), *Early Intervention Grant: Technical Note for 2011–12 and 2012–13*, London, DfE, 2011.
13 K. Sylva et al., *The Effective Provision of Pre-school Education (EPPE): Findings from the Pre-school Period*, London: DfES/Institute of Education, University of London, 2003.
14 Department of Education (DfE), *Supporting Families in the Foundation Years*, London, DfE, 2011.

Index

Note: alphabetical arrangement is word-by-word.

The Political Quarterly © 2012 The Political Quarterly Publishing Co. Ltd